Handbook of Structured Techniques in Marriage and Family Therapy

Handbook of Structured Techniques in Marriage and Family Therapy

by Robert Sherman, Ed.D.
&
Norman Fredman, Ph.D.

Queens College, New York

Brunner/Mazel, Publishers
New York

Library of Congress Cataloging-in-Publication Data

Sherman, Robert, 1928–
  Handbook of structured techniques in marriage and
family therapy.

  Includes bibliographies.
  1. Marital psychotherapy — Technique — Handbooks,
manuals, etc.   2. Family psychotherapy — Technique —
Handbooks, manuals, etc.   I. Fredman, Norman,
1932–   . II. Title.   III. Title: Structured
techniques in marriage and family therapy.
RC488.5.S49   1986   616.89'16   85-32064
ISBN 0-87630-424-2

Published by
BRUNNER/MAZEL, INC.
19 Union Square West
New York, New York 10003

10 9 8 7 6 5 4 3

Contents

Acknowledgments   *viii*

Preface   *xi*

CHAPTER 1   DEVELOPMENT AND USE OF TECHNIQUES   3

CHAPTER 2   FANTASY AND IMAGERY   11

INTRODUCTION   11
1.   EARLY RECOLLECTIONS   16
2.   FAMILY PHOTOGRAPHS   19
3.   FAMILY PUPPET INTERVIEW   23
4.   POETRY AND SONG LYRICS IN COUPLES GROUPS   26
5.   "IF I WERE"   29
6.   CREATING ANALOGOUS SITUATIONS   33
7.   SENTENCE COMPLETION   36
8.   VALUES CLARIFICATION: THE "MOM ALWAYS SAID . . .
     DAD ALWAYS SAID . . . " VALUES SENTENCE COMPLETION FORM   38
9.   VALUE ASSESSMENT COMPARISON   42

10. THE USE OF DREAMS IN FAMILY THERAPY   44
11. DRAW A DREAM   48
12. THE ROLE OF DREAMS IN SEX THERAPY   50
13. IMAGERY, SHAPING, AND ORGASM IN SEX THERAPY   53
14. IMAGERY: EVENTS IN THE FAMILY OF ORIGIN   55
15. GUIDED IMAGERY: THE INNER ADVISER   58
16. COUPLE IMAGES   62
17. THE EMPTY CHAIR IN FAMILY THERAPY   64

CHAPTER 3   SOCIOMETRIC TECHNIQUES   69

    INTRODUCTION   69
18. SCULPTING   73
19. FAMILY CHOREOGRAPHY   79
20. THE GENOGRAM   82
21. ROLE CARD GAME   90
22. THE ECOMAP: MAPPING A FAMILY NETWORK   96
23. THE STRAW TOWER   102
24. THE FAMILY FLOOR PLAN   105
25. THE FAMILY SOCIOGRAM   109

CHAPTER 4   STRUCTURAL MOVES   115

    INTRODUCTION   115
26. TRACKING   120
27. SUPPORTING GENERATIONAL BOUNDARIES   123
28. ALLYING WITH A SUBSYSTEM   127
29. STRATEGIC ALLIANCES   131
30. THE FAMILY RITUAL   134
31. THE VACATION   137
32. ROLE REVERSAL   140
33. THE COMPLEMENTARITY CHALLENGE   143

CHAPTER 5   BEHAVIORAL TASKS   147

    INTRODUCTION   147
34. THE COUPLE CONFERENCE AND FAMILY COUNCIL   151
35. THE MARRIAGE CONTRACT GAME   155
36. CARING DAYS   158

37. WITHIN-SESSION STRUCTURED TASKS   161
38. POSITIVE EXCHANGES   164
39. READING ALOUD AS AN INITIAL ASSIGNMENT
     IN MARITAL THERAPY   168
40. TEACHING CHOICE AWARENESS   172
41. SYMBOLISM AND GIFT GIVING   175
42. STRUCTURED COMMUNICATION TRAINING   181
43. THE SQUEEZE TECHNIQUE IN SEX THERAPY   186

CHAPTER 6   PARADOX   189

INTRODUCTION   189
44. REFRAMING   197
45. PRETENDING TO HAVE THE SYMPTOM   200
46. ILLUSION OF ALTERNATIVES   202
47. THE PARADOXICAL LETTER: BRINGING A RESISTANT
     FAMILY MEMBER TO THERAPY   205
48. CONTAMINATING THE SUICIDAL FANTASY   207
49. THE THERAPIST AS DIRECTOR OF THE FAMILY DRAMA   211
50. PRESCRIBING INDECISION   215
51. THE WINNER'S BET WITH ADOLESCENTS   218
52. JOINING THE OPPOSITION: PARADOX WITH AN OPPOSITIONAL
     ACTING-OUT CLIENT AND HIS COMPLIANT FAMILY   221
53. PUTTING THE CLIENT IN CONTROL OF THE SYMPTOM   225

CHAPTER 7   ALTERNATIVE MODELS   229

INTRODUCTION   229
54. CO-THERAPY   230
55. VIDEOTAPE PLAYBACK   233
56. TELEPHONE CALLS WITHIN THE SESSION   236
57. HOME VISITS   238
58. TIME-EXTENDED FAMILY INTERVIEWING   240
59. THE SURROGATE FAMILY GROUP   243

CHAPTER 8   EPILOGUE   247

Acknowledgments

We are deeply indebted to many people for their assistance in the preparation of this book. We are particularly grateful to Leonore Hanson, Esther Koenigsberg Chagigi, and Gaston Weisz for their assistance with research and editorial services.

We wish to thank the following individuals, former graduate students, for their help in identifying and describing many of the techniques included in the book: Stephen Abrams, Carole G. Beckford, Gania Bialer, Phyllis Carter, Carmen L. Cedeno, Ida Cooper, Kandy Diamond, Mark Drexler, Marion Fleischer, Lyn Halper, Steven L. Jones, Karen C. Kitler, Dorothea S. Lewis, John Linhardt, Trinidad L. Lum, Jill M. Meyerson, Carole C. Moleti, Eloise B. Nicholson, Virginia Orgel, Lloyd M. Peckman, Alice Pinhas, Judith R. Reinhauer, Debra A. Sahm, Anthony Stanici, Joyce M. Stillman, and Patricia Woods.

It is a privilege to receive permissions to adapt or directly quote the copyrighted work of other authors as follows in their order of appearance in the book:

Adaptations from "Family photographs: In treatment and training," by C. Anderson and E. Malloy in *Family Process*, 1976, 15:2, 259–264.
Adaptations and quotations from "Sentence completion as an aid to

sex therapy," by J. Gumina in *Journal of Marital and Family Therapy*, 1980, 62, 201–206.

Adaptations and quotations and a copy of the instrument "Mom Always Said . . . Dad Always Said Values Sentence Completion Form," by Richard Krajeacki and John Linhardt, unpublished.

Adaptations and quotations from "Values assessment comparison (VAC)," by H. H. Floyd in *Family Therapy*, 1982, 9:3, 280–288.

Adaptations from "Draw a dream: An intervention promoting change in families in conflict," by B. J. Tonge in F. W. Kaslow (ed.), *The international book of family therapy*, 1982, pp. 212–225. Copyright © 1982 by F. Kaslow. Reprinted by permission of Brunner/Mazel Publishers.

Adaptations and quotations from "The role of dreams in sex therapy," by A. N. Levay and J. Weissberg in *Journal of Sex and Marital Therapy*, 1979, 5:4, 334–339.

Adaptations from "Imagery techniques in family therapy," by J. K. Morrison in *The American Journal of Family Therapy*, 1981, 9:2, 52–56.

Adaptations from "Family choreography," by P. Papp in P. J. Guerin (ed.), *Family therapy: Theory and practice*, pp. 455–471. Copyright © 1982 by P. J. Guerin. Reprinted by permission of Gardner Press.

Adaptations and quotations from "Evaluation of family system and genogram," by P. J. Guerin and E. G. Pendagast in P. J. Guerin (ed.), *Family therapy: Theory and practice*, pp. 455–462. Copyright © 1976 by P. J. Guerin. Reprinted by permission of Gardner Press.

Adaptations from "When a family needs therapy," by G. Ogden and A. Zevin. Copyright © 1976 by G. Ogden and A. Zevin. Reprinted by permission of Beacon Press.

Adaptations and quotations from "The family floor plan: A tool for training, assessment and intervention in family therapy," by E. Coppersmith (Imber-Black) in *Journal of Marital and Family Therapy*, 1980, 6, 141–145.

Adaptations and quotations from *Families and family therapy*, by S. Minuchin. Copyright © 1974 by S. Minuchin. Reprinted by permission of Harvard University Press.

Adaptations and quotations from "Strategic approaches with resistant families," by M. M. Breit, W. Im and S. Wilner in *The American Journal of Family Therapy*, 1983, 11, 51–58.

Adaptations and quotations from *Family therapy techniques*, by S. Minuchin and C. Fishman. Copyright © 1981 by S. Minuchin and C. Fishman. Reprinted by permission of Harvard University Press.

Adaptations from "Family problem solving training," by E. A. Bleichman in *The American Journal of Family Therapy*, 1980, 8, 3–22.

Adaptations from "Gestalt approach to family therapy," by R. Bauer in *The American Journal of Family Therapy*, 1979, 7:3, 41–45.

Adaptations from "Choice awareness: An unlimited horizon," by R. C. Nelson in *Personnel and Guidance Journal*, 1976, 54, 462–467. Copyright AACD. Reprinted by permission.

Adaptations from "Marriage enrichment through choice awareness," by R. C. Nelson and W. P. Friest in *Journal of Marital and Family Therapy*, 1980, 6:4, 399–407.

Adaptations and quotations from *Human sexual inadequacy*, by W. H. Masters and V. E. Johnson. Copyright © 1970 by W. H. Masters and V. E. Johnson. Reprinted by permission.

Adaptations and quotations from "The therapist as director of the family drama," by M. Andolfi and C. Angelo in F. W. Kaslow (ed.), *The international book of family therapy*, pp. 119–132. Copyright © 1982 by F. W. Kaslow. Reprinted by permission of Brunner/Mazel Publishers.

Adaptations from *Strategic family therapy*, by C. Madanes. Copyright © 1981 by C. Madanes. Reprinted by permission of Jossey-Bass Publishers.

Adaptations from "Use of paradoxical techniques in a school setting," by J. M. Williams and G. Weeks in *The American Journal of Family Therapy*, 1984, 12:3, 47–56.

Adaptations from "Some co-therapy techniques with families," by J. Hannum in *Family Process*, 1980, 19, 161–168.

Adaptations from "Expanding uses of the telephone in family therapy," by E. Coppersmith (Imber-Black) in *Family Process*, 1980, 19, 411–417.

Adaptations from "Time extended interviewing," by D. B. Breslow and B. G. Hron in *Family Process*, 1977, 16, 97–103.

We owe our thanks to our editor, Ann Alhadeff, whose guidance, assistance, and patience were invaluable.

Although we received help from many persons and sources, we take full responsibility for the final outcome.

To our wives, Judith Sherman and Micheline Fredman, for the best part of a good life: the acts of love and kindness.

Preface

While running professional conferences and training programs, we found a great demand for practical "how-to" information in making diagnoses and interventions. What do you do after "the Master's" single dramatic demonstration? How do you accomplish and maintain the desired behavior change—the hard job of the working-through process? Many methods can be adapted to a given therapy situation. It is certainly good to invent new methods but unnecessary to reinvent already existing convenient ones.

Rapid expansion of the field of couple and family therapy and education fosters increased attention to research, theory building, and the invention of and experimentation with new techniques. Some of these developments are published; some are not.

The veritable explosion of technique and instrument development now in process is fueled by the following factors:

1. There is an increasing need for the public to deal with the breakdown in couple and family relationships and interpersonal behavior.
2. There are increasing numbers of professionals struggling with the challenges of prevention, life cycle changes, and treatment.
3. The profession is trying to obtain government and public recognition of its competence and services by raising standards for train-

ing, accreditation of practitioners, and accreditation of training and service facilities.

4.   Many theorists wish to demonstrate the relative validity and effectiveness of their theories.

There are growing numbers of clinicians and counselors trained in individual therapy who increasingly are including couple and family work. They seek practical methods and instruments to assist them in their therapy.

The purpose of this handbook is to provide a single convenient source to which practitioners, researchers, and trainees may turn to find descriptions of the techniques and instruments suited to their needs. The book is designed for quick reference. Readers may easily identify what they need by category of technique.

Chapter 1 deals with the process of creating techniques, choosing techniques, what is being done in the field, and the usefulness of currently available resources.

Chapters 2 through 7 focus on special techniques for diagnosis and intervention. The rationale for a technique is given, followed by a description of the procedure, illustrations of use, discussion of possible uses and outcomes, and sources of further information. The reader can find such diverse techniques as sculpting, the genogram, the family floor plan, early recollections, the couple conference and family council, reframing, the therapeutic counterparadox, and behavior rehearsal. These are organized into six major categories. A chapter is devoted to each category — for example, Fantasy and Imagery; Structural Moves.

We are very much aware that a list of techniques can be nothing more than a bag of tricks. All the listings in this handbook, though potentially powerful tools, need to be used appropriately: A selected technique is employed in relation to a theoretical framework in a situation where it can achieve a specified purpose in relation to a desired goal with a particular person or population. The user needs to know why she* is doing this, to whom, and with what anticipated consequences. Each category of techniques is discussed in a brief theoretical introduction, which also provides some background on the areas of projected usefulness of the category.

The techniques as presented are general working versions. The descriptions cannot include the refinements in application to a particular case and situation. This must be the responsibility of the therapist. Also, timing and presentation are very important in the delivery of a good

---

*For the sake of simplicity, in this book we use the female pronoun primarily to refer to the therapist, and the masculine pronoun primarily to refer to clients of either sex.

technique. Techniques are tools. Their ultimate effectiveness depends greatly on the hands of the craftsmen utilizing them.

There has been considerable growth in the number and quality of these techniques. This has been the result of the interchange of ideas at conferences and in journals and the evaluation of these ideas by universities, therapy centers, and journal review boards. New technologies, such as the VCR, make possible new techniques.

Most of the listings in this handbook are *not* carefully standardized processes. Therefore, there is much room for creativity to adapt the ideas, and to modify and refine the methods to meet your own needs and desired outcomes. This handbook may well stimulate readers to their own creativity as they interact with and think about the material within their own theoretical background and with their own clients in mind.

Chapter 8 identifies trends in and needs for development of techniques in couple and family therapy. One of the trends noted is that many techniques are particularly designed to overcome client resistance to change, especially those techniques in the paradoxical intervention category. What are the ethical implications for use of such procedures? There is growing use of fantasy, imagery, and metaphoric techniques and adaptations of hypnotherapy methods to family counseling. There is a movement toward greater use of right brain hemisphere functioning in working with clients that reflects a dramatic change in the therapeutic process.

This is a very exciting and creative time in the field of family therapy. We hope this book captures some of that excitement.

R.S.
N.F.

Handbook of
Structured Techniques
in Marriage and
Family Therapy

1

Development and
Use of Techniques

George is a therapist working with Mr. & Mrs. F. They are engaged in a constant power struggle characterized by conflict and bitterness between them. George would like to defuse that power struggle. For him there are many techniques available including the couple conference, the couple choreography, and positive exchanges.

Elana is a therapist struggling with the S. stepfamily. Married for 10 years, they have two adolescent children from a previous marriage who are "out of control." She would like to find ways of strengthening the parents' position and gaining the cooperation of the children. She can employ such techniques as the Family Council, Family Floor Plan, the Straw Tower, or paradoxical techniques.

We often notice as supervisors that therapists are able to establish useful goals but many times don't know how to reach them. The number of training cases supervised does not begin to open up for the therapist the rich lode of techniques invented by their colleagues. Supervisors themselves may not go beyond a limited number of favored techniques, especially in the time available.

The worker needs a variety of alternative methods to determine what is going on and what it means. The problem becomes more acute in the working-through process as the therapist tries to implement a behavior change. Although most theory texts provide case illustrations, these cases are not exactly the same as those faced by the practitioners. Finally, clinicians have to design their own behavior change interactions. The ability to design such a plan is the difference between a technician and a professional.

To facilitate that process, many clinicians have described in the literature methods and instruments they have developed. Many techniques — probably most — have never been published.

"How-to" techniques and objectives do not constitute a bag of tricks. They are carefully designed plans of action founded on theory and observation of behavior. Each has a particular purpose, and each must be chosen for use by the worker for the appropriate time and circumstances. Theory and clinical judgment determine which techniques to use, when, and how. Techniques are the means for converting ideas into practical use. They operationalize the theory.

To help the reader determine which techniques to choose, each chapter has a theoretical introduction to the category of techniques that follows. In turn, each technique is described in terms of its rationale and appropriate usefulness.

Clinical techniques and objective instruments exist on a continuum of formality from clinically subjective to statistically objective and standardized. In the middle are instruments that are questionable to categorize. Is the use of a sociogram a test or a technique? Is a structured inventory that has not been subjected to validity and reliability studies but has clinical value a technique or a test?

We propose the following definition of a technique.

What Is a Technique?

A technique is "a systematic procedure by which a complex or scientific task is accomplished" (Morris, 1970). In this book a technique is considered a complex move, prescription, or suggestion made by the therapist. It requires that the client perform a series of actions which will yield greater understanding of their existing behavior and/or stimulate them toward behavior change. In this book we do not include as techniques brief interactions or momentary tactics such as changing the seating order, asking a single question, or making an empathic or validating comment.

Techniques described in the literature are numerous. There are many books on family therapy that include the word "techniques" in their titles. Each family therapy theory usually includes a body of 6–12 major techniques commonly used in the application of that theory. For example, Minuchin (1974, 1981) describes in detail the joining process, Adlerian therapists (Manaster and Corsini, 1982) the early recollection and family council, and strategic therapists (Weeks and L'Abate, 1982) different types of paradoxical interventions. Techniques of that complexity have been selected for inclusion in this work. The techniques presented are also divided into categories based on the principal medium used — imagery, structural moves, behavioral tasks.

By doing this we hope to provide the possibility for cross-fertilization of ideas among the different theories.

How Are Techniques Invented?
It is interesting to speculate how timely jokes are created and in various versions quickly become known over wide geographic areas. It seems techniques emerge the same way, often with originators unidentified, until, finally, someone publishes one or more versions. However, since techniques are related to scientific tasks, we can speculate with some precision about how they are invented.

We begin with a hunch about human behavior. If A is going on and a sequence of events called B is introduced (the technique), then outcome C occurs. Many variables are involved in the ongoing interaction process. Those variables can be manipulated in an organized, systematic way to create a new technique or change an existing one. Each variable is a potential ingredient in the construction of techniques.

Adding to the possibilities for development of new techniques are the invention of new technologies such as mechanical audio and video systems; one-way-vision mirrors; computers; telephone systems; rapid transportation systems; and copy machines. A huge number of toys and games is available. The abundance of literature, music, dance, art, and crafts, with tools and instruments to produce and use them, also present intriguing possibilities.

Following are some of the more common variables used in developing techniques:

1. *Expanding or reducing the number of members in the therapeutic system.* This enables new modalities to be created such as a co-therapy, multiple family groups, surrogate family groups, family network groups, group of the family and all professional systems working with the family; and meeting with different subsystems.

2. *Varying the time frame for meeting or tasks.* Sessions can be any fixed time, on demand, open-ended, once a week or month, an entire weekend. The number of sessions can be limited by contract or left open. Tasks can be assigned open-ended or on a fixed, regular schedule.

3. *Changing the place in which therapy meetings or tasks occur.* The therapy office, client workplace, client home, school, community center, resort, or church are among the most common possibilities.

4. *Altering the activity or introducing a new one.* Clients can be invited to lunch, play games, draw pictures, write a marriage contract, enact

a drama, or sculpt the family. Alternatives are limited only by the imagination.

5. Engaging different levels of consciousness and thought processes. The therapist can engage various thought functions through reasoning and planning, or through dreams, fantasy, imagery, and metaphor. Meditation and hypnosis are among other choices.

6. Structuring the patterns of communication. The therapist can suggest or prescribe rules for communication. Some examples are: who can speak with whom, when, about what, and in what order. The rule might be speak only for "the" self, or the therapist may engage in circular questioning in which the members answer about other members rather than for themselves. The therapist can also design therapeutic double bind communications.

7. Altering or reversing the place or roles of members of the system. Maneuvers such as reversing roles, disengaging a child from parentlike activities, forming alliances, empowering parents, changing seating arrangements, and validating an adolescent's desires for more independence and responsibility are examples. The therapist can prescribe a change of roles such as putting an overly responsible spouse in charge of family fun or teaching a passive person to be more assertive.

8. Varying the therapist's mode of interacting with clients. The therapist can listen, question, react, probe, interpret, dramatize, underplay, lead, follow, take a one-up, one-down, or equal position, encourage or restrain actions. She can be empathic, sympathetic, self-revealing. She can present herself as kindly or assertive, loose or structured, supportive or demanding.

Many variables and tactics make up a complex technique. However, one or two usually stand out. This permits us to identify categories of techniques. They have enough similarity in the way they are organized and implemented to enable us to group them together. Thus, techniques organized around changing members' places and roles in the system can be thought of as "structural moves." Techniques centered around sequential structured activities and tasks can be grouped as behavioral tasks. Of course there is some arbitrariness to making these groupings. We believe, however, that they serve a useful purpose in identifying alternative techniques based on somewhat similar operating principles.

Choosing and Using Techniques
Scientifically, the best way to use a technique is to implement a strategy determined by a theoretical and practical understanding of a situation in order to accomplish a particular goal. Thinking holistically, the tech-

nique is thus part of a larger planned process of therapeutic strategy. Some theories incorporate a sequence of prescribed categories of techniques, (i.e., in structural therapy joining, enacting, restructuring, etc.).

A technique is chosen on the basis of the clinical judgment of the therapist who believes this is the right thing to do at this point in the work. Clinical judgment is based upon logical, scientific thinking and also on analogical, intuitive understanding. It is art as well as science. Originators and publishers of a technique generally recommend when and how it is best used.

To be successful the therapist needs to feel comfortable with the medium and style of the technique as well as with its theoretical rationale. If the therapist is unassertive, behaving prescriptively may be difficult. If the therapist is structured, the use of more ambiguous, projective methods may present problems. A passive type of person may have difficulty with more action-oriented methods.

We are often enthralled watching a master colleague in action in vivo, on videotape, or described in a textbook using a given technique with apparent, almost magical results. The technique befits both the master and the particular situation. We recognize that they cannot always do what Minuchin, Papp, or Satir can do and get the same result. The personality of the therapist is a critical element in the use of a technique. Further, authors rarely report incidents in which the technique either did not help or hindered the therapy.

Techniques are designed as tools to accomplish therapeutic goals. Unlike the objective standardized format of testing instruments, they are intended to be used with greater flexibility based on clinical judgment and the creativity of the therapist. Therefore, a given technique that has emerged within one theoretical framework often may be adapted readily for use within a different theoretical system.

How Do We Know If a Technique Works?

This flexibility of techniques, which is such a positive asset, is also a major deficit: Without standardization, it is difficult to determine how well the technique works. On a case-by-case basis, the therapist can observe carefully whether the specified goal is attained after implementation of the technique. If so, then probably the technique contributed toward its attainment. For example, if after sculpting the family is realigned in terms of each person's place in the family organization and members express different attitudes toward one another and toward the family and have established different ways of communicating with one another, we can assert (but not prove) that the sculpting process probably contributed to those changes.

We can observe specific changes in organization or behavior. For example, how often does the symptom appear in a given time sequence?

How often is a new behavior expressed by a member? Does a member respond differently than before to an act that previously produced unwanted symptoms? Is there evidence that resistance has been reduced; for example, do the family members carry out the recommended behavior? Do members speak together directly who previously communicated only through an intermediary?

Similar criteria can be formulated by any therapist to determine if the technique is succeeding in its purpose of facilitating a particular change. Most of us look for such changes as we work through a case but rarely subject our observations to more formal measurement. Formal outcome research is a difficult area in all types of psychotherapy. The number of objective measuring instruments in the field is growing, and some can well be used to determine the relative effectiveness of particular complex techniques. (See the *Handbook of Family Therapy Inventories* [Brunner/Mazel, 1986, in press] by the authors of this book. The *Handbook* describes over 30 instruments representative of those currently available and examines the state of the art.)

Techniques are also used for diagnostic purposes; they provide valuable feedback about the clients. However, how do we know if the information obtained is accurate, typical, or central to the issues involved? Any technique is but a small sample of client system behavior. Is the behavior observed merely an artifact of the technique itself and not really representative of the clients' patterns?

We can check directly with the clients to verify if this event is typical of their functioning. We can use a second alternate procedure to see if we get similar results. We can compare our observations with data obtained by tests and inventories. When clients are confronted by observing their own behavior, there is often a recognition reflex expressed in the eyes, by the body, or verbally.

Using appropriate techniques, we can obtain a great deal of data from our clients. After all, they have lived many years and have experienced much. The criterion is not the volume of data, but seeking selected data that will be significant in explaining and understanding the symptoms. The data are also needed to describe exactly what is being done by whom with what effects on each that keeps it going.

We choose techniques diagnostically not just to acquire more information, but rather to get at the most relevant information desired. We would like to observe the essence of the interaction process. For example, family myths, rules, metaphors, and rituals provide good clues. The direction of the behavior and its effect on the various members (the consequences of the behavior) can help us to determine its purpose and meaning. The way the therapist is incorporated into the sequence and its effect upon the therapist is another factor that may provide additional understanding of what is happening.

A technique used as a diagnostic tool, then, can be designed not only to gather more data, but to help us focus in on the method, purpose and meaning of the interactive pattern.

We would guess that the typical therapist employs those techniques that she knows about which befit her personality and skills. She feels comfortable with them. She tends to use repeatedly a limited repertory of techniques used before which she believes are successful in her practice. She has faith in them. The criterion is how useful do they seem to be clinically. Some of them were probably carefully taught during her supervised training. Others she invented herself—a few carefully designed, others impromptu in a moment of inspiration. Though the therapist uses many techniques in her work, they are only a small fraction of those she knows and a much smaller percentage of those available.

Use of This Handbook

The major innovation of couple and family therapy is thinking about the couple or family as an organized unit and as the client unit, while not losing sight of individual members. This difference in concept requires the invention of new tools to understand the unit under study and to facilitate changes in its organization. Moreover, the idea that there is a problem in the organization has led us away from thinking in terms of the origin, care, and treatment of individual psychopathology. Instead, we tend to focus more on such systemic concepts as attraction, cohesion, alliances, boundaries, power, roles, rules, differentiation, fusion, enmeshment, disengagement, loyalty, legacy, contracts, and conflict resolution. Careful definitions and tools to deal with those constructs become imperatives of the field.

The purpose of this handbook is to gather in one place examples of the current state of the art in the development of techniques and instruments. These are the ways in which theory is applied. In addition, these are the techniques that inspire the instruments that assess the validity and value of our theories.

Resources are provided at the end of each chapter introduction and each technique. Some give additional information on the techniques. Others provide more information on the underlying theoretical framework for such techniques. And some are listed because they include related techniques.

Our theory is holistic and so this handbook must be regarded as part of a larger whole. It provides us with some aspects of the how-to-do-it part of our professional activity. That part in turn is related to theoretical concepts.

Readers may find here a useful compendium of techniques. Researchers and clinicians may also use the current state of the art as a way of brainstorming new ideas and inventing new techniques and instruments to solve problems that are not described here.

Examination of the wide range of techniques presented in the following chapters may perhaps help those practicing or preparing to practice in the field to expand their repertories and solve some of the more difficult problems they encounter in diagnosis and facilitation of behavior change. The reader may find just the technique to get beyond an impasse in the work.

RESOURCES

Dreikurs, R. *Children: The challenge.* New York: Hawthorne, 1964.

Fredman, B. and Sherman, R. *Handbook of family therapy inventories.* New York: Brunner/Mazel, in press.

Minuchin, S. *Families and family therapy.* Cambridge, MA: Harvard University Press, 1974.

Minuchin, S. and Fishman, C. *Family therapy techniques.* Cambridge, MA: Harvard University Press, 1981.

Manaster, G. and Corsini, R. C. *Individual Psychology.* Itasca, IL: Peacock, 1982.

Morris, W. (ed.) *American heritage dictionary of the English language.* Boston: Houghton Mifflin, 1970.

Weeks, G. R. and L'Abate, L. *Paradoxical psychotherapy.* New York: Brunner/Mazel, 1982.

2

Fantasy and Imagery

INTRODUCTION

The richness of the human imagination has provided inventive psycho-therapists with many fruitful tools for diagnosis and behavior change. Such diverse schools of therapy as psychoanalysis, behaviorism, hypno-therapy, encounter group therapy, games theory, and art and dance therapy have developed a variety of techniques based on client imagina-tion. Family therapists, too, have seen the advantages of utilizing pro-jective and expressive behaviors formulated in the imagination. Some of the techniques based on these behaviors are described here.

Virtually all people use their imaginations (Singer and McCraven, 1961), which is why imagery is such a popular tool for those interested in human behavior. Among the diverse techniques invented or adapted for couple and family work are family photographs, puppetry, poetry readings and writings, imagery, and analogical metaphors. Each appears in multiple variations to serve different purposes.

The power of imagination has fascinated humankind throughout his-tory and can be observed in parables, fairy tales, myths, epics, tribal dances, and cultural rituals (Bettelheim, 1976). Shamans, faith healers, writers, and orators make extensive use of imagery. The methods are designed primarily to change the behavior of people in the real world through some form of symbolic suggestion.

An image is not real in an objective sense. It is a representation or mental symbol of something real or fancied (Morris, 1970, p. 657). Like word symbols, images can be shared among people, although with subjective differences in shades of meaning. We symbolize in imagination the experience of the five outer senses: sight, smell, hearing, taste, and touch. Each person will image using favored sense modalities.

According to Araoz (1982, p. xx), imagery is a cognitive process akin to hypnosis. It is "any mental activity which is more experiential than critical, more subjective than outer-reality oriented, more primary process than secondary process thinking, more right hemispheric than left hemispheric."

This world of ideas is a subjective creation of the human mind based on the person's own *impressions* of reality, a personal mythology. These myths then are used both to explain objective reality and to take actions in the real world in the service of the myths.

Shared myths influence the actions of nations: "manifest destiny," "keep the world free for democracy," obtaining, maintaining or protecting a "national homeland."

People and families also create images of themselves in the world and guide their actions according to such images. The images are not only myths that capture the meaning of past experiences but lead to anticipation of future events. A family myth that says "we are an economically poor family, and victims of the 'establishment'" may lead to exceptionally frugal behavior, distrust of social institutions, and a picture of being "the little guy" long after the family has achieved affluent socioeconomic status. Family members continue to interpret the world and behave as if they were socioeconomic victims.

Many of these myths take the form of assumptive, unquestioned values and expectations that cannot be realized in the real world or with one's real partner or family. These myths may contribute to a severe narrowing of options and flexibility in the dysfunctional family. The therapist's pointing out of the rigidity or indicating new options may not be sufficient for the family to overcome the power of such myths, which are deeper than digital logic and more compelling. Araoz (1982) calls this process *negative self-hypnosis*. Through negative imagery, clients work themselves into bad feelings, frustration, pessimism, and anger, thus inhibiting constructive change. What therapists often encounter as resistance is the force of negative images expressed as habitual behavior.

Moving from experiences to imagery and from imagery to behavior constitutes a two-way translation process: It is typical that in making translations some transformations take place by adding to, omitting from, or distorting the original. Children enjoy the game of telephone in which a sentence is whispered into the ear of each child of a line of children who then wait with glee to see what sentence will come out at the end. The movie *Rashomon* presents another example of how different witnesses and participants perceive the same event.

Bandler and Grinder (1975) are among those who study those translation processes with respect to psychotherapy. They identify three processes through which experience is transformed into something different from the original reality or the symbolic reality: generalization, deletion, and distortion.

1. Generalization — the process of extracting one part of an experience and using it to represent the whole experience and all other experiences in the same category. For example, a graduate student who had difficulty in ninth-grade algebra concludes that he is unable to do any math, must fail statistics and testing, and couldn't possibly do his income tax return because he has no facility with numbers. Or think of the couple who gave birth to a firstborn learning-disabled child who decide not to have any more children because all their offspring will suffer from brain damage.

2. Deletion — "the process by which we selectively pay attention to certain dimensions of our experience and exclude others." Consider the depressed person who imagines that her whole life is a failure and believes she can do nothing worthwhile. She cites the example of not putting her best foot forward at a recent job interview as evidence that she can never get a job, ignoring the jobs she has successfully obtained in the past. Or, consider the couple who complain they no longer have any interests in common. They ignore their joint love and hopes for their children, shared religious values, common friendships, and their collection of antiques.

3. Distortion — "The process which allows us to make shifts in our experience of sensory data," such as the artist's rendering of a landscape modified by his own impressions, or the parents' notion that their baby is a genius who must be a prophet in her time.

Helping therapist and clients become more aware of the underlying images that guide behavior and creating positive images that will lead to more constructive behavior change are among the purposes of the use of imagery techniques.

Techniques based on imagery, fantasy, and metaphor depend operationally on projective/expressive behavior. The therapist sets up a stimulus situation with which the clients identify. The clients then project their own thoughts and ideas onto the situation and thereby represent themselves and their interaction in the process. This enables us to gain a better diagnostic understanding of the system. Similarly, by asking clients to go further and project new possibilities in the situation we can facilitate movement toward desired changes.

According to Rabin (1960) there are four main types of projective productions.

1. Associative. Clients are asked explicitly or implicitly to respond to a word, image, idea, or story. Explicitly it may be an immediate response, as in a word association test. Implicitly, the therapist may seek no overt response but tells the client metaphoric stories, analogies, and jokes, a common practice of Milton Erickson and his followers (Zeig, 1980). These are told as analogies without explanation. It is believed that the clients may be affected at some subconscious, right hemisphere level leading to behavior change.

2. Constructive. Clients are encouraged to make up stories, fantasies, family sculptures, poems, a particular kind of drawing (your family, your home). They can write a script of their own arguments. The construction is of their own invention but in response to a direct request by the therapist.

3. Completion. Clients are asked to complete an incomplete product such as sentences ("As a man I must . . . ; as a woman I could . . . "); finish a story; add to a fantasy or daydream initiated by the therapist, group, or another member of the family.

4. Expressive. Clients are given free expression in play, arts, crafts, writing, drama, puppetry, or dreams to represent themselves and their experience in any way they wish. They can be also asked to select and bring in "important" pictures from the family photograph album or recall early memories.

Clients reveal themselves in all forms of expressive behavior—posture, dress, the way a family seats itself in the first session. The metaphors of speech are equally eloquent. "I'm carrying a heavy burden"; "We're locked in"; "I'm all washed out"; "Everything I do stinks."

Family systems theorists believe that the presenting symptom, properly understood, is itself a metaphor for the needs of the family system (Papp, 1984). The problem for the therapist is to translate the metaphor found in the symptom into the underlying functioning of the system and its purpose.

There are some powerful advantages available to those therapists who use the techniques of imagery and metaphor:

1. Imagery and metaphor are not bound by the ordinary rules of space, time, and movement. We can be and do anything, anywhere, any time, in any combinations. We can be out in space or traveling through the body exploring inner space; be self as a child and simultaneously our adult self playing with the child; be in a mother's womb or talking with a deceased parent.

2. Imagery and metaphor are not bound by the rules of linear logic. We can think in any direction, skip from one idea or event to another with seeming caprice in any order.

3. Imagery and metaphor are suggestive. New ideas, options, and actions can be invented by the clients or suggested directly or indirectly by the therapist. The therapist can request that family members envision a scene that represents the best of all marriages, families, or worlds. They describe the scene. They are asked to enact the scene together or in imagination. The therapist assists them to restructure the scene in a way that includes new constructive relationships in the family. Clients can work out issues in the family of origin by imagining themselves as children in that family. With the help of the therapist they examine and relive those situations and family relations with greater effectiveness than they did while growing up. The therapist can help turn discouraging images and scripts into optimistic, encouraging ones.

4. Imagery and metaphor are safe experiences. Clients can experiment with any idea, option, or behavior. They can take any risk with any person or situation without the danger of external consequences. They can evaluate, erase, correct, or refine the script before translating it into behavior in the real world.

5. Imagery and metaphor are empowering and lead to greater self-control. Clients are producing the images out of their own inner resources. They learn that they can control their thoughts. Self-control makes one feel more powerful and encourages a different experience of self in world. In turn this gives one a sense of being more in control in the world.

6. Imagery and metaphor are surprising. Asking clients to be creative and imaginative poses an unexpected challenge for which they have few, if any, entrenched defenses. It is also better to hear that you have a creative mind than that you are sick or disturbed.

As with all categories of techniques, those that follow in the next chapter are not a bag of tricks. They are to be used within a theoretical framework at an appropriate time and place within the therapy. Those described illustrate the wide spectrum available and may well trigger the readers' imagination to invent new adaptations and new techniques.

RESOURCES

Ahsen, A. *Basic concepts in eidetic psychotherapy*. New York: Brandon House, 1968.

Ansbacher, H. L. and Ansbacher, R. R. (eds.) *The individual psychology of Alfred Adler*. New York: Harper & Row, 1956.

Araoz, D. L. *Hypnosis and sex therapy*. New York: Brunner/Mazel, 1982.

Assagioli, R. *Psychosynthesis*. New York: Hobbs, Dorman & Co., 1965.

Bandler, R. and Grinder, J. *The structure of magic*. Palo Alto, CA: Science and Behavior Books, 1975(A).

Bandler, R. and Grinder, J. *Patterns of the hypnotic techniques of M. H. Erickson* (2 vols.) Cupertino, CA: Meta Publications, 1975(B).

Bandler, R. and Grinder, J. *Frogs into princes: Neuro-linguistic programming.* Moab, UT: Real People Press, 1979.

Bettelheim, B. *The uses of enchantment.* New York: Knopf, 1976.

Bonime, W. *The clinical use of dreams.* New York: Basic Books, 1962.

Bry, A. *Directing the movies in your mind.* New York: Harper & Row, 1978.

Erickson, M. H. and Rossi, E. L. *Hypnotherapy: An exploratory casebook.* New York: Irvington, 1979.

Journal of Mental Imagery, 1977 to present.

Kroger, W. S. and Fezler, W. D. *Hypnosis and behavior modification: Imagery conditioning.* Philadelphia: Lippincott, 1976.

Morris, W. (ed.). *American heritage dictionary of the English language.* Boston: Houghton Mifflin, 1970.

Papp, P. *The process of change.* New York: Guilford Press, 1984.

Rabin, A. I. (ed.) *Projective techniques with children.* New York: Grune & Stratton, 1960.

Segal, S. J. (ed.) *Imagery, current cognitive approaches.* New York: Academic Press, 1971.

Sheehan, P. W. *The function and nature of imagery.* New York: Academic Press, 1972.

Sheik, A. *Imagery — Current research and application.* New York: Wiley, 1983.

Sheik, A. A. and Shaffer, J. T. (eds.) *The potential of fantasy and imagination.* New York: Random House, 1979.

Singer, J. L. *The inner world of daydreaming.* New York: Harper & Row, 1975.

Singer, J. L. and McCraven, V. Some characteristics of adult daydreaming. *Journal of Psychology*, 1961, *51*, 151–164.

Singer, J. L. and Pope, K. S. (eds.) *The power of human imagination.* New York: Plenum, 1978.

Yuille, J. C. *Imagery, memory, and cognition.* Hillsdale, NJ: Lawrence Erlbaum Associates, 1983.

Zeig, J. K. (ed.) *A teaching seminar with Milton Erickson.* New York: Brunner/Mazel, 1980.

1 | EARLY RECOLLECTIONS

Rationale

Early recollections are basically a projective tool invented by Alfred Adler (in Manaster and Corsini, 1982) to help assess the life style of the client or client system. The technique thus is originally formulated within the constructs of Adlerian psychology. Since perception is subjective and selective, and since we have a vast store of memories, any specific memory chosen for recall will be important and relevant to the client in the present moment. The way the client describes the event will highlight particular personality characteristics and goals of the person's life style, such as important themes, beliefs, attitude toward life, and preferred sensory modalities to cope with life.

Procedure

Request client, couple, or family members individually to recall the first and earliest incident that comes to mind and to describe it as if it were occurring *now*. Sample questions might be:

"Can you recall the earliest incident that comes to your mind as a very young child?"
"Can you recall the first incident that comes to your mind at an early age about your mother (father, sibling, school, etc.)?"
"Can you recall the first time you met your spouse? What happened? What impressed you? What attracted you?"

The therapist then asks, "What stands out most vividly in the recollection? What does it feel like right now as you recall this incident? Are you happy, sad, anxious, excited, etc.?"

The recollection is written down verbatim or recorded. The therapist may request a series of recollections. Each is then carefully analyzed for its manifest content. Every word is taken at face value, ignoring unconscious symbolism.

Each memory is examined for its thematic content to see what the concerns of the person are. Verbs describe such themes as passiveness, action, withholding. The objects of the actions (verbs) are likely to be related to the major goals and purposes of the person's behavior. Adjectives and adverbs describe the qualitative beliefs of the person. Those of the five sense modalities the person favors will be evident by actions of looking, touching/experiencing, hearing, and so on. Such attitudes toward life as optimism, pessimism, or being for, against, or withdrawn from people, are usually evident.

Example: Early Recollection by a Couple of Their First Meeting

Mary's recollection.

Mary: I see Tom at the other end of the room. He is dressed in a very colorful and handsome way. He is neatly dressed, not like so many of the others. Most men are creeps. He comes over and introduces himself. We talk for a long time. He is interested in what I have to say and pays a-lot of attention to me. He helps me make some decisions that I am struggling with. He wants to go out with me.

Therapist: What is most vivid?

Mary: That he pays attention to me even when other people are around.

Therapist: What do you feel when you remember this now?

Mary: Sad. He doesn't do that now.

Mary's recollection reveals several themes: (1) she is relatively passive and waits for others to initiate; (2) she wants others to pay attention to her and be interested in her; (3) she wants others to help her; (4) she enjoys the intimacy of talking over problems; (5) physical appearance is important; (6) neatness is important; (7) she is more pessimistic about life and others than optimistic (men are creeps, struggle with decisions); (8) she tends to look down on men; (9) her favored sense modalities are vision and hearing.

Tom's recollection.

Tom: I noticed that this girl is looking at me. I think she's attractive, so I go over and introduce myself. She's easy to talk to and doesn't hassle me. She seems to respect me and asks for my advice. I ask her to dance and she agrees. I ask her out and she agrees. She doesn't compete with me. When we're dancing she holds me nicely. There is a warmth about her that I like.

Therapist: What is most vivid for you?

Tom: Her warmth and the way she holds me.

Therapist: How do you feel remembering this now?

Tom: It feels good, pleasant.

Several themes come to light here: (1) physical attraction is important; (2) he wants the other person to do what he says and not hassle him; (3) he is willing to take risks and is an initiator, an active person; (4) he likes being in the superior position of helping others and being needed; (5) warm, physical contact is important; (6) he expects criticism and competition in the world and would like to protect himself from an impersonal relationship.

From the foregoing samples the therapist can assess important life style characteristics, personal needs and expectations, the complementarities and similarities between Mary and Tom. This particular use of early recollections also enables the therapist to identify the original contract between the couple. In this case he will pay attention to her, make her special, initiate things to do, and help her. These will make her feel good. She will be warm, friendly, physically close, needy of him, and agreeable, allowing him to be in a one-up position. Violations of that contract cause disappointment, anger, and hurt. We can infer that she wants more to look and to talk. He wants more to act and to touch. They need to learn one another's languages of satisfaction.

The clients can be asked to interpret their own recollections or the therapist can interpret by asking "Might it be that you are the kind of person who . . . ?"

Uses
The technique can be used with any person (except with very young children) capable of remembering and talking.

It can be used early in the therapy as a diagnostic tool; later to help make structural changes by interpreting back to the client aspects of the individual, couple, or family life style; and periodically to assess changes in the person's beliefs and perceptions as the therapy progresses. As a basically projective method, it can help resistant clients get past or around areas of difficulty that occur during the interview.

RESOURCES
Christensen, O. C. and Schramski, T. G. *Adlerian family counseling*. Minneapolis; Educational Media Corp., 1983.
Dinkmeyer, D. C., Pew, W. L., and Dinkmeyer, D. C., Jr. *Adlerian counseling and psychotherapy*. Monterey, CA: Brooks/Cole, 1979.
Dreikurs, R., Grunwald, B. B., and Pepper, F. C. *Maintaining sanity in the classroom*. New York: Harper & Row, 1971.
Manaster, G. J. and Corsini, R. J. *Individual psychology*. New York: Peacock, 1982.
Mosak, H. *On purpose*. Chicago: Alfred Adler Institute, 1977.
Nikelly, A. *Techniques for behavior change*. Springfield, IL: Charles C Thomas, 1971.

2 | FAMILY PHOTOGRAPHS

Rationale
The universal appeal of nostalgia and reminiscence makes the family photograph technique a helpful instrument for studying the impact of the past on the present. Family photographs provide a vehicle for the study of family structure, communication, and styles, as well as the roles of family members. There is an array of techniques designed to elicit certain past experiences or bring members of a family in touch with feelings toward one another that sometimes are carryovers from the past. Underlying the interventions is the assumption that the therapist's knowledge of the family's history and interactive patterns can be beneficial in understanding the family as it is now, and that the members of the family,

reexperiencing their past together, will be better able to understand one another's feelings and learn to deal with unresolved conflicts. Specific examination of family photographs can yield a wealth of data about the family's developmental history and the relationships of its members to each other. Family cutoffs can be both identified and ameliorated.

The therapist can observe many important behaviors: which pictures were shown first and last; who in the family was left out; how quickly or slowly each picture is presented; how much interest or anxiety is aroused; and how much joking and laughing accompanies the presentation. Pictures can be examined to determine closeness and distance of each family member to others and the general atmosphere of the photographs. Usually, alignments, splits, role behaviors, boundaries, communication processes, and family structures are thrown into sharp relief in this process. Customs, traditions, and special times together often are revealed.

Procedure

The procedure is described by Anderson and Malloy (1976).

If a therapist is having difficulty "reaching" a family, or a family seems to be blocking on recall about significant past events and "important others," they may be asked to bring in photographs.

A warm-up exercise which involves some sharing is recommended. The family discusses the process of obtaining and selecting photos. Difficulties often occur. Common problems may include the inability to find any picture of the entire family, inability to make a selection, and surprised reactions to what does or does not exist. Sometimes the process or problems the family expects to encounter are more significant than the photographs themselves. For example, when a family album contains no picture of the father, his nonparticipation in the life of the family is a likely issue, or he may be the only "worthy" photographer.

Looking at the photographs jointly with the family may continue over several therapy sessions. Families usually respond favorably to the request, since it shows a sign of interest in them and their heritage and generally is easy and pleasant to fulfill. It is not complex and usually does not seem to evoke much anxiety; rather it proves of high interest value. Prodding memories by using family photographs helps elicit much repressed material and evokes forgotten affect attached to specific occurrences and people. The therapist asks questions about the individuals and places in the pictures, as well as questions about mood and atmosphere. Sample questions may be:

"Who are the people in this picture?"
"Do you remember where so and so was at this time?

"How did it feel to be together on that day?"
"Who took this picture?"
"What happened after this?"
"Tell me about this room."

The following procedure often is recommended.

Each family member is asked to bring in a specific number of family photographs that say something important about the family relationships. The therapist does not give any instructions about the composition of the photographs.

She limits the number of pictures to be brought in. The pictures chosen thus have more significance because the individuals need to go through the process of selection to arrive at their final choice.

The length of time available for the exercise as well as the goals (e.g., assessment, therapy) are the best determinants of the number of photographs to be brought in as well as the span of time which is covered by the photographs. As a rule of thumb, three photographs can provide a sufficient amount of material to establish basic themes and can generally be covered within a time allowance of 15 minutes per person. If the family member is going to examine three-generational themes, a larger number of photographs and considerably more time may be required.

It is important to create a climate in which everybody feels comfortable dealing with intimate themes, since the discussion of developmental stages and themes of family life may arouse strong feelings.

The therapist needs to impose a structure to ensure the distribution of time per person and the number of photographs.

Each member of the family in turn presents the chosen photographs and tells the rest of the family members why they were chosen, the meaning they have, and the individual's feelings about them. The order and style of the presentation may be significant. Such things as which picture is presented first (or last), the speed with which the photos are shared, the level of interest or anxiety about each, and the amount of joking or seriousness of manner are of particular note. The content of each photo is also discussed, exploring the closeness and distance between family members, the degree of formality, as well as present or absent members to assess various aspects of the family system. In this process alignments, role behaviors, boundaries, communication processes, and family structures can be examined. Sometimes even the care that has been taken of the snapshots can add to our understanding of these issues.

As the person presents the photographs, other family members are encouraged to respond to the presentation with questions and observations leading to increased self-awareness and new perspectives of family patterns.

Example

The following example is from an article by Anderson and Malloy (1976).

Mr. and Mrs. C. came for help with their marital problems. Mrs. C. had been diagnosed as schizophrenic with repeated hospitalizations on psychiatric units. With each successive hospitalization their marriage seemed to deteriorate further. Though Mrs. C. was functioning reasonably well, the stigma of her illness remained as the sole focus of the marital relationship, he accusing and she bemoaning. At the time of the assessment both partners were locked in a discouraging interaction defining their life together as all bad. It became clear that their negative focus left little hope for change or the formation of reasonable goals. It was at this point that Mr. and Mrs. C. were asked to select three family photographs to bring to the next session.

Both Mr. and Mrs. C. arrived at the next session with more animation and enthusiasm than ever before. Their report of the selection process revealed a degree of communication they had thought impossible. They had unearthed an old family album and claimed to have had their first enjoyable time together in years. Mrs. C.'s previously "defective" memory was stimulated in the process of reminiscing, as each of them recalled happier times. One of the snapshots she had chosen pictured her in an outfit she had sewn. As she described the photo, her pride swelled. Remembered competence further chiseled away at the negative image she now carried as a sick patient. Mr. C. chose a picture of his wife in an evening gown which emphasized her sexuality. She was embarrassed by his choice and unable to respond positively to the complimentary statements he made. This interchange and the discussion that followed graphically demonstrated conflict and confusion in their sexual expectations and communications. Both were relieved that the issues were in the open and readily agreed to make this area the business of future sessions.

Uses

This technique can be used with any family with verbal members. It can be used to study the family structure, roles, communication, and relationships. The impact of the past on the present can be studied, and what is important for each member today can be determined by each one's selections and resulting discussions.

To study families of origin or three-generational themes, the assignment can be modified to request one to three photos from each of three generations, or a larger number of photos of significant members of the extended family.

Specific themes can be explored: power, dependency, intimacy, anxiety, male and female roles. Family members are asked to bring in pictures which relate to how they have worked out these issues over the years.

To help clarify disappointments, disparities, and goals for the future two photos would be requested: one that represents the ideal (how they wish the family was) and one the reality (how the family is).

Photographs may stimulate the family members to question family myths, rules, belief systems, and roles played by each family member. Subjective misunderstandings of past relationships can be called into question ("My mother always ignored me").

Recognizing oneself in a mirror or a photograph can be a rewarding discovery. Consequently, positive responses to one's own image are found even among the severely disturbed. Although no dramatic cures have been noted, pictures may serve as a vehicle for increased socializing between hospital personnel and patients.

RESOURCES

Akert, R. U. *Photoanalysis*. New York: Wyden, 1974.

Anderson, C. and Malloy, E. Family photographs: In treatment and training. *Family Process*, 1976, *15*(2), 259–264.

Bodin, A. and Ferber, S. How to go beyond the use of language. In A. Ferber et al., *The book of family therapy*. Boston: Houghton Mifflin, 1973.

Corlentz, A. L. Use of photographs in a family mental health clinic. *American Journal of Psychiatry*, 1964, *121*, 601–602.

Entin, A. The use of photographs and family albums in family therapy. In A. Gurman (ed.), *Questions and answers in the practice of family therapy*. New York: Brunner/Mazel, 1981.

Ferber, A., Mendelsohn, M., and Napier, A. *The book of family therapy*. Boston: Houghton Mifflin, 1973.

Kaslow, F. W. Family therapy: Viewpoints and perspectives. *Clinical Social Work Journal*, 1973, *1*, 196–207.

Kaslow, F. W. and Friedman, J. Utilization of family photos and movies in family therapy. *Journal of Marriage and Family Counseling*, 1977, *3*(1), 19–27.

Martin, A. Nostalgia. *American Journal of Psychoanalysis*, 1954, *14*, 93–104.

Paul, N. L. and Paul, B. B. *A marital puzzle*. New York: Norton, 1975.

3 | FAMILY PUPPET INTERVIEW

Rationale
The family puppet interview provides many opportunities to observe the visible as well as the covert ways that family members communicate with each other. The puppet choices, the conflicts expressed in the fantasy,

the postplay discussion when members are invited to associate to the story, the inquiry about the relationship of the story to the family's functioning — all give important clues about the family and the available ego strength for confronting problems.

As a family fantasy gets played out through the dramatization of a story, conflict emerges within the characters' interactions. The form and content of these family fantasies usually center around one or more themes that often seem to be an additional, symbolic response to the therapist's initial question to the family, "Why did you come for therapy?"

Procedure

This procedure is described by Bing (1970) for use with a child or an entire family.

In an individual interview, the child is asked to select a number of hand puppets from a representative variety and then is asked to use these puppets to make up a pretend television story. Following the child's story, the clinician gathers associations to the material by "interviewing" the puppets and/or the puppeteer, much as one interviews a performer after a show. In the postplay puppet interview the child is encouraged to associate to portions of his story as the therapist seeks to validate clinical hunches or clarify portions of the material. In the final part of the assessment the therapist talks with the child about the story itself and possible relationships to his real-life situation.

In a family interview each family member is asked to define the problem as he sees it. Most frequently, the family consensus identifies one member as the "problem." An important outcome sought in this initial joint family task is to help members begin to view their family as an interactional system in which each is involved with the others.

To present the rationale and task of the puppet story the therapist asks the family to play together for a while and presents them with a basket of puppets. The family may take a few minutes to look through them and choose a few that interest them. The therapist encourages the family members to leave the formality of their chairs, giving tacit permission for them to "regress" together in a play situation. As the family members select their puppets, the therapist observes their individual behaviors and their interaction, noting which puppets are selected, rejected, avoided, and so on. Sometimes one member intrusively selects puppets for another while others seem to wait for subliminal feedback about their choices. The puppets may represent some aspect of the self or significant others. The idiosyncratic meaning the puppet has for the puppeteer, however, may become clear through the interaction and conflict portrayed within the story as well as through the poststory discussion when members are asked to think about which puppets they chose and why.

When the puppets are put away, the members return to the discussion circle where they are encouraged to associate to the story they have just played. Each member might be asked to think of a title for the story; a theme, moral, or lesson that one might learn from the story; the character each would most want to be; the character each would least like to be. Family members are asked to comment on ways in which the story is representative of their family. The therapist then tries to help the family connect the story with issues that seem relevant to the conflict areas for them.

Example

The A. family was selected for the puppet diagnostic interview because of the parents' tendencies to intellectualize and deny feelings, especially aggressive ones. The family listened wordlessly as the directions for the task were given. When the puppets were put on the floor, however, Mr. A. asked for clarification, "Are there certain kinds of puppet we should choose?" Told he could pick any he liked, he anxiously pursued the therapist with such questions as "Is this to be nonverbal, or what?"

In contrast to his father's anxiety, Tommy, age 12, inspected the puppets and quickly chose the devil and the skeleton, "I know what the story's gonna be . . . 'The Haunted Castle' . . . and the devil and the skeleton are gonna be in charge. . . . " His father laughed, "Oh yeah?"

The identified client Stephen, age 10, picked up the pirate with the patched eye and scarred face. Holding it over his face, he said to nobody in particular, "Hi, folks . . . gimme all your money." He laughed softly to himself.

Mother chose two furry puppets, a lion and a dog, and absent-mindedly rubbed their soft fur against her face as she waited for the others to finish. The lion, she said, was "reformed, he's not fierce anymore" and the dog, . . . "Well, he was like Joe, the family dog, who had been put to sleep." Tears filled her eyes as she talked.

Louise, the 14-year-old, fingered the puppets in a bored, desultory way, then chose the witch and the queen. Later she related the story of the wicked witch trying to kill Snow White because she was jealous of her beauty, a theme of jealousy and rivalry that was later evident in interaction with her mother.

Father was the last to finish. He chose two females and emphasized emphatically that they were "kind, not mean, ladies . . . they have caring eyes, they play tricks, but nice tricks not mean tricks."

In spite of the parents' tremendous efforts to control the plot line and eliminate any trace of conflict, the children succeeded in playing a story filled with rage, competitiveness, and self-destruction. The parents' fear of aggression, their attempts to control the process as well as the plot of the story were evident in their initial approach to the task.

Questions are raised for consideration:

1. Does father have a great need to be "right" and please authority figures? Does he believe that females play tricks and need to be watched or are they all prostitutes "turning tricks"?
2. Does mother identify herself with Joe and see her husband as a lion in need of taming?
3. What is the purpose of the rivalry between mother and daughter?
4. How are anger, competition, and conflict expressed in this family if you are not allowed to do so overtly and directly?
5. What is the purpose of such a strong need for control and possibly revenge?

Uses

In clinical work with children the use of puppets can be valuable both diagnostically and therapeutically because of the richness of the symbolic material elicited in spontaneous play. The therapist can enter the puppet play directly, through questions, or by suggesting and redirecting the flow of interaction in order to produce systems changes. Structural therapists use the technique as a part of the "enactment process" of the therapeutic strategy. Families unskilled in putting thoughts and feelings into words or who manipulate others with intellectualization can use the puppet drama to cut through defenses and examine family dynamics in a nonthreatening way. This technique is most useful for families with children aged 5 to 12 who may find it difficult to talk to the therapist directly about family problems.

RESOURCES
Bing, E. The conjoint family drawing. *Family Process*, 1970, *9*, 173–194.
Minuchin, S., Montalvo, B., Guerney, B., Rosman, B., and Schumer, F. *Families of the slums*. New York: Basic Books, 1967.

4 | POETRY AND SONG LYRICS IN COUPLES GROUPS

Rationale
Poetry has always been a doorway to the soul, to the truths that underlie facts and experiences. It is a way for individuals to get to the essence of their lives and feelings by creating their own poems or through identification with the works of poets who better articulate those meanings.

Poetry therapy has long been in use. Recent adaptations have been made to work with couple groups.

Poetry affords a method of facilitating group process and breaking down resistance with couples. Couples often come to therapy with an inability to relate to each other effectively. Communication remains a primary factor in marital dysfunctioning.

Mazza and Prescott (1981) describe the use of poetry as a therapeutic tool giving couples the opportunity to express themselves in unique and nonthreatening ways. As they increase their abilities to express emotions verbally, they develop more positive identities as well as move from indirect to more direct, effective communication. Poetry is also helpful to the therapist in breaking through initial resistance and facilitating constructive communication.

Procedure

All of the following material is based on the method developed by Mazza and Prescott (1981). There are many ways of employing poetry with a single couple, a couple group, or a family. The following methods are primarily directed toward a couple group.

1. A poem may be read to the group by the therapist or a group member, who then invites reactions that can be directed to the poem as a whole or a particular line or image.
2. The group is asked to construct a collaborative poem in which each member contributes lines to the poem. This requires the therapist to determine a theme or feeling in the group and proceed to develop it through the poem.
3. The group is presented with a poem or song. Couples are then asked to move to separate areas of the room and develop a two-line statement about the meaning of the poem to them. Couples later have the opportunity to share the two-line poems when the group is brought together again.
4. Utilization of poetic images or symbols may be derived from group members' dialogue.
5. Clients are encouraged to bring to sessions a poem or song which they found helpful.

Mazza and Prescott say, "The actual introduction of poetry into group sessions may be as simple as the therapist expressing a wish to share a poem with the group. Another means of introduction is to connect the content or image of a poem with the dialogue in a session" (p. 54).

Examples

Mazza and Prescott describe how poetry was utilized as a technique in a short-term couples group designed to help couples committed to developing a relationship or rediscovering ways to make the relationship more rewarding. The goals included the growth of the individual as well as the couple.

The primary theme of the opening session was the maintenance of space in relationship. The therapist planned to use the lyrics of John Denver's song "Looking for Space" to introduce the theme and facilitate discussion. However, the group was already dealing with this issue. The poem/song proved to be helpful in connecting the individual expressions and providing closure for the sessions.

A couple was married for five years and was experiencing the strains of dual career demands. Carol King's song "Bitter with the Sweet" was brought in to share with the group. The lyrics elicited common themes from the entire group. They agreed that taking time and space for themselves was all right. Some members recognized the fact that there are both bitter and sweet aspects of their relationships.

A theme that grew out of the discussion and interaction centered on trying to feel complete, which then became the title of the group's effort toward a collaborative poem. The reading of this poem provided further cohesion and validation. Group members responded to the poem as an indication of what they were feeling. They were able to provide images and metaphors that served as an instrument for self-disclosures.

Stephen Crane's poem "If I Should Cast Off This Tattered Coat" was shared with the group by the therapist. The purpose was to deal with the risks and anxieties in new experiences. Subsequently, each couple shared and discussed the poem. They were later brought together and constructed couplets, which proved to be particularly helpful in pointing out differences in the way that the partners viewed various issues. It pointed out the similarities of their thinking and feeling, thus validating their relationship.

Simon and Garfunkel's song "The Sounds of Silence" was helpful in dealing with many of the unspoken concerns of the group. This selection provided the transition to termination issues. One member shared a closing poem/song by Gilberto Gil entitled "Here and Now." It provided a validation of the group and its relationships. The members reminded each other of the importance of dealing with the here and now.

Uses

Poetry as a medium in therapy offers the potential to generalize feelings that clients may be apprehensive about revealing or to capitalize on childhood fantasies. It can provide a nonthreatening means to express feelings. As a starting point in group interactions, poetry therapy affords an opportunity for therapists to observe patterns of communication.

Clients who are inarticulate may have trouble with this technique. Consideration of time and appropriateness in using poetry as a technique is essential. Introducing poetry may serve the needs of the therapist better than those of the clients. The therapist should be prepared with a few poems but should also be ready to discard them if they are not applicable in a particular session.

Finally, the group's ability to get past the poem to a focus on the development of interpersonal skills may prove a major determinant in choosing poetry as a medium.

RESOURCES

Blanton, S. *The healing power of poetry*. New York: Crowell, 1960.

Buck, L. A. and Kramer, A. Poetry as a means of group facilitation. *Journal of Humanistic Psychology*, 1974, *14*(1), 57–71.

Edgar, K. F. and Hazley, R. Validation of poetry therapy as a group therapy technique. In J. J. Leedy (ed.), *Poetry therapy: The use of poetry in the treatment of emotional disorders*. Philadelphia: Lippincott, 1969.

Gladding, S. T. The creative use of poetry in the counseling process. *Personnel and Guidance Journal*, 1979, *57*(6), 285–287.

Lerner, A. (ed.) *Poetry in the therapeutic experience*. New York: Pergamon Press, 1978.

Leedy, J. J. Principles of poetry therapy. In *Poetry therapy: The use of poetry in the treatment of emotional disorders*. Philadelphia: Lippincott, 1969.

Leedy, J. J. (ed.) *Poetry the healer*. Philadelphia: Lippincott, 1973.

Lessner, J. W. The poem as catalyst in group counseling. *Personnel and Guidance Journal*, 1974, *53*(1), 33–38.

Mazza, N. Poetry: A therapeutic tool in the early stages of alcoholism treatment. *Journal of Studies on Alcohol*, 1979, *40*(1), 123–128.

Mazza, N. and Prescott, B. U. Poetry: An ancillary technique in couples group therapy. *American Journal of Family Therapy*, 1981, *9*, 53–57.

Schloss, G. A. *Psychopoetry: A new approach to self-awareness through poetry therapy*. New York: Grosset & Dunlap, 1976.

5 | "IF I WERE"

Rationale

The technique as it is described here has been adapted for family therapy by Esther Koenigsberg.*

The technique, "If I Were" is a projective sentence completion game. It has been used with individuals, groups, and families. Members of the family imagine themselves or one another as some sort of inanimate object which serves as metaphor for that person. It helps family members zero in on certain feelings they are having about how a person really is or ideally can be. It helps the therapist gain understanding of each person's

---

*Koenigsberg, E. Graduate student in family therapy, Queens College, 1984.

perceived role and place in the family and in society. It spotlights issues in interaction such as how do a rabbit and a lion communicate? The therapist can use it to break through difficulties with a nonverbal family or control the talking in a family that overintellectualizes.

Procedure

The "If I Were" technique can be used in a variety of ways. It is often used as a fast-moving game. The therapist initiates the game by starting a sentence and having the family finish it. As soon as they are finished with one round the therapist says another "incomplete" sentence. This can be done for several rounds, covering a variety of inanimate objects. Sentences are invented by the therapist to include metaphors that include different sensory and thought modalities and begin as follows:

If I (he, she, this family) were a vehicle, I (he, she, it) would be. . . .
If I were a state in the United States, I would be. . . .
If I were a fruit, I would be. . . .
If I were a color, I would be. . . .
If I were a mood, I would be. . . .
If I were a sin, I would be. . . .
If I were a tool, I would be. . . .
If I were an animal, I would be. . . .
If I were a form of transportation, I would be. . . .
If I were a famous person from literature or history, I would be. . . .
If I were an odor, I would be. . . .
If I were a food, I would be. . . .

The game should move quickly, and members should have little time to ponder. It is suggested that the game be recorded so that it can be replayed to the family and they can react. A member might also have a comment about somebody else's sentence.

Clients may also be asked to qualify their choices with appropriate adjectives — *pale* blue, a *cuddly* teddy bear, a *large* station wagon. They can be asked what the metaphor means to them. "A stallion is proud, powerful and fast. He leads and protects the herd."

Examples

Mr. and Mrs. O. started therapy several months after their first child was born. They were both feeling very tense and anxious. After the second interview the therapist felt that the couple were not talking about their feelings but rather spending much energy on recounting details of their arguments. The therapist briefly explained the game and instructed the couple to complete the sentences.

Therapist: If I were a color I'd be . . .
Mr. O: I'd be light blue.
Mrs. O: I'd be pale yellow.
Therapist: If I were a car I'd be a . . .
Mrs. O: I'd be a four-door Ford.
Mr. O: I'd be a station wagon.
Therapist: If I were an animal I would be . . .
Mr. O: I'd be a homing pigeon.
Mrs. O: I'd be a puppy.
Therapist: Would you react to one another's choices?
Mr. O: I like that you said pale yellow. That is something about you I like. Sort of subdued, but very special. But I don't picture you as a Ford. You're more like one of these new convertible Volkswagens, sporty and practical.
Mrs. O: I am so surprised to hear you say that. I imagine that you picture me as "old reliable." The unattractive person who you are stuck with. Homing pigeon! How do you see yourself as a homing pigeon?
Mr. O: Well you know, I go out on my "missions" every day, but I return to my nest. And I like it. To my warm, sexy puppy. Too bad she is snappy.

The game helped the therapist open up an honest dialogue between Mr. and Mrs. O. Both were encouraged from the warm way they responded to one another. Mrs. O., who was feeling negatively about herself both physically and emotionally since the birth of their baby, was encouraged by her husband's response. She was enthused that her husband saw her as attractive and special. The couple discussed their similarities (both pale colors) and their differences (Mrs. O. was feeling rejected as if her husband was tired of her). The O's discussed both their strengths and weaknesses and also their difficulty in discussing apprehensions together. They discussed their need to have a "perfect" marriage and their fear of arguing. The game helped the couple see that much of their nervousness resulted from lack of communication. Each was unsure about how the other felt and conjured up many negative thoughts. The therapist had to deal with their inability to exchange compliments freely. The "game" helped them praise each other in an indirect manner. Once the barrier was broken and their feelings were out in the open, the therapist was able to build on the positive framework, explore many issues, and help the couple develop more productive ways of communicating.

A variation might be asking clients to complete the sentences for another member of the family. This helps the therapists as well as the family gain insight into how each perceives the others and to discover the degree of congruence in perceptions.

The meaning of the choices by or about a given person can be put together to form an interesting profile of how that person is perceived.

Metaphor	Choice	Meaning of Choice
Animal	Stallion	Proud, strong, protective leader
Color	Red	Strong, aggressive
Geographic feature	Ocean	Big and deep, makes waves, erodes shoreline
Tool	Knife	Sharp, cutting, dangerous, can be useful
Famous person	Napoleon	A dictator, very bright, built many things

The therapist might conclude the game with a reflective statement, such as, "It appears that you think of yourself as someone who is strong and aggressive, intelligent, and able to do many creative things. Apparently, sometimes your strength and enthusiasm overlap the boundaries of others in the family, making moves for them, and can be risky or painful for them."

Uses

Having family members complete sentences is useful when a family is having difficulty opening up. Using inanimate objects to portray feelings about self and others is a nonthreatening way for people to express both positive and negative feelings. Because every image can be interpreted in many ways, a clever therapist will use the symbols to reframe certain situations and will use symbols as themes that can be dealt with in sessions. Positive attribution to certain images can help strengthen a person's self-image or raise the status of a family member.

The technique may be used in as many ways as the therapist's imagination permits. Sentences to be completed might be given as a homework assignment. The therapist might examine the choice of answers and look at other dynamics in terms of completing an assignment.

In terms of family interaction, a therapist may also look at each person's "object" in relation to the others. What does it feel like to be a fish in a family of land animals? How is it that one family member is a huge watermelon while the others are very small (e.g., nut, grape, strawberry)? Does everybody in the family have to be the same (e.g., are they all sport cars?). Many family dynamics are brought to the therapist's attention much more quickly than they would be through standard questioning.

Therapists from a variety of backgrounds may benefit from the use of the "If I Were" technique. Depending on the thinking of the particular therapist, the direction of the "game" will differ.

RESOURCE

Hiebert, W. J. De-escalating couples' power struggles. In A. S. Gurman (ed.), *Questions and answers in the practice of family therapy*. New York: Brunner/Mazel, 1981, pp. 431–434.

6 | CREATING ANALOGOUS SITUATIONS

Rationale
The use of metaphoric interventions can help a client (family or individual) both to define a problem more clearly and to aid in the problem's resolution. Metaphors are useful ways of talking about human experience and may succinctly symbolize complex communication or behavior patterns by suggesting one statement or description that resembles something else that is going on within an interactive system. By focusing on the analogy, the behavior change may occur spontaneously in line with the goals of the therapy.

Techniques involving metaphors are rooted in the strategic class of therapies exemplified in the works of Haley (1973, 1976), Watzlawick, Weakland, and Fisch (1974) and Erickson (Zeig, 1980). Augustus Napier and Carl Whitaker (1978) and others who work in the symbolic–experimental mode use metaphors to invade and challenge family relationships and to playfully "unstick" persisting dysfunctional patterns.

Procedure
Once the therapist clearly understands the family problems, she can select an activity or situation that resembles the problem area but is relatively anxiety free. She may talk about it, gathering additional information and engaging the family members. A task is assigned in this area which has the desirable outcome in both the problematic and trouble-free areas. Thus a discussion of labor–management negotiations or the dangers of nuclear war might be helpful for a family at war. Tending a garden might be a useful experience as an analogy for childrearing. Teaching a pet new behavior could serve in a situation where one partner is determined to change another.

In a completely different way metaphors can also be used to dramatize symptoms. A person who continuously complains can be characterized as a "tragedy queen" or "disaster chaser." The family always looking back can be described as "Lot's wife."

The therapist does not at any time explain the metaphor in relation to the original problem area. The message is an indirect suggestion for new ideas and behaviors.

Examples
The following example is given by Milton Erickson in Haley's (1973) *Uncommon Therapy*.

A couple enters therapy and one of their problematic areas is their sexual relationship. The wife feels her husband is not sensitive to her needs. She feels ignored and is dissatisfied with her husband's technique. The therapist chooses another situation in which the couple spends time together that includes processes resembling sexual activity but is more easily talked about. Erickson's example of having the couple talk about having a meal together is excellent for this purpose. During the discussion the therapist may ask if there is a time they have a meal without children, just the two of them; he may comment on how different people approach eating in different ways; some may start out slowly enjoying an appetizer and lingering over a bowl of soup, and others may like to dive right into the meat and potatoes. He can also say how "some husbands compliment their wives on how nice everything looks and others just don't notice; so their wives then don't really bother to try." The therapist makes sure that as the discussion proceeds the couple doesn't overtly connect to their sexual difficulties. The purpose is to have the connection unconsciously planted. The therapist encourages the couple to choose a night and together plan a dinner. They are to show appreciation for each other's taste and to bring up only pleasant topics during the meal. They are encouraged to stimulate each other's appetites. The likelihood of this sensual, positive mood carrying over the sexual relations is enhanced.

The expression, "It's as American as motherhood and apple pie" can provide an analogy to explore the connections and relationships within a family and to communicate concepts that relate to properties of baking a pie as a family pie metaphor. Rule (1983) describes many uses of this metaphor. Elements like the parts or slices contribute to the whole, the ingredients for good taste, varying the cooking recipes, which can be passed down for generations, etc., lend themselves to entrance into the symptomatic systems that families may present. Questions suggested by Rule (1983) for stimulating problem resolution may be:

"What ingredients in the pie need to be changed for everyone in the family to enjoy it more?"

"What key ingredient is missing from this family pie?"

"Whose responsibility is it to see the pie doesn't burn?"

"Let's say this pie represents the family problem; who should get the biggest slice?"

"What size slice should each member get based on what he or she contributes to the problem?"

Uses

The therapist's use of metaphoric communication serves as an intervention technique designed to stimulate new ways of couple and family communication, both verbally and behaviorally. Because it is indirect it is less likely to stimulate resistance or threaten the existing order.

Another use of metaphor is in the total assessment and understanding of a family or couple's current life situation in which a symptom is viewed as a metaphor for the total set of family dysfunctions. The metaphor is identified and tracked and problem resolution is geared around changing perception and behavior. In Minuchin's videotape *Taming Monsters*, Taming Monsters is the metaphor for the family's difficulties in which each member views every other as a monster who won't do what he or she is supposed to do.

The therapist's use of metaphor is most effective when it is in line with the flow of an individual's or family's unique representation modality (i.e., visual, auditory, kinesthetic) for its greatest impact. In example 1 above, planning and eating a dinner with its sensual and cooperative components is used as a visual and kinesthetic analogous metaphor for the couple's sexual dysfunction.

RESOURCES

Barker, P. *Using metaphors in psychotherapy.* New York: Brunner/Mazel, 1985.

Haley, J. *Uncommon therapy.* New York: Norton, 1973.

Haley, J. *Problem solving therapy.* New York: Harper & Row, 1976.

Madanes, C. *Strategic family therapy.* San Francisco: Jossey-Bass, 1981.

Madanes, C. *Behind the one way mirror.* San Francisco: Jossey-Bass, 1984.

Napier, A. Y. and Whitaker, C. A. *The family crucible.* New York: Harper & Row, 1978.

Rule, W. Family therapy and the pie metaphor. *Journal of Marital and Family Therapy*, 1983, *9*, 101–104.

Watzlawick, P., Weakland, J., and Fisch, R., *Change: Principles of problem formation and problem solution.* New York: Norton, 1974.

Zeig, J. K. (ed.) *A teaching seminar with Milton H. Erickson.* New York: Brunner/Mazel, 1980.

7 | SENTENCE COMPLETION

Rationale

Sentence completion is both a diagnostic and a therapeutic tool. It is believed that clients reluctant to share their feelings would more easily do it through their responses to open-ended sentences. Open-ended sentences are ambiguous stimuli which encourage the clients to project a response from within. Because the clinician can invent any sentence stems appropriate to the case and is not using a standard form, we include sentence completion here as a technique.

The client's responses express his inner perception of events, people, and surroundings. By the way the client completes the sentences, both his conscious and unconscious ideas can be better understood. Clients are often surprised by their own answers or pattern of answers.

Clients' responding verbally in front of their spouses encourages interaction. They learn of each other's thoughts and feelings. They see the difficulties and the issues that concern each other and their relationship. Similarities and differences between them become evident.

Procedure

The therapist introduces the technique as a means to help the clients' understanding of themselves and their relationship and to improve their communication. After getting their approval to try it, the therapist seats the clients facing each other. Gumina (1980) suggests the following instructions to the clients:

Therapist: I am going to give you a series of openings to sentences. For each such opening, you are asked to take turns in completing them. You should go on taking turns until I change the sentence. Obviously, you may change your ending as your turn comes again, even when it is the same sentence you have already completed before. You may say anything that comes to your mind. Please be as free as possible, and do not interpret your, or your spouse's, endings. When we finish with the whole series of sentences, we will discuss their content. Do you have any questions?

Among the kinds of stems the therapist can use are:

I must . . .
I wish I could . . .
When I am angry I . . .
I show my love by . . .
I am significant when . . .
If I were to change, the danger would be . . .

If I had the courage, I would . . .
If you knew me, you would . . .
The person I love must . . .
My mother (father) is . . .
My favorite person is . . .
The best time of my life is when . . .

The stems chosen by the therapist may vary in degree of ambiguity from "I must . . . " to "My favorite person is. . . . "

During the process the therapist may ask the clients to repeat important endings or encourage them. An interesting ending given by a client may be used to construct the next stem. "I MUST *be a good girl*" can be followed by "A GOOD GIRL MUST. . . . "

Example
The following example is quoted from Gumina, 1980 (pp. 203–205).

Tom: IF I WEREN'T SO ANGRY I might listen to you.
Joan: IF I WEREN'T SO ANGRY I wouldn't pressure you.
T: IF I WEREN'T SO ANGRY you might like me more.
J: IF I WEREN'T SO ANGRY we could have fun together.
T: IF I WEREN'T SO ANGRY I'd be happier.
J: ONE WAY I PUNISH YOU IS to withhold my feelings.
T: ONE WAY I PUNISH YOU IS to be angry a lot.
J: ONE WAY I PUNISH YOU IS to do things without you.
T: ONE WAY I PUNISH YOU IS to not have sex with you.
J: IF I TRUST YOU I MIGHT spend more time with you.
T: IF I TRUSTED YOU I MIGHT not worry about your screwing other men.
J: IF I TRUSTED YOU I MIGHT share more of myself with you.
T: IF I TRUSTED YOU I MIGHT be able to have an erection.
J: THE GOOD THING ABOUT NOT HAVING SEX WITH YOU IS that I don't have to perform.
T: THE GOOD THING ABOUT NOT HAVING SEX WITH YOU IS that you won't compare me to your lover.
J: THE GOOD THING ABOUT NOT HAVING SEX WITH YOU IS that I can masturbate more.
T: THE GOOD THING ABOUT NOT HAVING SEX WITH YOU IS that I can, too.
J: IF WE WERE CLOSER I'd show you how much I really care about you.
T: IF WE WERE CLOSER I wouldn't keep punishing you for having an affair.
J: IF WE WERE CLOSER we would be able to solve our problems.

T: IF WE WERE CLOSER, I'd stop threatening to divorce you; we'd work things out.

(Many other sentences can be completed prior to the wrap-up sentences, which occurs in this example below.)

J: I'M BEGINNING TO SUSPECT that we have a lot of work to do together.
T: I'M BEGINNING TO SUSPECT that we can save our marriage if we want to.
J: I'M BEGINNING TO SUSPECT that we'll both have to make some changes.

In this example, the clients gained some insight into each other's expectations and better understanding of their problems and feelings. They better saw each other's needs and gained an idea of what they had to do in order to improve their relationship. They became closer and more attuned to each other.

Uses
The sentence completions technique can be used in marital, sex, and family therapy. It can provide insight and new perceptions resulting in changed feelings. By listening to each other and to oneself, it can help the participants see the direction of change in order to improve their relationship. It can be used to break an impasse in communication or to get beyond a power play. Since the therapist makes up the stems, sentence completion is more useful after the therapist already knows something about the client system.
    Children are also capable of responding to this technique.

RESOURCE
Gumina, J. M. Sentence completion as an aid to sex therapy. *Journal of Marital and Family Therapy*, 1980, *62*, 201–206.

8 | VALUES CLARIFICATION:
THE "MOM ALWAYS SAID . . . DAD ALWAYS SAID . . . "
VALUES SENTENCE COMPLETION FORM

Rationale
Adapted from group work, the "Mom Always Said . . . " sentence completion form by Krajeacki and Linhardt (unpublished) is completed by each participant in the therapy. It elicits the perceived values of one's

parents and the values of the parents themselves as they report them. It is somewhat similar to obtaining the "scripts" and "tapes" of families in Transactional Analysis. As with all sentence completion techniques, it is a projective device. It is adapted here for couple and family therapy by John Linhardt.* We include it as a technique because it is a clinical device rather than a statistically reliable and valid measuring instrument.

Being able to identify, label, discuss, and compare values is a way in which a family can better understand its members and itself. Seeing the degree of congruence between what one person says are the other's values and the list prepared by the other is also instructive. Looking for similarities, differences, and complementarities in values helps us better evaluate the system. The behavior observed makes more sense, and possibilities for correction of misunderstandings are improved as the existing values are clarified.

Values show what we tend to do with our limited time and energy and are thus central to the actions of the family. They are the results of hammering out a style of life in a certain set of surroundings such as the family system. After a sufficient amount of subjective experiences with life, certain patterns of evaluating and behaving tend to develop. Some things are regarded as right, desirable, and worthy, and others as wrong. Other people are expected to conform to our values and beliefs, at least to some extent. Many of the conflicts in the family are based on a failure to meet those expectations or to reward what each person considers to be "right" behavior. False assumptions about another person's values supported by actions in the service of those assumptions are also a source of conflict.

The symptom itself may be in the service of family values. For example, a value found in many dysfunctional families is that it is okay to be sick to reduce tensions, but it is not okay to be angry.

Procedure

The children, or identified child, are asked to fill in the "Mom Always Said . . . " values sentence completion form and follow the directions. If a child is too young to write the answers, the therapist can write them in. Each parent is asked to complete a form at the same time. Values expressed by each parent are recorded on the form and whether or not the respondent agrees or disagrees with the value is circled.

A discussion follows completion of the forms to identify and clarify

---

*The "Mom Always Said . . . " instrument is unpublished and was invented by Richard Krajeacki, 456 Spruce Street, Morgantown, West Virginia 26505 and John Linhardt, Queens College. The procedures for the use of the instrument and the example were developed by John Linhardt, a graduate student at Queens College.

the values described. Similarities, differences, and complementarities are explored by the family. Questions can be posed such as:

"What values do you have in common?"
"Are they of similar importance?"
"Which values are different?"
"Do they cause conflict?"
"Which values are reciprocal so that they complement one another?"
"Which values surprised you?"

   Misunderstandings are reviewed and corrected. Participants may well insist that their perception of another person's values are right and the other person's perceptions of his own values are wrong. In such a case the therapist can inquire of the first person: "Do you agree that this is how it seems to the other person?" The therapist then asks the second person: "Can you agree that you seem to come across this way to the first person, regardless of what is intended?" By making each right and accepting of the other's position, the meaning and outcome of the reciprocal behavior can now be realistically discussed.

Example
The R. family came in with the presenting problem of an acting-out adolescent. Tom, the adolescent, was asked by the therapist to fill out the blanks on the "Mom Always Said . . . " sheet and follow the directions. While Tom was completing the assignment, his parents were seen for a therapy session. When Tom returned to the room, his parents were given a blank sheet of the instrument. Each was asked to respond orally to the categories. (It was interesting to note that Tom had written almost the exact wording of his parents' responses.) After each parent spoke, Tom's answer was read out. A copy of the form with his responses follows below.

Tom's Responses on Mom Always Said . . .

Most parents tell their children a lot of things (often over and over again). Below are 10 areas of life and under each area are sentences to complete.
Example: *MONEY*
Mom always told me "Save your money for a rainy day." _____A   D
Dad always said "Have fun with your money."_____A   D
(Complete the sentence using what your parents would have said. Then circle (A) if you agree or (D) if you disagree. P.S. As you can see from the example, moms and dads don't always agree.)

ECOLOGY
Mom always said "Make good use of what you have."   (A)   D
Dad always said   "   "   "   "   "   "   A   D

SEX

Mom always said "You're too young for it."   A   D

Dad always said: "You're too young for it at this age, but . . . "   (A)   D

RELIGION

Mom always said "You've got to go to church Sunday."   (A)   D

Dad always said "You've got to go to church Sunday."   A   (D)

LEISURE

Mom always said "You should spend your time doing something."   A   (D)

Dad always said "Why don't you relax for a change."   (A)   D

POLITICS

Mom always said "Everything is politics these days."   A   (D)

Dad always said "You got to know someone to get places."   A   (D)

WORK

Mom always said "I don't think you're old enough to work."   A   (D)

Dad always said "   "   "   "   "   "   "   A   (D)

FAMILY

Mom always said "We should do more family things."   (A)   D

Dad always said "We should do more family things."   A   (D)

OTHER RACES OR GROUPS

Mom always said "You shouldn't worry about others."   A   (D)

Dad always said "You should always try to stay ahead."   A   (D)

SELF-IMAGE

Mom always told me I was "Always negative about things."   A   (D)

Dad always told me I was "Not a good listener."   A   (D)

FUTURE

Mom always said I would end up as doctor or dentist   A   (D)

Dad always said I would end up as lawyer, engineer,   A   (D)
                                   involved in computers

A discussion followed. The focus of much of it was on areas in which Tom had disagreed with his parents.

The parents were amazed that YES, Tom did hear what they had said many times. Tom as a teenager did hear, but often had his own value system. The parents were unaware of Tom's values or feelings and no negotiations were taking place.

Apparently Tom was more amenable to some parental values when expressed by one parent, but not by the other, and it varied according to categories (see, for example, ecology, religion, and family).

Tom disagrees with his parents' vocational plans for him. Mom and Dad disagree on whether Tom should be doing something or relaxing, thus giving him a double and opposite message. The parents' value about politics indicates that they feel powerless and probably enact the same powerlessness with their son, hoping that a more powerful authority, the therapist, will help them get somewhere with him. Tom feels more powerful and is rebellious. He believes he is old enough to work and choose his own career.

Further examination of similarities, differences, and content enabled the family to improve their patterns of relationship and to reconsider some of their values.

A variation is to have the family negotiate a single answer to each question while the therapist carefully observes the process.

Uses

The values sentence completion form is used to identify the existing values and how they combine systemically. It can be used with couples and families. The content of the values is also instructive in understanding the life style of the family and the presenting symptoms. Since values are in effect priorities, it enables the therapist to understand and predict the flow of energy in the system. However, stated values may be at variance with what people actually do — manifest values. Therefore, what is reported on the instrument and what is said in discussion should be compared with what the participants actually do. Adolescents, particularly, may state or agree with idealistic or parental values and yet behave quite differently. (See also the "Value Assessment Comparison" technique which follows.)

9 | VALUE ASSESSMENT COMPARISON

Rationale

The technique is based on an interactionist/system approach, assuming that any interactional relationship can be viewed in a holistic way and can give insight into the persons who make up the system. It can be used in the family system as well as in a couple relationship.

The technique assumes that values and social roles are part of a social-psychological process. The technique is built on the perceptions and interpretations of the individual members of the couple or family. It elicits awareness and expression of the values that affect the relationship. The technique gives the therapist and the clients access to similarities, complementarities, differences, and problems.

Procedure

Floyd (1982) describes a particular method for using this technique.

A minimum of two family members must participate in the process. An individual assignment is given to be completed at home, which is discussed in the next session.

Introducing the exercise may be done as follows:

Therapist: I am going to give you an assignment that deals with values. When thinking about values, think about objects, events, or activities you consider most important to you. Each of you will prepare two lists of values; one list represents your own values, and the other list represents what you think are your spouse's values. Please place them in the order of their importance. There are no restraints on the content of the values or their length. Do not discuss these values between you before the next session.

In the next session the clients are asked to read their lists aloud, in the order written, and the therapist records them on a single sheet, clear enough to make it possible to read and be compared by all.

While the participants are evaluating the lists, the therapist looks at issues such as: possible sources of the values represented, contradictions within and between the lists, differences in content, client accuracy in their perception of the other's values, etc.

The clients are asked to express their impressions of the lists, and questions are drawn from the above issues and others that emerge.

Example

Husband's List		Wife's List	
My Values	*Her Values*	*My Values*	*His Values*
1. family	1. cleaning	1. good health	1. work
2. business	2. family	2. happiness	2. money
3. sex	3. friends	3. family	3. sports
4. jogging	4. work	4. sex	4. being loved
5. traveling	5. religion	5. friends	5. family
6. friends	6. go to parties	6. studying	6. traveling
7. reading	7. sex	7. work	7. sex
8. learning new things	8. shopping	8. sport	8. eating
		9. religion	9. friends

Some of the issues that can be raised in the discussion are:

- The importance of "family" to the husband is not seen by his wife.
- Neither spouse is aware of how high sex ranks for the other partner.
- Cleaning, going to parties, and shopping were not mentioned by the wife, but mentioned by the husband as part of his wife's values.

- The importance the wife puts on religion is less than seen by her husband.
- They have many interests in common — family, learning, sex, travel, sports, friends.
- Values relating to time alone or time with each other are not included.
- Reasons for the inaccurate perception of the rank of values.
- The perception of each other's values are related to one's own.

Uses
The technique can be used in both marital or family therapy. Although more complex, it can be used by any number of people in a family or for transgenerational work. Some of the more productive areas for using the technique are: helping family members participate in the interaction; clarifying and challenging the assumptions or "taken for granted" perspective of individual family members. The technique can be applied in early sessions, when family members feel that they have no order in their relationship, or when individuals feel indifference or depression.

The technique reveals information about individuals, but also about the social-psychological system they form — the relationship itself. It provides indications of interpersonal perception, communication, and system balance. (See also the preceding technique, "Values Clarification: Mom Always Said . . . Dad Always Said. . . . ")

RESOURCE
Floyd, H. H. Values assessment-comparison (VAC): A family therapy technique. *Family Therapy*, 1982, *IX*(3), 280–288.

10 | THE USE OF DREAMS IN FAMILY THERAPY

Rationale
Parents, parental figures, and "significant others" mold, expand, and influence the intellectual and emotional development of the growing child; they have impact and are integrated in the dream life of all of us. The presence of the family in therapeutic sessions enables dream material to assist in the examination of dysfunctional communication among family members and affords the possibility of the restructuring of family relationships. Bynum (1980) describes how dreams can be used within a systems approach. This method is taken primarily from Bynum's work.

This approach is process rather than content oriented. It focuses on forms and styles of relating rather than specific symbolic meaning. Each family member views significant events in a particular way, which allows the therapist to see how the network of family relationships is contained. The dreams of one particular family member may reflect his views of the family conflict. The dynamic structure of dream work can elicit the unconscious understandings and assumptions about how the family system functions. The therapist can view each member of the family as being in touch with underlying feelings of the other members even though the particular situation may not be obvious.

Thus, through dream work, misguided attempts at problem solving can be restructured and given new directions.

Procedure
Families are encouraged to maintain a log of their dreams to be used when appropriate. Very little tabulation of dreams is necessary to provide rich clinical material. Several methods can be applied to this approach.

One method is for members to compare their respective interpretations of one particular family member's dream. To avoid reinforcing the identified client's role, such dreams are not generally focused on the identified client in the early sessions. In later sessions, the therapist may reflect to the family that the "sick role" is not necessarily fixed on the identified client. Various members might also use free association in this dream work. Similarity of associations can suggest the extent to which fusion or enmeshment exists in the family system.

Another design is to have all family members state what the dream signifies, paying particular attention to the fact that they are reflecting upon themselves and not upon what it means for the member who had the dream. This provides the opportunity for each member to individuate and differentiate from the family by encouraging exploration of ideas, associations, and affects. This approach also reinforces each member's ability to utilize exploratory and expressive behavior.

A third method involves all family members telling about a dream which may or may not be their own and working extensively on its meaning and significance. This enables the therapist to draw a working hypothesis of the various aspects of the family communication and provides data for the restructuring of the family relationships.

Examples
In one family, a son had recurring dreams about constantly running to his mother's bedroom after arguing with his father. It seems that the son had continual arguments with his father over money matters and with his mother over her constant intrusion into his private life. The dream reflects a dependence relationship between parents and son and suggests

the indication of triangulation within the family in which the son is placed between the parents and occupies their attention.

A teenage girl had recurring dreams about escaping from her parents' home and taking their car. As she drove away, her father ran after the car and each time he got closer, the car would go faster until, finally, she drove the car into a telephone pole and killed herself.

Themes of autonomy and separation with erupting anxiety prevailed during the family's therapeutic sessions. It was also found that many arguments ensued over the teenager's involvement with a young man; she constantly felt dominated by and rebellious toward her father. When she stayed away from home too long, she experienced somatic problems and wanted to "lose herself" in other males.

This teenager's younger sister revealed a similar theme. In a recurring dream, some large "awful man" screamed at her, her sister, and her mother. The man would then step on them, but would not kill them. It was found that the father had a manic-depressive psychosis. The mother is an extremely religious, compulsive woman. All three females complained of somatic cramps, gas pains, migraine headaches, and frequent depressive episodes.

In this next example, strong, unresolved dependency needs are observed in a parent–child relationship. The mother of an identified patient has been confronted a number of times by her children, who complain that she is constantly overinvolved with them. Whenever any child is involved in arguments either in school or at home, the mother becomes agitated and blames the middle child. She keeps a tight rein on her children. On several occasions, she dreamed that she was in a storm by herself. Nobody spoke to her and she was trying to find her way home on dark, windy streets.

Implied here was a sense of isolation and abandonment. Her reaction to separation was demonstrated in another dream where she let one of her children go with a strange man, her girlfriend, and a little boy to a school. The mother had a disagreement with the other mother, insisting they should follow and catch them. The ambivalence over separation was reflected in the psychological split of the mother and the "other mother." The "stranger" was associated with the father of the family, indicating that distance has grown between the marital couple since the children were born and the more recent problems adjusting to the children leaving home. Fear of change and shifts of power in the marital transaction brought on the scapegoating of the identified client. During sessions, the mother was particularly agitated and depressed. The possibility of separation between the marital pair might be a consideration, although they were not overtly aware of it.

One client reported that he recurrently dreamed that his younger, new-born brother turned into a large bird in his crib and flew away. Although this appears to be a common sibling rivalry dream, the difficulty was that the child's younger brother died suddenly as a result of crib death and he was overcome by guilt and grief. The mother felt guilty also. She reported that she dreamed that her mother took the dead child away and tried to help it. The issue of grief and guilt had not been expressed until now and, as such, treatment was based on an extensive period of grief work.

Dreams often reflect intense marital difficulties and the role of the identified patient in the family system. One adolescent described recurrent dreams in which his mother and father were in the process of leaving the house. Whenever the adolescent cried or screamed, his parents would return to the house and stay together. As soon as his crying ceased, his parents would, again, prepare to leave. This dream reflects the dilemma of the marital relationship as well as the adolescent's situation.

Uses

Dreams provide a meaningful source of material suitable for an understanding of one's intrapsychic, interpersonal, and family–social life. Dreams are of particular value in a family systems context and can be used to reflect, explore, and clarify dependency and triangulation relationships; themes of autonomy and separation; somatic problems; marital conflict; suppressed rage, grief, and guilt; issues reflecting specific family life cycle stages; role expectations, distortions, family alliances, and sibling constellations; and fusion and enmeshment.

RESOURCES

Beck, M. J. Dream analysis in family therapy. *Clinical Social Work Journal*, 1977, *15*, 53–57.

Bynum, E. B. The use of dreams in family therapy. *Psychotherapy: Theory, Research and Practice*, 1980, *17*, 2.

Freud, S. *The interpretation of dreams* (1900). New York: Avon Books, 1965.

Garfield, P. I. Keeping a longitudinal dream record. *Psychotherapy: Theory, Research and Practice*, 1973, *10*, 3.

Greenleaf, E. Senoi dream groups. *Psychotherapy: Theory, Research and Practice*, 1973, *10*, 3.

Markowitz, I., Taylor, G., and Bokert, E. Dream discussion as a means of reopening blocked familial communication. *Psychotherapy and Psychosomatics*, 1968, *16*, 348–365.

Piaget, J. *Play, dreams and imitation in childhood*. New York: Norton, 1962.
Simkin, J. S. The use of dreams in gestalt therapy. In C. Sager and H.
    S. Kaplan (eds.), *Progress in group and family therapy*. New York: Brun-
    ner/Mazel, 1972.

11 | DRAW A DREAM

Rationale
Open hostility and quarreling in the family, particularly when the child
is involved in the parental conflict, are likely to be damaging to the child.
The stress on the child can be further aggravated when there is a lack
of warmth and affection shown to the child and when the conflicts are
prolonged over time.

What is less certain is the role the child's behavior may play in reducing, maintaining, or aggravating the parental conflict. The child's symptoms often are reinforced because they play a central role in family conflict avoidance.

If the child is the identified patient, frequently it is difficult for the therapist to gather information that the family members may not consider
relevant. The Draw a Dream technique as described by Tonge (1982)
is a projective tool used to help assess the child's distress and his or her
perception of the family problem. It is also seen by the child to be a form
of play and often helps the child relax and establish a meaningful relationship with the therapist.

Procedure
Much of the following material was developed and described by Tonge
(1982).

In making a simple drawing of a child in bed with an associated large
cartoon balloon, the therapist says that the child is having a bad dream
and asks the child to draw the dream. If the child's name is Bill, the therapist will say, "Here is a boy named Bill having a bad dream—perhaps
it is even you. I wonder if you could draw that dream for me." Linking
the child's dream drawing to real life events, such as his or her parents'
quarreling, may help the child understand the meaning of his or her dis-
tressing feelings and behavior. This understanding often brings immediate relief.

The therapist then suggests that they show the dream drawing to the
parents (with the child's consent), since it may enable them to understand their child's feelings and problems. The therapist gives the child
the choice of staying with her when the drawing is discussed with the
parents and is linked with family problems. This discussion can have a
profound effect on the parents when the child is presented as the prob-

lem because the parents often are unaware of their own involvement in the child's difficulties.

The child's dream may appear weird and unexpected, but the effect of the dream image on the family is to move the emphasis away from the focus on the symptom. The child's dream drawing acts to reframe the conceptual understanding of what is happening in the family. The problem is redefined by the child in concrete terms and the covert problem becomes overt. This reframing of the problem is even more effective because it is the child's reframing and imagery that are presented to the parents.

The child is also given some safety and security because it is only a dream, but the directness of the message and the dream imagery confronts the family with an unavoidable and new understanding of their conflicts which may circumvent previous patterns of conflict avoidance.

It could be argued that the therapist, by aligning herself with the child, may be inappropriately undermining the power of the parents in the family. This is avoided if the therapist simply conveys the child's drawing and message to the parents as a go-between, emphasizing that it is their child's message to them as parents, which therefore pushes the parents to take responsibility for the implications of that message.

The technique of Draw a Dream can be used in any family counseling orientation and is extremely useful in settings that focus on children.

Example

The following example is provided by Tonge (1982).

"Marcus, eight years old, was referred by his school because he was increasingly aggressive towards other children and . . . disobedient towards the teachers. . . . Marcus and his parents were resentful about the referral. The father said that Marcus was timid and withdrawn at home, not listening to what he was told, which made the father angry" (p. 217). No other problem was presented.

The therapist drew the dream balloon "and commented that it was a boy called Marcus, maybe even him, who was having a bad dream. He hesitated, then started to draw a 'home' that was being 'broken up by an angry giant man' who was then going to leave. . . . The worst part of the dream for Marcus was when the giant man grabbed him and shook him" (p. 217).

The therapist then suggested to Marcus that maybe things happen at home like in the dream and perhaps his father was like the giant sometimes. Mark looked very sad and stated that his parents had "terrible fights" and "broke things" and that his father had left home for several days after one of these fights.

The therapist suggested that the dream be shown to Marcus' parents and maybe this would help them understand what worried him. Mark agreed and decided to stay while the therapist talked with the parents. The dream drawing was explained by the therapist, linking it to events at home.

Marcus' father put his hand on his son's "shoulder and admitted that over the past year relationships at home were as Marcus described. Mother wasn't coping and was very depressed, and she was irritable and emotionally unavailable to her family. . . . The father asserted that he didn't want his home to break up and asked for help" (p. 217).

The parents, when confronted with their child's dream picture, were provided with a powerful representation of the parental conflict and its impact on the family. This was an experience that the parents could not easily ignore, and it therefore provoked a response toward change.

Uses
The use of the technique Draw a Dream elicits from the child a graphic picture and statement of what is really happening, and sharing this with the parents may produce change in the family system. When the child is presented as the patient having symptoms, the parents have tried various solutions directed at the child's behavior and they seek help from the therapist, asking the therapist to also focus on the child's behavior and attempt to change it. By using the Draw a Dream technique, the therapist steps outside the parent–child problem perspective and provides the child with a means of expressing what is really happening in his world in a graphic and concrete manner.

RESOURCE
Tonge, B. J. Draw a Dream: An intervention promoting change in families in conflict. In F. Kaslow (Ed.), *The international book of family therapy*. New York: Brunner/Mazel, 1982, pp. 212–225.

12 | THE ROLE OF DREAMS IN SEX THERAPY

Rationale
Dream interpretation is a valuable tool used by psychoanalysts. Psychoanalytically oriented sex therapists can utilize this tool in understanding the unconscious factors responsible for sexual dysfunction. Clinical psychoanalytic studies have shown that it is crucial for successful sex therapy to work through unconscious phenomena, such as unresolved conflicts, transferential distortions, and resistance (Levay and Weissberg, 1979). Although presented here within a psychoanalytic framework described by Levay and Weissberg, dreams can obviously be used within many other theoretical models. For example, Adlerians would concentrate on

the manifest content of the dream, regarding the dream as an effort at problem solving. Some Gestalt therapists would see each element in the dream as representing some aspect of the self that needs to be owned and integrated into the larger whole.

Encouraging and examining the dreams of each spouse can be helpful in understanding the sexual interaction between them.

Levay and Weissberg (1979) take issue with behaviorally oriented sex therapists who, they believe, influence their clients' dreams by creating conflict in the superego. The therapist's task is to promote sexual pleasure. This is in direct conflict with the function of the superego, which is responsible for controlling instinctual desires. The conflict generates dream activity. The authors contend that the intense relationship fostered during therapy combined with an increase in sexual responsiveness play "an activating physiological and psychological role with regard to dream content" (p. 335). The dreams "tend to be vivid, to illustrate underlying conflicts in a relatively undisguised way, to be strongly charged affectively and to be linked to the events of the previous day" (p. 335).

Levay and Weissberg further divide the manifest content of the dreams into four types: erotic, affective, cognitive, retrospective, and interactional themes which may help identify both preferred methods of arousal and areas of inhibition. Affective dreams inform the therapist of emotions such as anger, fear, or loss that are stimulated by the sexual exercises commonly prescribed during the therapy. These dreams also point out signs of developing resistance and conflict. Cognitive dreams indicate the unconscious basis of conscious symptoms. "Retrospective dreams reveal the developmental roots of sexual conflict. Interactional dreams suggest how material from the patient's childhood affects current sexual relationships" (p. 335).

Procedure
The theory and process of dream interpretation are too extensive to report in this brief segment. Therefore, this technique is appropriate for use by those who possess this knowledge and can apply it to sex therapy.

The therapist encourages clients to record their dreams in detail immediately upon awakening after a sexual encounter, especially if they are following a therapeutic prescription. Suggesting in advance that they will probably have dreams and that they should write them down immediately will often have the effect of stimulating clients to recall their dreams.

During the next session, the therapist asks the couple to share their dreams in turn in the presence of the partner. Both are then asked to provide associations to the dream, particularly in relation to the events of the day previous to the dreams or anticipated imminent events.

The sex therapist makes use of dream material differently than the psychotherapist, according to Levay and Weissberg (1979). The sex therapist's relationship with patients is less intense. Both spouses are treated together, and the focus is on sexual and interpersonal behavior change. The sex therapist elicits dream material, associations, and the day's events in the classical way after asking the participant to record the dream immediately upon awakening. However, once the information is elicited, specific goals are set. The therapist points out the relevance of the dream to the current phase of therapy. She exposes the patient only to as much insight as can be immediately absorbed. "The therapist helps the patients to redefine or suppress dream material that may stir up undue anxiety or resistance for the good of the therapy and the marital relationship" (p. 338). The therapist will elicit dreams of both partners that were a result of their sexual experiences of the previous day. The similarities and differences in their processing of experiences afford the therapist insight into the couple's inner relatedness and covert needs. "The use of dream interpretation is very helpful with clients who are not psychologically minded, find the material too emotionally charged, or are sexually inhibited" (p. 338).

Example

Levay and Weissberg (1979) report the following case:

> An impotent man married a sexually active and responsive woman. Both felt they could work out their sexual problem. The wife had a history of sexual relationships with a series of grossly inappropriate men. When the husband developed some erectile capacity in sex therapy, the wife managed to avoid his overtures, being either too tired or ill. He continued to be solicitous and thoughtful in an almost apologetic way. In this context he reported the following dreams:
>
> Dream 1: He and the therapist, in Storm Trooper uniforms, were driving his parents and some other people to Auschwitz.
>
> Dream 2: He was taking a bath with his mother and something sexual was going on. He pulled the plug and, with the water, the mother went down the drain.
>
> Dream 3: A fat woman was standing in front of a toilet. He pushed her head into the bowl and was about to approach her sexually when he woke up.
>
> This series of dreams illustrated the extent and depth of this client's aggression toward maternal female figures. He was so angry and intent upon being destructive while sexual that it was difficult for him to be affectionate and sexually functional at the same time. He was extremely concerned with the retaliatory consequences of his aggression. (pp. 336–337)

Similarly, the wife's dreams were interpreted and the reciprocity between them was interpreted to the couple. It is clear that avoiding sexual intercourse was in the interest of both partners. They were then led to examine their internal conflicts and to help one another to resolve them.

Uses
This sex therapy technique can be used by any therapist who is skilled in dream interpretation to reveal both the unconscious conflicts and the manifest efforts to solve them within the dreams. By encouraging the couple to engage in sexual activity, dream about it, and then report on the dreams, the therapist can gain immediate entrée into the dysfunctional forces involved and their meaning. Analysis and interpretation of each partner's dreams reveal the basis for their reciprocal sexual behavior and how each reinforces the behavior of the other. Dreams are also used to resolve conflicts. The therapist can analyze how the dreamer handles the situation and the final outcome in the dream.

Another variation is to have the dreamer dramatically enact the dream, assigning roles to his partner and to the therapist and, if necessary, using objects in the room to represent other persons or objects in the dream. Dealing with the dreamer dramatically in the conscious state provides opportunity for the couple to deal with the issues both affectively and cognitively during the session. By repeating the enactment, different solutions to the conflict can be explained and examined (Gold, 1983). (See also the other dream techniques described in this chapter.)

RESOURCES
Adler, A. *Understanding human nature*. Greenwich, CT: Fawcett Books, 1927.
Blum, H. P. The changing use of dreams in psychoanalytic practice, dreams and free association. *International Journal of Psychoanalysis*, 1976, *57*, 315–324.
Gold, L. The dream o'drama. (Unpublished.) Presentation and demonstration, Regional Convention, North American Society of Adlerian Psychology, New York, March 24, 1983.
Levay, A. and Kagle, A. Recent advances in sex therapy: Integration with the dynamic therapies. *Psychiatric Quarterly*, 1978, *50*, 1.
Levay, A. N. and Weissberg, J. Role of dreams in sex therapy. *Journal of Sex and Marital Therapy*, Winter 1979, *5*, 334–339.

13 | IMAGERY, SHAPING, AND ORGASM IN SEX THERAPY

Rationale
The use of imagery as a shaping device in sex therapy is developed by Nims (1975). Shaping is a technique used by behaviorists to teach a complex skill or response pattern. Learning requires moving from a previously

learned or unlearned reflexive response to the new learned response. This is usually accomplished by the gradual addition of increments. Imagery is covert behavior within the central nervous system. Imagery is a normal component of sexual functioning. It refers to any thematic, sensory, ritualized, romanticized, or visualized accompaniment of sexual activity. A typical form of sexual imagery is fantasy. Subjects have reported sexual responsiveness due to appropriate imagery. Both men and women utilize imagery. Men are more apt to fantasize sexual scenes, while females report images around music, colors, and romantic themes.

Since imagery is an important factor in masturbation, it is believed that careful shaping techniques can be incorporated with imagery to increase both excitatory and orgiastic capabilities during intercourse.

Procedure

The use of imagery has been recognized by John Marquis (1970). He directs nonorgasmic patients to masturbate and at the point of orgasm the patient is to focus upon imagery of penile thrusting. This procedure has been found to be effective in men and women. Shaping is accomplished through fantasy and rehearsal, which is incorporated into intercourse.

Another form of shaping is to direct the patient during intercourse and to recall the imagery used during masturbation so as to enhance the possibility of orgasm. Some inhibited patients will be unable to recognize their imagery patterns. It is necessary for the therapist to be directive to help the patient become aware of his fantasies during masturbation. The therapist might ask for the patient to make notes of images and fantasies that are stimulating to the individual. However, this can result in creating considerable anxiety for the patient, and the therapist must be cautious to respond appropriately.

Example

> A 27-year-old woman was orgasmic during masturbation when utilizing a classical "bondage and discipline" fantasy. (This patient was offended by the term sadamasochistic, which she felt was "sick." She said, "I enjoy being hurt, but I don't like it when you call it pain.") In her fantasy she was forcibly gang-raped by several rough men, then finally saved by one strong but gentle man who drove the others off, swept her into his arms, and declared his love. Her orgasm was triggered by the declaration of his love, without specific imagery at that instant. (Nims, 1975)

The woman was told to concentrate on the image of penile thrusting while reaching orgasm. During intercourse she was told to follow her bondage and discipline fantasy. After several weeks the patient became orgasmic during intercourse. Her partner was coached to say "I love you" at the proper moment.

Uses
Use of this procedure is well suited for men or women who are able to be orgasmic during masturbation and not during intercourse. It can be used as a purely behavioral sex therapy technique in the early stages of treatment. Though described in this article as an individual technique, it could also be used in couple therapy. A therapist might choose to explore an individual's sexual fantasies in the presence of his spouse as a way to open the channels of communication and heighten awareness of the mate's needs.

RESOURCES
Friday, N. *My secret garden.* New York: Trident Press, 1973.
Hartman, W. E. and Fithian, M. A. *Treatment of sexual dysfunction.* New York: Long Beach, Center for Marital and Sexual Studies, 1972.
Nims, J. P. Imagery, shaping, and orgasm. *Journal of Sex & Marital Therapy*, Spring 1975, 1(3).

14 | IMAGERY: EVENTS IN THE FAMILY OF ORIGIN

Rationale
Imagery is used to recapitulate events and relationships that occurred during childhood. Children tend to understand their parents in a simplistic, distorted manner. Some family systems may even perpetuate these distortions over generations, resulting in the development and continuation of dysfunctional roles. Distortions may take many forms. They may involve deep feelings of hurt, fear, or abandonment. They may place a parent in a highly idealized position, which no person — partner or child — could hope to emulate.

Imagery is not the same as memory. Imagery taps into the person's subjective impressions of how things were and may reveal the feelings, beliefs, and goals that are derived from those impressions. Imagery techniques often elicit strong repressed feelings, which may be hidden under defenses producing further distortions. Imagining events from childhood can be utilized by multigenerational theorists to identify family legacies, loyalties, guiding lines, myths, and triangles. Cognitive theorists may find such a technique helpful to clients in identifying, challenging, or integrating deep underlying beliefs and assumptive values. Imagery helps clients get to the core of the problem with less defensiveness than other methods may elicit.

Some of the following material on this technique is adapted from the work of Morrison (1981, pp. 52–56), including the case example and uses.

Procedure

Imagery is utilized by the therapist as a guided experience for the client(s). After obtaining permission to use imagery, the clients are asked to relax themselves and, if comfortable to do so, to close their eyes. They are then asked to imagine themselves as children at a particular age. Next they are asked to form images of their parents and other family members. Based upon what the therapist is looking for, she will now suggest that the clients create a particular scene involving such situations as being treated unfairly, getting caught in the middle between the parents, or something that made them feel angry or abandoned. They might be asked specifically to imagine a scene with the opposite-sex parent and to carefully describe that parent's behavior and attitude.

Those clients who perceive themselves as victims might be asked to create scenes of good times — affectionate moments, parties, praise, presents, fun, or adventure — to help them gain a more balanced impression of their lives.

The feelings and beliefs, the patterns and themes of interaction, and the goals expressed can now be discussed as they are related to present family organization and interactions.

Even children can be asked to imagine scenes of when they were younger. They can all do it simultaneously in silence and write down the scene and then read it to the group; or they can report their experience in turn orally. Or the technique can be used with any subsystem.

Examples

The examples are from Morrison (1981).

A couple with marital difficulties sought help. Presenting problems were depression, anxiety, and related symptoms such as sexual difficulties, sleeplessness, and an inability to express anger. The focus in therapy was on their poor level of communication. Very little progress was made after many sessions. Although the couple had learned to communicate more effectively, they had difficulties applying the skills. So the therapist suggested an individual session for each spouse, to which they agreed.

During the individual sessions, the clients were asked to close their eyes and picture the opposite-sex parent. After generating a clear image, each spouse was asked to imagine the other standing next to that parent. Each spouse was then asked to describe the imaged person's similarities and differences.

The male client discovered the similarities between his mother and his spouse. His mother, having been a controlling, dominant woman, blamed him continually. This image enabled him to understand his feelings for his wife and to take responsibility for attempting to change her in a futile attempt to win his mother's love. He therefore stopped treating his wife as if she were his mother. His relationship with his children also benefited.

The female spouse, through her imagery session, discovered the similarities between her father and her husband, both of whom were weak and passive. Her father had never clearly demonstrated his love for her. She was then able to take responsibility for dominating her husband just as her mother dominated her father. Her image of her mother enabled the wife to reduce her dominant role, and she began to view her husband and children more positively.

After these individual imagery sessions, both husband and wife improved a great deal, and family therapy was able to progress smoothly.

A couple could not make progress in their relationship until the wife discovered that her idealistic image of her deceased father was interfering. Her expectations for her husband were too unrealistic.

In her imagery session, the wife was asked to picture the circumstances surrounding her father's death and funeral. This was enough to help her elicit sufficiently negative feelings regarding her idealistic image of her father. Subsequently, the couple's progress in therapy improved.

Uses
Imagery of the family of origin can be used when:

1. Couples are ineffective in overcoming their difficulties and dysfunctional roles, even when they may have clear insights.
2. Couples have a problem understanding their feelings for one another in family therapy.
3. Couples or spouses continually find themselves in cross-generational roles.
4. Strong feelings have not become evident and need to be expressed in therapy.
5. Couples or spouses need to understand the dynamics of how their feelings about their parents interfere in the spouses' relationship with each other.
6. Spouses need to understand situations from their children's viewpoint.
7. The hopes of one or both spouses need a boost in family therapy.
8. Spouses and couples need to stop blaming one another and, instead, understand the other person's viewpoint.
9. Parents need to understand conflicts with their children that stem from their own conflicts as children.
10. There is a difference between what is being said and what is being done.
11. There is a need to help one or more members integrate early experiences into their present conscious behavior and circumstances.

12.   The therapist would like to bring impressions of the past into the here and now to work on them.

RESOURCES

Ahson, A. *Eidetic psychotherapy: A short introduction*. New York: Brandon House, 1965.

Ahson, A. *Basic concepts in eidetic psychotherapy*. New York: Brandon House, 1968.

Ahson, A. *Psycheye: Self-analytic consciousness*. New York: Brandon House, 1977.

Morrison, J. K. *Changing artistic style through the reconstructive use of mental imagery*. Unpublished manuscript, 1978.

Morrison, J. K. Emotive-reconstructive therapy: Changing constructs by means of mental imagery. In A. A. Sheikh and J. T. Shaffer (eds.), *The potential of fantasy and imagination*. New York: Brandon House, 1979, pp. 133–147.

Morrison, J. K. The use of imagery techniques in family therapy. *American Journal of Family Therapy*, 1981, *9*, 52–56.

Sheikh, A. Mental images: Ghosts or sensations? *Journal of Mental Imagery*, 1977, *1*, 1–4.

Sheikh, A. *Imagery — Current theory research and application*. New York: Wiley, 1983.

Yuille, J. C. *Imagery, memory and cognition*. Hillsdale, NJ: Lawrence Erlbaum Associates, 1983.

15 | GUIDED IMAGERY: THE INNER ADVISER

Rationale

Guided imagery is a projective method of communicating with internal processes that occur outside of our conscious awareness. This internal exchange of information can be used in different ways. First, information about subtle physiological processes can be brought to conscious awareness as an aid to diagnosis. Second, the power of the imagination can be evoked to promote specific physiological changes as an aid to therapy. Third, cognitively, unlabeled ideas and feelings can be brought into conscious thinking.

The use of positive images to reinforce health has been an integral part of many healing traditions. Around the turn of the century, Emil Coué, a French pharmacist, initiated a clinic modeled on the use of positive imagery as a method of attaining maximum health. Coué believed that imagining an outcome would do far more to bring it about than willing or forcing oneself to do something. By imagining the endpoint, such as some specific career or life goal, the mind is carried in that direction without one's willing it or forcing oneself to desire it. This is especially important when a person may be imagining or expecting a negative outcome or condition. Helping a person to see his situation more positively through his mind's eye may have a significant effect on the response to treatment. The power of positive suggestion plants a seed which redirects the mind and body toward a positive goal.

Clinicians are experimenting with many creative uses of mental imagery in behavior rehearsal, hypnosis, dream-a-drama, and many other techniques. One of the most dramatic techniques, popularized by Oyle (1976) and by Samuels and Bennet (1973), is called the Inner Adviser. By creating and interacting with an inner adviser, a person learns to gather important information from his subconscious and is able to feel comfortable and familiar with parts of himself that had been previously inaccessible to conscious awareness.

Procedures

Imagery techniques are most frequently used within a state of relaxation. Inducing a relaxed state is the first step. There are different methods for doing this: a hypnotic induction; meditation; progressive relaxation of the body muscle systems from toes to head; imagining a quiet, pleasant, relaxing scene; concentrating on one's breathing or a phrase such as "I am at peace," while letting all other thoughts slip away; or recalling a wonderful vacation spot or past memory. The image stimulates the body to relax and inhibits muscle activity and verbal thoughts, thereby allowing mental images to become dominant. For the minority of clients who have difficulty in attaining this state, biofeedback training may also be helpful. Once a state of relaxation is attained, the client is then guided to create a picture in his mind's eye of what he wishes his body and mind to do.

One method is for the therapist to choose a scene that she believes indicates the client's conflict, fear, or desire for change. She requests that the client project himself into that scene and describe it aloud. The therapist then picks up on something or someone alive in that scene other than the client. The client is asked to get in touch with that "alive" being to be used as an inner adviser. She has the inner adviser reframe the pain or problem unto itself and away from the client, seeking his agreement to do so. Then the client is requested to return to his usual state from his relaxed state.

A second method is to ask the client to imagine a room in which the people connected with his problem are waiting for him to enter and work out the problem. He is to formulate a plan for doing so and then enter the room and execute the plan. He leaves that room and is asked to imagine a second room in which there is a very wise being who knows him well, knows his problem, and who has observed the events in the preceding room. He enters the room of the wise being who tells him what to do.

Example

The following example is taken from Weisz (G. Weisz, personal communication, 1985).

Roberta frequently developed migraine headaches in the evenings and therefore had trouble sleeping. The therapist explores with her the various aggravating thoughts which she experiences at night, especially those in which her mother-in-law is criticizing her.

The therapist decides to help her contact an inner advisor. She tells her to relax and imagine a pleasant, relaxing scene.

Roberta thinks of a quiet, serene field. There is a small pond with clear water. The air smells clean and there are no unpleasant sounds or distractions.

The therapist asks her to imagine another living creature in the scene and to give it a name.

Roberta: There is a wolf right next to me. I just noticed him. He says his name is Gary Wolf.

Therapist: Ask him if it's OK to stroke him and ask him if he'll be your friend.

Roberta: He says it's OK and he'll be friends with me since I'm not scared of him. All I have to do is never try to hurt him and stroke him once in a while.

Therapist: Ask Gary as a sign of his friendship if he can help you get rid of that nasty headache right now.

Roberta: He says I should drink from this peaceful pond and my head will be settled. It's an old remedy known to wolves.

After imaging drinking the water, Roberta is assured by the wolf that the headache will go away now and that she will sleep soundly that night.

Roberta: The pain is gone.

In the following weeks there were a few nights where Roberta had no headaches. She became more aware of her ability to control her tension.

In another session she asked the wolf how she might handle her overcritical mother-in-law. Gary explained to her that many of the animals he knows get angry with each other when one takes the other one's territory. Maybe her mother-in-law was angry because she lost her territory over her son to Roberta and she just wanted to punish Roberta. Gary suggested that Roberta let her mother-in-law know that she has a place in her son's life and that Roberta won't try to keep her away from him.

Roberta began forming a better relationship with her mother-in-law and her husband, allowing her husband to share more time with both his wife and mother.

Uses

The Inner Adviser technique can be used whenever the client is having trouble with the way he is handling a situation or the making of a choice or plan. This technique can be used when the client is stuck in a creative impasse.

If the client is trying very hard but cannot seem to perceive his situation very well or find ways to deal with it, this procedure can be helpful in opening up his inner creativity and getting at relevant subconscious information.

In addition to its use as a problem-solving technique, the Inner Adviser encourages self-reflection, creative living, and trust in one's own resources. It is a relatively nonthreatening technique since the client can imagine whatever he chooses without any pressure. The inner adviser might be an alter ego for the client and this technique provides an opportunity for integrating that alter ego. If the client is very dependent and sees the therapist as the expert, this procedure has the benefit of framing the client as a resourceful person in the therapeutic relationship.

People may become imprisoned by their own belief systems. This happens not only on the conscious level, but subconsciously as well. So, if quite unknowingly, a patient envisions himself as a hopeless, helpless victim of emotional or physical pain, it is essential for him to become aware of that and to adopt a new belief system that will facilitate healing. The inner adviser technique can help a person become intimately connected with his subconscious mind and can tell him how well he is incorporating new beliefs, new expectations, and new habits.

Putting the person in touch with his own inner resources is an empowering process that gives the person the sense that he "can do." He feels stronger and more competent.

The inner adviser can suggest ways in which the person can improve relationships with a spouse, children, parents, employers, or employees; differentiate the self from other family members and problems; heal emotional and communication "cutoffs"; and improve one's sense of self.

RESOURCES

Araoz, D. L. *Hypnosis and sex therapy*. New York: Brunner/Mazel, 1982.
Coué, E. and Brooks, C. H. *Self-mastery through conscious auto-suggestion by the method of Emil Coué*. Winchester, MA: Allen & Unwin, 1984.
Oyle, I. *Time, space and mind*. Berkeley, CA: Celestial Arts, 1976.

Samuels, M. and Bennet, H. *The well body book*. New York: Random House, 1973.

Shorr, J. E. and Sobel, G. E. *Imagery: Its many dimensions and applications*. New York: Plenum, 1980.

Wolpe, J. *The practice of behavior therapy*. New York: Pergamon Press, 1969.

16 | COUPLE IMAGES

Rationale

The technique of couple images is one in which the nature of a relationship is explored. Through the use of imagery each spouse identifies and discusses a "form" that feels like an appropriate characterization of the other spouse. This type of technique can explore an individual's perception of himself, his mate, and their interaction together in a nondirect, nonthreatening manner. A therapist can obtain information about how the couple is actually feeling rather quickly and without much direct questioning. After the couple present the images, they act them out. This can "loosen up" a difficult situation. It is helpful when a therapist senses that a couple is having difficulty presenting and exploring their patterns of interactions. Through the use of couple images the couples present their perceptions of their relationship and the therapist is able to intervene accordingly.

This technique is similar to the couple fantasy or couple choreography.

Procedure

The therapist starts by asking the couple or couples to close their eyes. They are told that they are going to express themselves in images. They are to consider their relationship with their partner and concentrate on what they feel is characteristic of their relationship. They should then present this characterization by imagining each other taking some non-human form. It can be any form whatsoever, animate or inanimate, heavy or light, large or small, anything at all that might illustrate what is unique in the relationship. They should then let their thoughts flow and try to notice the associations that come up. They should not be too critical and throw out the first idea, even if they think it seems unusual or meaningless. Then they are to imagine these two forms or things on the floor of the therapy room. The therapist instructs each person to use his or her partner to present physically what he or she imagined. When the couple or couples have enacted their dream images the session is concluded without any comments. During the next session the therapist will concentrate primarily on regarding the couple as participants in a self-confirming circular interaction. Viewed this way, couple's problems can be considered as unsuccessful attempts on each side to resolve relationship difficulties. The therapist will then try to break up this circular interaction by giving each of the partners tasks that suggest alternative behaviors.

Example

Lisa and Tom were in a couples' group. Lisa shows us a little lamb. Tom is the little lamb grazing quietly in the pasture. Lisa is a wolf going around in circles on a hilltop a little way off, trying to worry the lamb. The lamb calmly watches the wolf. Lisa explains the wolf knows it won't get anywhere with this lamb, so it disappears over the hills. The lamb continues to graze and, as Lisa explains, has defended itself very well by not doing anything.

Tom places Lisa with her arms straight out from her sides. She is a compass and he is a mountaineer. The visibility is bad but he knows intuitively in which direction he is to go. The compass, on the other hand, always shows an orientation completely at odds with the mountaineer's. So Tom goes his own way yet keeps the compass. He also keeps glancing at the compass, which makes him uncertain. He believes there is something wrong with it, but he is not sure. So he drags Lisa across the room while her arms are always pointing in another direction than the way he is taking her. It shows he is always in doubt, wondering whether he is to follow his own intuition or the direction of the compass.

In the following session the therapist states that she is going to start by studying the relationship Lisa has with her husband, so she can find out which tasks each partner will be given to carry out at home. These tasks will be used to find out whether it is possible to create any changes in the partner's behavior. The therapist separates the couple and asks Lisa what makes things difficult for her. It is concluded that she pushes Tom away because she feels he clings to her and threatens to suffocate her. A different type of behavior for her was assigned. She is to prepare a nice meal for Tom, splurge on candles, food, and wine. She is to do this three times before the next session without his knowing beforehand. If Tom asks why she is doing this, she is to explain that they are both aware that the marriage is emotionally ruined, so why sulk, let's just be nice to one another.

The therapist then talks to Tom and it is concluded that Tom feels Lisa is interested in everything but him and he believes she is about to leave him. To prevent this, he concentrates all of his efforts on her and the family. His own life has been put on a shelf. His task is to buy an Indian philosophy book and on six separate occasions pick it up and sit as if he is completely absorbed in it. He is to show no interest in Lisa or the children. After half an hour, he is to share with Lisa the deep truths he has found. If she tries to change the subject, he is to pretend not to notice.

The couple went through their tasks but not fully. For the next few weeks the couple continued to do these tasks and others until they got them right. When the couple left therapy, they saw that there were other options of ways to interact. In a six-month follow-up the therapist was pleased to find that the couple had stayed together and worked on their marriage.

Uses
This technique alone is only a steppingstone to working with a couple or couples. Following through with tasks for behavior changes is a crucial part and can be accomplished in different ways. The therapist and/or group must be creative and come up with tasks for the couple. The tasks are designed to change the existing pattern revealed by the couple images. If the tasks are not followed up by the couple and there is much resistance, other interventions might be indicated. Paradoxical work is highly recommended.

In this technique the members are presenting ideas about the nature of their relationship. What is showing is their underlying images of themselves and their partners. These images form the basis of what Caille calls the "mythical model" of a couple's relationship. This technique gave the therapist information concerning the structure of two of Lisa and Tom's fundamental truths. Using this technique the therapist can gain an understanding of the "truths" of a given couple and help them find new alternative ways to interact.

RESOURCES
Caille, P. How therapeutic intervention does create the prerequisite of change in human relations. *Journal of Marriage and Family Therapy*, 1981, *3*, 281–290.
Caille, P. The evaluation of systemic family therapy. *Journal of Marriage and Family Therapy*, 1982, *1*, 29–39.
Watzlawick, P., Weakland, J., and Fisch, R. *Change: Principles of problem formation and problem solution*. New York: Norton, 1974.

17 | THE EMPTY CHAIR IN FAMILY THERAPY

Rationale
The use of the empty chair technique was originally popularized by Frederick Perls in his *Gestalt Therapy* (1951). The object of the technique was to help an individual get in touch with and "own" parts of the self that have not previously been integrated into the whole self.

The process is based on the assumption that the parents' internalized object relations are played out with their children. The parents' internalized relational difficulties result in boundary and contact problems for the members of the family, such as scapegoating, enmeshment, and projective identification by the child. This technique affords the members of the family the opportunity to carry on dialogues with significant individuals who are not present or who are asked to observe rather than respond.

As children, we internalize our experience of others. In this process of introjection we become aspects of the other. We internalize not merely the object but the mode of relating—a dramatic relational polarity. We consciously identify with one side of the dialogue, disowning or splitting off the other side—the "not me" part. The cut-off, disowned, unconscious, aspects of the dialogue may be either acted out or, often within the family system, projected onto the child or parent. This then leads to miscommunication and often to bitter feelings and unresolved interactive problems.

In couple and family work the goal is to stimulate the person to own those feelings and beliefs that he projects onto other members. The projections create a distortion of reality in the system. The family is organized around those distortions. By integrating the feelings into the self, a more realistic pattern of interaction can emerge.

Procedure
Bauer (1979) describes the empty chair procedure. The therapist will have the parent enter into dialogue with the child in the empty chair. She will ask the parent to role play both sides of the split while sitting in chairs which face each other. The instructions may be: "Your child is sitting in that chair opposite you. Please sit in that chair now and give your child a voice. Speak for the child to yourself in the chair you just left." After some significant expressions in the role of child, the client is asked to switch chairs and speak for himself to the child. The client continues to alternate roles until some important integrations take place. The therapist may interject interpretive comments such as "You mean you are very angry and you want to kick this person?" Or the therapist might assume the role of alter ego and briefly express what she thinks the client is really experiencing and then watch the reaction.

By having the parent give a voice to the child, the parent begins to reown some of the projected parts. Eventually, the focus will shift from the parent and child dialogue to dialogue within the parent himself or possibly between the parent and his own imagined parent in the empty chair. In this way the experience is located historically within the family of origin.

Example
Bauer (1979) provides the following example.

When Mrs. C. was a child she experienced a sadomasochistic relationship with her father. She internalized the drama of victim and victimizer and plays out this drama in her present family life.

She perceives her son as vindictive and exceptionally aggressive as he reaches adolescence, while she experiences and identifies herself as all good and placating.

Therapist: Mrs. C., could you please imaging your son sitting in that chair? (She nods.) Would you tell him what you think about him and how that makes you feel?

Mrs. C.:   Tom, you don't give a damn about anyone else. You always do things to hurt me. You don't listen, you curse me, you do lousy in school. You're a big disappointment. You're just big trouble.

Therapist: Now could you sit in that chair and give a voice to Tom. Let him speak to you in this chair (the one she is leaving).

Mrs. C.:   That's right, you hate me! You're always wanting me to do things I don't want to do because they're good for me. Brief silence.

Therapist: (As Tom's alter ego) And so I fight you because I want to decide what I want to do. You're always trying to push me around. Please go back to Mom's chair and speak to Tom.

Mrs. C.:   You make me do that because you're always doing the wrong things.

Therapist: Please go back to Tom's chair and speak for Tom.

Mrs. C.:   (As Tom) I can never do anything right for you.
(Aside to therapist:) That's how it was with my father. He always criticized me and I could never do anything right in his eyes. It used to make me so mad that I wanted to do things for spite, but instead I always tried to please him. It never worked.

Therapist: Is it that your father was angry and aggressive toward you and that you are angry and attack your son; then your son becomes angry and hurts you?

Mrs. C.:   It seems that way. I didn't realize I was doing that with my son some of the same things my father did with me.

Therapist: Please imagine that your father is in that second chair and speak to him. Tell him how angry you are.

When she enters into a dialogue with her aggressive adolescent via the empty chair, Mrs. C. begins to reown her own aggression and when the dialogue shifts to one between her aggressive self and her passive weak self, she further assimilates her aggression. There may be another shift to the past as Mrs. C. recounts her experience of powerlessness with her father. The dialogue is again amplified between Mrs. C. and her parent, enhancing the reowning. It is by integrating her own aggression that she can deal directly with her aggressive child.

Uses

The Gestalt technique of the Empty Chair is a useful strategy for working with projection. To interrupt the process of projection this technique may assist the parent in reowning and assimilating the disowned part of himself. By reidentifying the disowned side of the dialogue, the parent is better able to see and relate to the child without projecting his disowned fantasy. The Empty Chair technique is used to shift the focus from between parent and child to within the parent. The person thus takes responsibility for his part of the difficulty in the interaction and is encouraged then to experiment with new behaviors in the family. The same can be done with the child or spouse.

In those clinical situations in which a parent projects onto a child, the therapist may interrupt the process of projection by having the parent use the Empty Chair technique. In this instance it is recommended typically to have the parent work on his projections separate from the children as the intensity and intimacy of the work may weaken generational boundaries. It is important for the spouse to be present. Seeing one's spouse work on his internal dialogues that are projected onto one's self supports differentiation, lessens projective identification, and often provides for a direct understanding of one's spouse as a psychological individual.

RESOURCES

Bauer, R. Gestalt approach to family therapy. *American Journal of Family Therapy*, 1979, 7(3), 41–45.

Bauer, R. Gestalt therapy strategies to reduce projection in families. In A. Gurman (ed.), *Questions and answers in the practice of family therapy*. New York: Brunner/Mazel, 1981.

Harper, R., Bauer, R., and Kannarkat, J. Learning theory and gestalt therapy. *American Journal of Psychotherapy*, 1976, 30(1), 55–72.

Perls, F. S. *Ego, hunger and aggression: The beginning of gestalt therapy*. London: Random House, 1969.

Perls, F. S., Hefferline, R. F., and Goodman, P. *Gestalt therapy*. New York: Julian Press, 1951.

3

Sociometric Techniques

INTRODUCTION

Sociometric techniques are methods for observing, measuring, and modifying social interactions. Role relationships and functions within a given social system are the major objects of investigation. To change behavior is to restructure the roles and functions in the system. Sociometry assumes a direct relationship between structure and function. The emphasis, therefore, is on each person's perceived place, what is being done, and how people feel about it. The objective is to reveal what is reciprocally being done repeatedly by whom, to whom, and how, as well as the purpose, meaning, and affect of the action. Because the focus usually is on repeating patterns, the behavior is observable, measurable, and predictable — major elements of any science.

Sociometry can be considered either a technique or a measurement. To the degree that it is used to chart and identify, sociometry must follow the rules scientists demand of instruments: agreement by independent observers, internal consistency, a likelihood that the same results will occur in the foreseeable future if there is no therapeutic intervention, and differences to give meaning to family relationships in responses.

When sociometry is used to modify social interactions it becomes a technique. Sociometric techniques are well suited to couple and family

69

therapy because of their effectiveness in vividly portraying each person's place in the system, the members' patterns of interaction, and their feelings about it.

Historically, Moreno and his followers (1940, 1945, 1946, 1951, 1966) introduced sociometric techniques to mental health clinicians, particularly the many techniques involved in psychodrama, sociodrama, and sculpting. Following their lead social psychologists and clinicians introduced many new techniques. Some examples are:

1. *The Sociogram* — a method for charting preferences and choices in role relationships.
2. *The Genogram* — a method for charting the family constellation and history.
3. *The Ecomap* — a method for charting the family's place in the extended family and community, influences operating on it, and resources available.
4. *The Family Floor Plan* — a method to chart the relationships among space, place, and emotions.
5. *Sculpting* — a method to physically position the members in ways that express their relationship in a given situation or ideally.
6. *Games* — Metaphors for enacting role behaviors by building a straw tower or a house from building blocks, or by completing a puzzle or solving a problem.
7. *The Role Card Game* — a method for identifying perceived and expected roles in the family.

These and other techniques are described in this chapter.

Adherents of different theoretical schools use sociometry to obtain the data and results consonant with their particular theory. For example, psychoanalysts obtain data on such forces as social influences, projection and identification models, the unfinished business or trauma in the family of origin, sublimation of frustrations, coping and adaptation mechanisms, and clues to the unconscious behavior of the identified patient.

Communication theorists seek out the lines of communication and faulty communication within the system. They are interested in determining who is the center of communication and who are the stars, isolates, blockers, supporters, questioners, followers, and so forth.

System theorists are concerned with the pattern and form of the interactional system; how it is organized in terms of power and decision making, boundaries, closeness and distance, alliances, collusions, roles, rules, complementarities, and similarities.

The therapist can feed this information back to the clients to increase their awareness and insight. She can intervene and reshape the structure through direct movement, coaching, questioning, interpretation, or direct prescription.

Sociometric techniques offer many advantages.

1. They move the therapy from an intellectual or emotional discussion to experimental enactment. This increases the active involvement of each member, which in turn often has the effect of increasing client spontaneity and reducing the resistance built up in the intellectual arena.

2. They place past, present, and anticipated future into a here and now operational framework. We can recall, but we cannot change the past. We can anticipate, but we cannot live in the future. By placing these in a here and now experience, clients can act on them immediately changing perception, understanding, planning, or behavior.

3. They contain an important element of personal identification and projection. Beliefs, feelings, and attitudes are behaviorally expressed in the interactional context so that they become overt and available for examination and modification. Projection adds a qualitative diversion to the facts portrayed. (See the Introduction to Chapter 2 for the advantages and qualities of projection.)

4. They expose and dramatize roles and role perceptions. The members observe what each does, how it is perceived, and how the roles are reinforced.

5. They are surprisingly different from what clients tend to expect in therapy. They may help avoid some of the resistances that might otherwise be encountered.

6. They are interesting. These techniques grab the attention of clients.

7. They constitute a form of meta communication. Reality and mythology are combined and new messages are formulated, sent, and received with no discussion. For example, when a family is sculpted and father is placed outside the family circle with his back to the family, there are many powerful messages in that event for husband, wife, children, and family as a unit.

8. They focus attention on the social unit and social interaction process. The isolation and alienated feelings of the "sick one," or identified client, are challenged as the family observes their reciprocal behaviors and positions. It becomes clear that one cannot lead if the other fails to follow; that one cannot be so helpless and survive if the other does not take over and do things for him. Such factors as intimacy, individuation, regulation of closeness and distance, and conflict management skills are observable.

The sociometric techniques reported in this chapter are a cross section of those available.

RESOURCES

Brodey, W. M. *Family dance.* New York: Doubleday, 1977.

Christensen, O. C. and Schramski, T. G. (eds.). *Adlerian family counseling.* Minneapolis: Educational Media Corp., 1983.

How to construct a sociogram. New York: Bureau of Publications, Teachers College, Columbia University, 1947.

Jennings, S. (ed.). The importance of the body in non-verbal methods of therapy. In *Creative therapy.* London: Pitman, 1975.

McAdams, D. P. and Powers, J. Themes of intimacy in behavior and thought. *Journal of Personal and Social Psychology,* 1981, *40,* 573–587.

Moreno, J. L. *Who shall survive?* Washington, D.C.: Nervous and Mental Disease Publishing Company, 1934.

Moreno, J. L. Psychodramatic treatment of marriage problems. *Sociometry* 1940, *3,* 20.

Moreno, J. L. (ed.). *Group psychotherapy: A symposium.* New York: Beacon House, 1945.

Moreno, J. L. *Psychodrama.* New York: Beacon House, 1946.

Moreno, J. L. *The theatre of spontaneity* (translated from the German *Das Stegreiftheater* by the author). New York: Beacon House, 1947.

Moreno, J. L. *Sociometry, experimental method and the science of society: An approach to a new political orientation.* New York: Beacon House, 1951.

Moreno, J. L., Friedemann, A., Battegay, R., and Moreno, Z. T. (eds.). *The international handbook of group psychotherapy.* New York: Philosophical Library, 1966.

Rosenbaum, M. *Group psychotherapy and psychodrama.* In B. Wolman (ed.), *Handbook of clinical psychology.* New York: McGraw-Hill, 1965, pp. 1254–1274.

Schramski, T. G. Psychodrama in Adlerian family counseling. In O. C. Christensen and T. G. Schramski (eds.), *Adlerian family counseling.* Minneapolis: Educational Media Corp., 1983.

The sociometry reader. Glencoe: Free Press, 1959.

Starr, A. *Psychodrama: Rehearsal for living.* Chicago: Nelson-Hall, 1977.

Thomson, E. and Williams, R. *Beyond wives family sociology: A method for analyzing couple data. Journal of Marriage and Family Therapy,* 1981, *44,* 999–1008.

Waynar, M. K. Using psychodrama for information gathering. *Social Casework,* 1981, *62,* 490–494.

Yablonsky, L. *Psychodrama: Resolving emotional problems through role playing.* New York: Gardner Press, 1981.

18 | SCULPTING

Rationale

A family sculpture is an arrangement of people or objects that physically symbolizes emotional family relationships at a particular time. It identifies each person's perceived place in the system. Each family member creates a live family portrait placing members together in terms of posture and spatial relationships representing action and feelings. The essence of one's experience in the family is condensed and projected into a visual picture. Papp, Silverstein, and Carter (1975), and Duhl, Duhl, and Watanabe (1975) are among the many strategic therapists who use this technique extensively.

One of the major advantages of sculpting is the ability to cut through excessive verbalization, intellectualization, defensiveness, and projection of blame. Families are deprived of their familiar verbal cues and are compelled to communicate with one another on a different, more spontaneous level. As triangles, alliances, and conflicts are depicted, they are made concrete and placed in the realm of the visual, sensory, and symbolic areas where there are different possibilities for communication of feelings in all their nuances. In this way, sculpting is a good diagnostic tool.

Another advantage of sculpting is the adhesive effect it has on families. For example, it compels them to think of themselves as a unit with each person a necessary part of that unit. It is impossible to isolate any one intense relationship without seeing the repercussions of it throughout the family. While uniting the family, the sculpting also individuates, since it requires each member to abstract his own personal experience, observe it, and interpret it.

Sculpting also provides the therapist with an opportunity to directly intervene. A structural therapist might help the family members rearrange their physical positions, creating more appropriate boundaries. In this way sculpting is used to produce change.

Procedure

Family sculpting may be appropriate at any point in diagnosis or therapy. One should preferably have at least three or four people present plus some readily mobile furniture or objects that may be used in place of additional persons. Either the family of the present or the family of the past may be represented and any number of extended family members may also be part of the sculpture.

The therapist explains to the family that this is a useful way to see what it feels like to be in this family. Sometimes it is easier to act out what happens than to relate it. Everyone in the family can show his or her own version of the family by sculpting it. Each member has a turn at ar-

ranging the other members of the family (or the people or objects substituting for them), one at a time, in the family life space so that postures
and spatial relationships represent actions and feelings (Papp, Silverstein,
and Carter, 1975). Papp suggests that the sculptor is encouraged to treat
each person as if he or she is malleable and made of clay in moving the
physical parts of the body to reflect the spatial arrangements, physical
actions, and emotional proximity or distance of the family members. The
sculptor places each person in a position that characterizes him or her
nonverbally. The therapist takes the physical position of the sculptor in
the family. Each person is positioned until the member setting up the
sculpture is satisfied that it reflects his family system. It is important for
the individuals in the family to let the sculptor arrange them in a way
that suits his interpretation of the family, with the understanding that
the others will also have a turn at portraying their own impressions.

After each member portrays how they experience the family members
at present, they can portray how they would ideally like it to be.

The therapist can intervene by coaching or suggesting possibilities.
Once this "ideal" is represented, reference can be made to it later in order
to evaluate movement in the therapy. What the therapist takes from the
form and content of the scene depends on what she knows about the family and where they are in the course of treatment. Incongruities between
one person's reality and another's can be crucial and they may be more
accessible in a sculpting situation than in a purely verbal one.

There are many variations of how sculpting can be used. Some therapists might ask the sculptor to assign to each member a word or phrase
that captures that person's typical behavior. The members are asked to
recite these words quickly in sequence after the sculpture is completed.
In this way the effect is not only visual but also auditory.

Some therapists might choose to explore the sculpture from multiple
points of view and discuss with the family its meaning, impact, implications, and ramifications. The therapist might also ask the following questions:

1. (of each person) How does it feel to be in that place in this family?
2. (of the family) Did you know that the sculptor perceived the family
    this way?
3. (of each member) Did you know the sculptor perceived you in this
    way?
4. (of the family) Do you agree that this is how the family functions?
5. (of the sculptor or the family) What changes would you like to see
    in how this family functions or organizes itself?
6. (of the sculptor prior to any other discussion) Can you give a cap-
    tion to this scene?

Other therapists might let the family integrate the experience on its own without in-session discussion.

Sculpting can also be used when working with an individual. Furniture can be used in place of family members. Though this is different from having each person portray his own position as assigned by the sculptor, it is still a dramatic technique. The sculpture can help clarify the individual's perceived position in the family. An ideal sculpture can be created the same way.

Sculpture should not be overinterpreted as describing the situation as it really is because the sculptor is simply representing his own subjective inner reality.

Example

The L. family was referred to therapy because their youngest son, Miguel (12 years old), had run away from home. The father, stepmother, and the three older sisters were all present. Though tension in the family was obvious, it was not clear what Miguel's anxieties were about. It was important for Miguel to protect his father and his sisters and he insisted that everything was fine at home. He said, "I don't know why I ran away." Miguel, holding back verbally, was a good potential candidate for sculpting, since he might be able to express his feelings in a mode that was less threatening to him than verbal discussion.

The therapist instructed Miguel as follows: "Imagine that you are a sculptor. I want you to make a sculpture of your family. Your family is made out of clay. You can place them anywhere, in any position. Go ahead and sculpt, I would like to see what the family looks like."

The therapist then began to help Miguel along with specific questions: "Here is mother. Should she be standing or sitting? How should she put her hands? Where is she looking? How about father—where is he? How is he standing? Is he touching mother? Where is he looking? Where is Lia standing in relation to mother and father? Move her shoulders so that it looks right at you. How about Maria? Where does she belong? Where is she looking? And Lydia, place her. Now put me in your place. Should I stand or sit? What kind of look do I have on my face? Does the sculpture look at you? Come here and trade places with me and see if it feels right. Is this what it feels like?"

Miguel initially hesitated but gradually was able to take the part of the sculptor. He placed his three sisters in a circle. It was clear that Miguel saw no room for himself in their circle. The parents were also represented as a closed unit. Miguel was standing alone someplace in the background between his parents and his sisters (see Figure 1). Through sculpting the sisters noticed that although they claimed that they felt close to Miguel, he felt like an outsider. All of the children depicted the paren-

Figure 1.   Miguel's Sculpture of His Family*

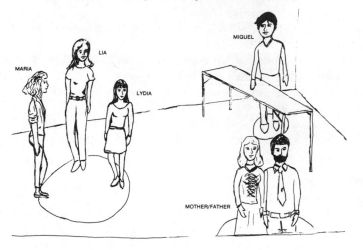

*Illustration by Gaston Weisz.

tal unit as closed, with their stepmother further away than their father. There was usually an object, like a table or newspaper, separating one parent from the children. Three of the children's four sculptures placed the father with his hands crossed. The father's sculpture showed Miguel with his arms crossed and not facing the family. Both the father and the stepmother reacted strongly to the children's sculptures. The parents were surprised at the distance that was placed between them and the children. When discussing the sculpture the parents said that they had never sensed their separateness. Lia said, "Maybe you just never were able to hear how I felt, now you can see it."

Each of the family members was asked to sculpt an "ideal" sculpture. Miguel placed each member substantially closer than in the original sculpture with himself part of the family circle (see Figure 2). In the ensuing discussion Miguel was able to express himself verbally in a way that was previously very difficult, and he discussed his feelings of being an "outsider." He sensed his sisters as a group and his parents as a closed unit. Miguel was able to come closer to owning his feelings of "not belonging." Lydia was surprised by Miguel's professed feeling of isolation, for she envied his special position of being the only son.

The sculpting and the sculptures helped the family members honestly assess their present positions. They were given the opportunity to pre-

Figure 2. Miguel's Sculpture of His Ideal Family*

*Illustration by Gaston Weisz.

sent in a nonverbal manner how they would like to be ideally. For a family that denied difficulties, the sculpting was accepted as a nonthreatening technique. Sculpting also promoted the family's working together and helped remove the focus from Miguel, the "bad-boy runaway."

Uses
Sculpting can be conducted with almost any meaningful unit, with an individual, with couples, with parent–child subsystems, sibling subsystems, with the whole family, with a co-therapy or other work team, or even with an entire corporation, although the staging and format will differ with the unit of choice. Sculpting is useful as an evaluative measure, interventive measure, or even as a mechanism for communicating to clients. It can be a powerful antidote to "blockage" and "dragging" in therapy.

Adolescents usually make excellent sculptors because of their insight into family truths and their natural relish in manipulating their elders. Latency children are also good natural sculptors, although what they produce may be somewhat idealized and stereotyped. Furthermore, so-called well siblings may express secret loneliness, fear, or hostility previously considered the sole domain of the "sick" child. It is harder for young children or parents to initiate sculpting, the former because of a lack of comprehension and the latter because of anxiety about their dignity. However, once the initial awkwardness is gone, they may show themselves very perceptive sculptors, and lively competition may develop among family members to present their own points of view.

As the family role pattern begins to emerge, triangles, alliances, and emotional relationships begin to appear as well as issues of power, closeness and distance, and boundaries. The technique of family sculpting is a way of observing these patterns more clearly and is useful with families who are skilled in verbal manipulation or who resist the traditional interview process.

Family choreography is an extension of family sculpting. See also the next technique "Family Choreography," in this chapter.

RESOURCES

Ackerman, N. W. *Psychodynamics of family life*. New York: Basic Books, 1958.

Christensen, O. C. and Schramski, T. G. (eds.) *Adlerian family counseling*. Minneapolis: Educational Media Corp., 1983.

Constantine, L. L. Designed experience: A multiple goal-directed training program in family therapy. *Family Process*, 1976, *15*(4), 373–387.

Duhl, B., Duhl, F., and Watanabe, S. Types of sculpture. Unpublished notes, The Boston Family Institute, 1170 Commonwealth Avenue, Boston, MA, 02134, 1975.

Duhl, F. S., Kantor, D. and Duhl, B. S. Learning space and action in family therapy: A primer of sculpting. In D. Bloch (ed.), *Techniques of family psychotherapy: A primer*. New York: Grune & Stratton, 1973.

Ferber, A. and Mendersohn, M. Training for family therapy. *Family Process*, 1969, *8*, 25–32.

Framo, J. L. Marriage therapy in a couple group. In D. A. Bloch (ed.), *Techniques of family psychotherapy: A primer*. New York: Grune & Stratton, 1973.

Framo, J. L. A personal viewpoint on training in marital and family therapy. *Professional Psychology*, 1979, *10*, 868–875.

Framo, J. L. Marriage and marital therapy: Issues and initial interview techniques. In M. Andolfi and I. Zwerling (eds.), *Dimensions of family therapy*. New York: Guilford Press, 1980.

Freud, S. *Group psychology and the analysis of ego* (1921). The Standard Edition of the Complete Works of Sigmund Freud, Vol. 18. London: Hogarth Press, 1955.

Hale, A. E. *Conducting clinical sociometric exploration: A manual for psychodramatists and sociometrists*. Available from author: 1601 Memorial Avenue, No. 4, Roanoke, VA, 24015, 1981.

Moreno, J. L. *Psychodrama*. New York: Beacon, 1946.

Papp, P., Silverstein, O., and Carter, E. Family sculpting in preventive work with "well families." *Family Process*, 1975, *12*(2), 197–212.

Satir, V. *Conjoint family therapy*. Palo Alto, CA: Science and Behavior Books, 1967.

Starr, A. *Psychodrama: Rehearsal for living*. Chicago: Nelson-Hall, 1977.

19 | FAMILY CHOREOGRAPHY

Rationale
Family choreography is an outgrowth of family sculpture developed by David Kantor and Fred and Bunny Duhl at the Boston Family Institute and Peggy Papp at the Ackerman Family Institute in New York City. It is a metaphor to describe systems theory as a physical form through spatial relationships. However, Peggy Papp felt that the term "sculpture" implied a static rather than a fluid state. She felt that since emotional relationships are always in motion, "choreography" was a more accurate term for a process that implied movement. A family member is asked to physically position the members of the family in a scene that expresses the relationship among them with respect to an event or the stated problem and then enact the scene.

Family choreography is an effective technique that can be comprehensible to any family, particularly those who have difficulty verbalizing easily. Problems and alternative solutions can be presented in terms of action, sight, and movement. Family choreography can change defensive, repetitive, and predictive patterns in dysfunctional interactions; it transcends language and thus can reveal the underlying emotional problems experienced in individuals, couples, families, and other groups. These problems then can be explored in terms of alternative solutions.

Family choreography relies primarily on the creation of new patterns. It means changing the system to which one belongs rather than experiencing or understanding that system. These changes are attempted through an exploration of alternative transactional patterns in terms of physical movement and positioning (Papp, 1976, p. 466). Its major value lies in its ability to physically reveal human relationships.

Procedure
The procedure tends to vary; it is flexible and can be modified depending on the particular interactional themes. Generally, family members are instructed to demonstrate nonverbally a physical and visual picture of the manner in which they view their current family functioning or couple relationships. They are then instructed to show how they would like the family situation to be.

Specifically, each family member is instructed to situate himself about the room in whichever manner best demonstrates the problem. The therapist then directs and assists the family members in describing through movement and positioning the manner in which they relate to each other nonverbally, acting out the entire scene. It can then be resculpted in the manner in which they would like their family to be.

Through positioning and enactment the therapist might ask one family member to show a picture of his family and then instruct this member to demonstrate what he would like to do or how he would like the family to be.

To further clarify the problem, the therapist might also instruct this member to give the others and himself a short, verbal statement which best describes or characterizes each one's position and function in the family. Each member would then, in turn, repeat their statements to the others. The therapist inquires of each how it feels to be in that place in this family and how he feels about the others.

In a different situation, the therapist might instruct family members or marital couples to enact and repeat, through movement and positioning, the dysfunctional sequences of their interactions trying harder each time to get what they want. If these repeated attempts prove futile, the therapist helps the partners or family members to explore alternative solutions through further movement and positioning.

Another variation is to ask the clients to fantasize first the others and then themselves each as some kind of animal or object. For example, the client envisages that he is a large, powerful lion with big jaws and sharp teeth. The person then fantasizes a scene involving these animals or objects and describes the scene in terms of color, light, space, and positioning. The action of each in the scene is described. Then the group is asked to assume the positions described and enact the scene.

Examples

The following three examples are adapted from Papp (1976).

A marital couple was having difficulties between themselves and with their two grown children. The family was clearly alienated. Hostility was evident between the son and daughter. Choreography was initiated as a means of cutting through the conflicting relationships. Each person was asked to show a visual picture of how he or she viewed the problem.

Through systemic questions and suggestions aimed at emphasizing the interactional patterns, the basic dysfunctional triangle was given a physical form and could be altered within that form. Each member positioned himself or herself in a manner that best described the rifts in the family: mother close to daughter; father close to son; daughter moving back and forth in an attempt to bridge the gap; brother caught between all three. The therapist asked the son to show his family the way he would like it to be. He placed them in a circle with his father and sister on either side of him and his mother opposite him. The therapist, focusing on the marital relationship, asked the father to take responsibility for doing something about the mother's unhappiness; he couldn't. The son immediately attempted to take over. The therapist asked the mother to show where she would like the father to be. She positioned her husband just outside the door. She stated that she was once close to her son as she positioned her son and daughter in front of her. The therapist asked the mother to show how close she meant. She embraced her son and sobbed. She was asked to have her husband come in. Shortly thereafter, she released her son and embraced her husband with one arm and her daughter with the other. The children were eventually excluded with mother and father left alone to confront one another and their unresolved issues, thus releasing the children from their entanglement. (pp. 466–468)

An 11-year-old girl was doing poorly in school. She entered the therapy session with her mother, her 15-year-old brother, and her 80-year-old aunt. There was very little communication from the daughter. The therapist asked her to make a picture, through positioning, of how her family lived together. She placed her mother and brother embracing each other and her aunt directly in front of herself. She stated that she couldn't get to her mother because her brother and aunt were between them. The therapist asked what she would like to do. She brushed past her aunt, pushed her brother aside, and, crying, embraced her mother. The mother, never being able to demonstrate such affection, clung to her daughter.

Verbal communication could never have graphically displayed this scene nor could it have changed it as dramatically. This choreography helped break through the conflict and instill hope in the mother and daughter. (pp. 468–469)

A husband comes home after disappearing for months at a time. This has been his habitual pattern. He walks into his bedroom. His wife approaches and attempts to make contact. He leaves the bedroom and walks from room to room as his wife continues to pursue him, but to no avail. She tries every device she knows until she eventually breaks down crying. Her husband feels trapped.

The therapist asks them to repeat this sequence with each partner trying harder to do what they habitually do. Their attempts prove futile. Different alternatives are explored through position and movement. The therapist instructs the wife to first greet the husband, then immediately walk away and get involved in activity. The husband responds with interest and curiosity. The sequence is then repeated; this time the husband enters the house and sweeps his wife off her feet. The habitual, dysfunctioning pattern is replaced by a new one. The couple was asked to practice this at home. (pp. 469–471)

Uses

Family choreography is useful for:

1. Realigning relationship in the nuclear family.
2. Connecting children's symptoms to family patterns by providing

them with a channel for expressing what they cannot express verbally.
3. Tracking and interrupting vicious circle patterns by providing a clear picture of the sequences leading to the escalation.
4. Training mental health and family therapy practioners by creating a graphic picture of family processes over time and helping them understand their own behavior by choreographing their own families of origin and current families.
5. Educating the public and other professionals by dramatically demonstrating the family system.
6. Utilizing an audience in groups which can both actively participate in the process and view it with detachment and objectivity, especially couple group and multiple family group.
7. Consulting by providing not only a different point of view, but a different form.

RESOURCES

Duhl, F., Duhl, B., and Kantor, D. Learning, space and action in family therapy. In D. Bloch (ed.), *Techniques of family psychotherapy*. New York: Grune & Stratton, 1973.

Papp, P. Family choreography. In P. J. Guerin (ed.), *Family therapy: Theory and practice*. New York: Gardner Press, 1976.

Papp, P. The use of fantasy in a couples group. In M. Andolfi and I. Zwerling (eds.), *Dimensions of family therapy*. New York: Guilford Press, 1980.

Papp, P., Silverstein, O., and Carter, E. A. Family sculpting in preventive work with "well families." *Family Process*, 1973, *12*, 197–212.

20 | THE GENOGRAM

Rationale

A genogram is a structural diagram of a family's three- or four-generational relationship system. It is particularly used by Murray Bowen (1978) and others who take a multigenerational approach to family therapy. Its aim is to show how patterns are transmitted and how past events such as death, illness, great success, or immigration have influenced current patterns and how they affect family dyads and triangles. It allows the therapist and the family to view these phenomena together. At times it brings "skeletons out of the closet" and in general it permits a rich vertical view of the family. This approach has some similarity to the more traditional history-taking approach, except that it is pattern and structure oriented and it is done by charting the data. In most cases clients involve extended family in the process.

The genogram uses specific symbols to illustrate the family relationship system. These symbols, together with other pertinent data, are used to show the relationships and positions for each family member. This diagram is a roadmap of the family relationship system. Once the names, the age of each person, the dates of marriage, deaths, divorces, and births are filled in, other pertinent facts about the relationship process can be gathered, including the family's physical location, frequency and type of contact, emotional cutoffs, issues that create conflict or anxiety, nodal events, and degrees of openness or closeness. Family themes, values, rules, and masculine and feminine guiding lines can also be elicited. Each of these facts will help the therapist form a diagram of the family characteristics and dynamics.

Procedure
The object is to obtain and diagram a history of the problem, nuclear family, and extended families of both husband and wife, preferably for at least three generations. The work is begun any time after the therapist has joined with the family members, and it is offered as a matter-of-fact method for collecting data to help understand and solve the problem. It is usually done in the presence of all family members old enough to listen and learn about their family. It is assumed that members are indeed interested in learning the details and observing the relationships that emerge in the process.

The evaluation begins by focusing on what the symptoms are, who has them, when they emerged, and what has been the clinical course. Physical, emotional, and social acting-out symptoms are all considered to be manifestations of disturbances in the family emotional process. The symptomatic person reflects something about the way anxiety is managed in the family. Exact dates of symptom's development and exacerbations later may be correlated with other events, for example, a death in the extended family systems. The family members may be so preoccupied with the immediate problem that they have lost sight of the influence of other events.

Next the history of the nuclear family is elicited, beginning with when the two parents met and coming up to the present time. Their ages when they met, what they were doing with their lives at that time, and the nature of their courtship, the marriage, the period before the birth of their first child, the impact on the family of the births of the various children, and some assessment of the present functioning of each child are all important areas. Where the family has lived and when any moves occurred are important, particularly if moves have taken the family significantly close to or away from the extended family. The health, educational, and vocational history of each parent is also collected in this part of the evaluation.

The history of husband's and wife's extended family is then discussed.

The husband's and wife's sibling position, some assessment of the emotional process in the families of each of their siblings, and an evaluation of the past and current functioning of their parents are minimal for this part of the evaluation. Basic data on the parent's health, educational, occupational, and marital histories, as well as similar data on siblings, are collected. Exact dates about extended family events are important because they may correlate with events in the nuclear family.

The therapist uses the structure of the genogram to spell out the physical and emotional boundaries in the family, the characteristics of the membership, the general degree of openness or closedness, and the multiplicity or paucity of available relationship options. Contextual issues are explored such as cultural, ethnic, and religious affiliations, cultural heritage, socioeconomic level, the way the family relates to the community, and the social network in which it lives. Ideally, by the end of the diagram the therapist should have a reasonably clear definition of the membership and boundaries of the family system and some beginning definition of the emotional process surrounding the presenting symptom.

As this information is obtained it is charted using words and symbols to express chronological events, roles, and relationships. Each therapist may invent symbols of convenience, but the following are commonly used:

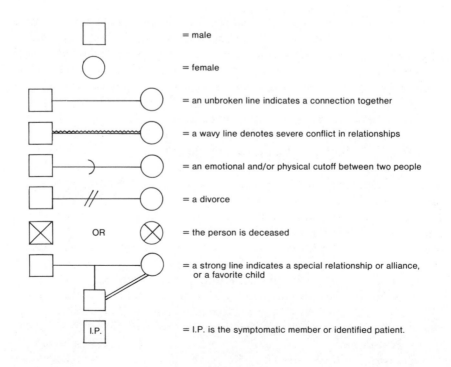

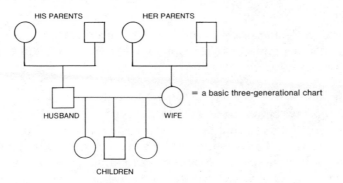

HIS PARENTS   HER PARENTS

HUSBAND   WIFE

CHILDREN

= a basic three-generational chart

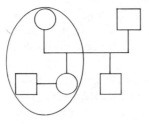

= a triangle identifies a relationship in
which a third person is brought into a
dysfunctional relationship between a pair
in order to reduce the anxiety or to
stabilize that dyadic relationship

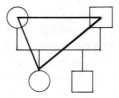

= a line around a combination of members
points out that these members are in
alliance or collusion

= child in utero

A

= abortion or stillbirth

d. 1972   = died in 1972

Example

Guerin and Pendergast (in Guerin, 1976) provides an example of the use of the genogram. The following case is abstracted from Guerin and Pendergast, 1976, pp. 455–464.

Tom . . . is 49 years old; his wife, Mary, is 41. From previous marriages they have between them a total of seven children. Mary called and asked if she and Tom could come in for consultation around the effect on the family of Tom's being out of work. In the initial phase of the evaluation interview the genogram was employed and the basic facts were gathered. One of the facts that surfaced early in tracking the genogram with this family was that both Tom and Mary had lost mates. Tom's first wife and Mary's first husband both died in the same year, a symmetrical emotional experience for the couple. Mary lost her husband through suicide; the therapist files away for some appropriate time a series of questions about how responsible Mary felt for her husband's suicide. If she did, then how did she deal with that? Whom can she talk to most openly about it? Later on, the therapist learns that his suicide is a major secret being kept from her children. Tom's wife died in childbirth, an unusual happening in this generation. The fact that she had died giving birth to a sixth . . . child leads to speculation about the degree of responsibility Tom felt for his wife's death. This family has sustained a number of losses in a very short period of time. (See Figure 3 for genogram of Tom's and Mary's families.)

The therapist organizes the information around significant areas: the family's operating principles, its operating principles in times of stress; the function of time in these relationships; generational and personal boundaries; the conflictual issues — sex, money, in-laws, kids; triangles; personal closeness, tenderness, and honesty; and the extended family's relevance to the stated problem.

The therapist turns to Mary for her view of the problem. She states that she has been feeling better just since making the appointment to come in. The fact that her mother has been visiting since the previous week is offered as the most recent disorganizing experience. The therapist decides to be untracked for a moment and find out just what position Mary's mother occupies in the present family structure. Mother is described as anxious, critical, and easily upset. The therapist probes the openness of that relationship by inquiring if Mary told her mother she was coming in for consultation. Mary replies that her mother couldn't handle that sort of information. The therapist, referring to his genogram, sees that Mary is an only child, and investigates the impact of that fact on the intensity of their relationship. Going further, she looks for three-

Figure 3. Genogram of Tom's and Mary's Families

IRISH IMMIGRANTS

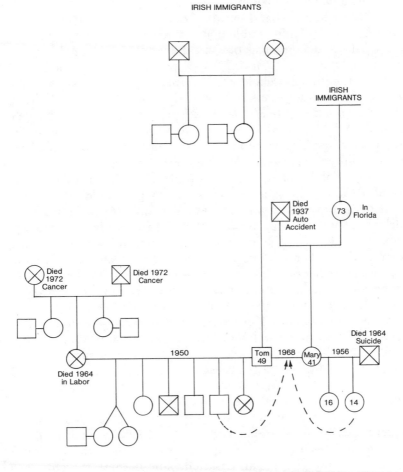

generational triangulation and asks, "Which of your kids is Grandma's favorite?" The answer is Nancy, who just happens to be the daughter Mary is most concerned about.

A number of things come together at this point. Earlier in the interview Mary remarked on how much Nancy reminds her of her father, Mary's first husband, Bill. One of her worries about Nancy, Mary reveals, is that Nancy might repeat her father's suicide. This revelation, combined with the therapist's observation that while this line of questioning is going on with Mary, Tom is relieved to the point of being pleased, causes the therapist to take a series of steps. She frames her move by first recalling Mary's concern for Nancy's possible suicide; then she gradually moves to open the issue of potential suicide in the marriage.

The first target of the therapist's questioning is Mary's feeling of responsibility for her first husband's death. Next the therapist checks on Mary herself. "With all of this trouble that you have been having recently with the children, and Tom's lack of work, have you ever thought of cashing in your own chips as a solution?" Mary replies that while she frequently feels that the entire household would improve greatly if she packed a bag and left, she does not see suicide as the answer to her problems.

The therapist then moves to cover the primary target and asks a reverse question. "You'd never find yourself worrying about Tom becoming so despondent about his own career that he would take his own life?" Mary's answer requires no period of deep thought. She says immediately, "Definitely. Quite often." This is then opened up with Tom and checked out with him. Tom does a disclaimer, stating that suicide is not his style; but he does admit being annoyed at not being able to reassure Mary. Much of the presenting problem as it appears from Mary's vantage point has been spelled out. She has never come to terms with her feelings of responsibility for her first husband's death. She is determined to prevent a recurrence in her daughter and present husband. She has virtually no one that she can talk to about her deepest worries in this regard. When she does let them out into the relationship with Tom, he rejects her intense feelings as unreasonable. Her mother, too, lost a husband prematurely. But the intensity of that relationship cannot contain Mary's emotions. In her isolation Mary is constantly taking Tom's emotional temperature, trying to deal with his children as well as her own, and feeling supported by no one.

Tom appears to be a calm, reasonable man who takes most things in his stride. He even appears to have the present state of affairs under control, and describes his situation with a half-smile and a gentle joking manner. The therapist observes this, and puts it together with the fact from the genogram that Tom is an Irishman, and perhaps therefore has inherited some of the cultural patterns of his forefathers. How much is his calm, jocular exterior related to the Irish manner of holding in feelings of rage?

Here is a man who is used to making $50,000 a year in an important job. Now his wife supports the family on considerably less. The therapist asks, "What are some of the problems you personally face around your present work difficulties?" "Frustration, mostly," is Tom's reply, "I mean, I never get violent or anything." The therapist remarks, "The Irish are famous for their underground rage." Tom laughs and admits that he does experience a significant degree of rage, and that most of the time he just does not know where to put that feeling. He tries hard to control it. He does doubt himself and his abilities. He worries daily, and sometimes feels that this constant internal battle will result in a loss of confidence in himself, so that when he does go to an interview, his embarrassment and lack of belief in himself will show, working against the impression that he makes.

The operating principles that each of this marital pair uses to govern his or her own individual action and reactions have been evident throughout the interview. The therapist knows, for instance, that Mary is a distancer when it comes to her mother, but a pursuer of her husband and children. She is the self-appointed protector of her charges who tries to keep them from all harm. She oversees everything from the laundry to her daughter's and her husband's depression index. Tom, on the other hand, distances from everything but his work. He used his work as a source of refuse when his first wife and baby died, and also later on, after the untimely and unfortunate death of his son. Here is a man whose major prop — the work in which he took pride — has been removed. In his own words, "Pride gets in my way and sometimes it colors my judgment about things. Sometimes I think that now it is my pride that I protect the most."

The problems that this couple have with their two middle daughters (one each from their former marriages), who strongly resemble their respective dead parents, point up the need to deal with the ghosts of these former spouses, so that the children do not indeed become pushed into repeating those parts of the family script. Much of this is revealed by the genogram (Guerin and Pendergast, 1976, pp. 455–464).

Uses

The genogram takes an enormous amount of verbal data and interpersonal behavior and presents them in a dramatic pictorial format on one or two large pages for all to see. Family members obtain much insight about who they are. They learn their place and job in the family, how they relate to one another, an awareness of their roots and how all of this fits into some larger, longer term pattern. Working through the genogram itself, the therapist may help the family repair cutoffs, reduce anxiety, break down triangles, and make all kinds of changes in their organizational pattern. Most particularly, the genogram is a powerful diagnostic tool adapted for use according to the principles and emphases of each theory. See also The Ecomap: Mapping a Family Network, in this chapter.

RESOURCES

Adler, A. *Understanding human nature*. Greenwich, CT: Fawcett, 1927.
Bowen, M. *Family therapy in clinical practice*. New York: Jason Aronson, 1978.

Carter, E. A. Generation after generation. In P. Papp (ed.). *Family therapy. Full length case studies*. New York: Gardner Press, 1977, pp. 47–67.

Carter, E. A. and McGoldrick, M. (eds.) *The family life cycle*. New York: Gardner Press, 1980.

Guerin, P. J., and Pendergast, E. G. Evaluation of family system and genogram. In P. J. Guerin (Ed.), *Family therapy: Theory and practice*. New York: Gardner Press, 1976, pp. 450–464.

Hollman, A. M. *Family assessment tools for understanding and intervention*. Beverly Hills, CA: Sage Publications, 1983.

McGoldrick, M., Pearce, J. K., and Giordano, J. (eds.) *Ethnicity and family therapy*. New York: Guilford Press, 1982.

21 | ROLE CARD GAME

Rationale

The role card game was designed by Gina Ogden and Anne Zevin (1970) as part of a series of procedures they use when working with a family. It is a nonverbal technique that illustrates the jobs and interactional roles each member has in the family. Using this technique, a therapist can ascertain the various roles of family members as well as note how the family interacts when working on a project together. By means of a card game, the members of a family choose the roles each performs within the system. This enables the family members to see what the jobs in the system are, and how the work is divided up. The skills, negative mechanisms, and family dynamics are examined. The technique described here is taken primarily from the work of Ogden and Zevin (1970).

Procedure

Members, without talking, pick out cards (listed below) for themselves and for each other. The cards describe household job roles during dinner-evening-bedtime, and certain kinds of interaction roles. Members have the opportunity to agree or disagree with the appropriateness of each card for each person in the family and a chance at the end to reject cards they do not want to keep.

Job Roles

Household Organizer	Drink Maker	Giver of Small-Kid Baths
Food Shopper	Cook	One Who Puts Kids to Bed
Meal Planner	Table Setter	Outdoor Worker
Floor Washer	Table Clearer	Holiday Manager
Big Filthy Job Handler	Dishwasher Unloader	Rule Maker
Errand Runner	Dishwasher	Disciplinarian
Fixer	After-Meal Cleaner	Person Responsible for
Cleaner Up After Snacks	Pet Feeder	Everything

Interaction Roles

Positive	Negative
Truthteller	Blamer
Helpful One	Placater
Understanding One	Computer
Creative One	Lone Wolf
Happy Person	Distracter
Negotiator	Victim
	Screamer

The point of this exercise is to find out in a nonthreatening card setting how the members see themselves and each other in terms of job and interaction roles. It is important to look for discrpancies between how a member sees himself and how others see him. The therapist is able to see how jobs are distributed and observes the family in a nonverbal, structured situation.

The equipment that is needed is a tape recorder, 36 role cards (each role statement above printed out on a separate card), a piece of paper, a pencil, and a rubber band for each member.

The directions to the family are as follows: "I am going to lay out a bunch of cards. I'd like each of you to pick up the cards that are accurate for you and lay them in front of you on the table so that the others can see them. If someone picks up a card you feel belongs to you, write it on the paper in front of you — this isn't a contest to see who gets the most cards. This is going to be a nonverbal game, so no talking please. These cards are not just for your family so all cards do not have to be picked up. You may think a card belongs to more than one person. If so write that on your paper."

Each person is also directed to check out the cards and see if they are all accurate. "If you are not in agreement that a certain card belongs to you or someone else say so into the tape recorder."

Each member is also instructed to talk into the recorder if he feels somebody else should take a role that he did not pick up. "If someone is given a card that you feel doesn't belong to him say so and put it into a 'wrong' pile." When each person has had a turn to check out his opinion of the others' cards, the family is given a chance to get rid of any roles that they do not like, even though they may be accurate. Then each member is instructed to put a rubber band around the ones he has kept.

The tape recorder is used by the therapist when evaluating the "game." The therapist listens to the tape and creates charts for each member of the family that help identify their roles and positions in the family.

Example

Sue and Douglas and their two adolescent sons were in therapy. Sue was dissatisfied with the communication with her sons and husband. She was often depressed and felt very frustrated with her family. The therapist suggested that the family sit around the table and participate in the role card game. The 36 role cards (listed earlier) were on the table face up. The family was instructed to look at the cards and for each to choose the roles that he felt belonged to him. Then the family was asked to discard roles with which they no longer felt comfortable. It became apparent that Sue was the "worker" in the house and had a disproportionate amount of jobs compared with the other members of the family. She was unhappy with her negative interaction roles and chose to discard these.

Because this was a nonverbal game, the family did not get caught up in their usual patterns of blaming and yelling. The atmosphere was controlled and calm and the family observed one another in a way that did not occur at home. Douglas, who usually said that he did his share by taking care of the backyard work, realized that it wasn't quite enough. When the boys saw graphically the inequity of the job distribution, they volunteered to take more on themselves. Because the rearranging took place during a quiet and peaceful family time and there was no blaming or yelling going on, members of the family were willing to honestly assess their roles in the family. Furthermore, it became clear to Sue that she had taken on many negative interaction roles. She felt caught up in her "screamer" and "blamer" roles and instead wanted to take on the roles of "creative one" and "happy one." Her husband and sons responded positively to her desire to alter her ways of dealing with other family members.

Certainly this does not solve all the role and interaction difficulties in a family but it does afford the therapist a nonthreatening way to deal with the issues of jobs and roles in a family. In addition, it helps the family to see the division of labor graphically. It is different from the usual way that job roles are discussed in a family, which is most often in the midst of an argument. It allows members to take on new roles and discard old ones in a cooperative atmosphere of a group working together.

Figure 4 (pp. 94–95) is a sample blank chart. On the chart is the member's name and seven columns. The following explains the column heads.

+ (for positive interaction roles)
– (for negative interaction roles)
Chosen (for roles the member chose for herself)
Laid On (for roles laid on one member by others, whether accepted or not)
Wrong (for roles laid on the member that he thinks are wrong and will not accept)
Not Belong (for roles others said were not accurate for that member)
Reject (for roles the member discarded at the end of game)

Uses
In assessing the role card game a variety of aspects should be examined.

Skills

1. *Shared facts, meanings, values*. Agreement among family members about the roles all pick for themselves and each other. Are most roles accurate — or are many "wrong" or "not belong"? Are there discrepancies between how a member sees himself or how others see him?
2. *Responsibility*. Look for job sharing and parents' modeling and teaching job sharing to the children. What kinds of jobs do the various members pick?
3. *Positive contact with each other*. Do members give each other positive roles during the game?
4. *Ability to play*. Are the members willing to play? Are they competitive? Do they have fun with the experience, or is it "deadly"?
5. *Accepting individual differences*. Is it possible for members to be different from one another or to change the accepted image of themselves? Members' ability and willingness to reject roles they do not want measure the family system's permission for members to be different and to change.
6. *Internally chosen roles*. Do family members tend to think of themselves positively, or do some members get singled out by the family as being the "bad" one, or the one who placates, distracts, or blames?

Negative Mechanisms

1. *Putdowns*. The negative interaction roles the family members give to one another, along with any putdowns that are heard while listening to tape.
2. *Self-putdowns*. The negative interaction roles members choose for themselves, along with any spoken self-putdowns.
3. *Other negative mechanisms*. Inappropriate jokes or unnecessary questions. (It is important to note who is doing the joking and who is asking the questions.)

Family Dynamics

1. *Sexism*. Are the jobs divided along the traditional sex lines? Does the husband/father automatically pick up the "rule maker" and "disciplinarian"? Can members cross traditional lines in terms of household chores?
2. *Scapegoating*. If anyone picks or is given the "victim" card, it is important to note if that person is being scapegoated by the family. Does the person accept the card? If so, who is the victimized and who is the rescuer?
3. *Power*. The game allows for examination of the power or lack of power in the family. One can note who does the most jobs, who assigns the most jobs to others, and who receives a great many jobs from others.

Figure 4. Role Chart

Role Chart

Name: Sue Jones

Role	+	−	Chosen	Laid On	Wrong	Not Belong	Reject
Dishwasher							
Household Organizer							
Food Shopper							
Meal Planner							
Floor Washer							
Errand Runner							
Cleaner-Up after Snacks							
Drink Maker							
Cook							
Table Setter							

Figure 4. (*continued*)

Role	+	−	Chosen	Laid On	Wrong	Not Belong	Reject
Table Clearer							
Dishwasher Unloader							
Holiday Manager							
Rule Maker							
Person Responsible for Everything							
Blamer							
Screamer							
Happy Person							
Creative One							
Understanding One							

4. *Family alliances.* Who shares jobs with whom? Do two people play against each other — that is, give many roles back and forth? Does one subgroup gang up on another subgroup to lay on negative roles?
5. *Anger.* It is important to note who is taking job roles from others and laying on negative roles. Sometimes the anger is obvious, other times it is underlying.
6. *Emotional support.* If a family shares jobs pretty equally, gives only positive roles to each other, and takes away only negative roles from one another, they are demonstrating emotional support or seeking to impress the therapist and look good.
7. *Hidden agenda.* Underground conflicts, unspoken in the family, about who a person really is and what he needs from others, may show up in the role cards.

Nonverbal clues are also to be noticed. Is the mood up or down? Is there shrieking, card grabbing, anger, or hilarity? Is there organization and calm? Do people arrange their cards so that others can read them or do they mess, hoard, hide, or drop them on the floor?

This technique can obviously be very useful in family therapy. It is a way for a therapist, in a short time, to gather a wealth of information about a family and its way of interacting. The exercise demonstrates graphically the number of jobs there are and who does them. It gives the family the opportunity to discuss new ways of dealing with the division of labor. All kinds of hidden attitudes about jobs can come out — both positive and negative. Though people might complain about a certain job, they might not be willing to discard it. The interaction, or non-job, cards, can provide insight into the way the family members relate to one another.

RESOURCE
Ogden, G. and Zevin, A. *When a family needs therapy*, Boston: Beacon Press, 1970.

22 | THE ECOMAP: MAPPING A FAMILY NETWORK

Rationale
The ecomap is a tool that is described by Atteneave (1976) and Hartman (1979). It was designed as a way to diagram a family and examine its needs. It graphically depicts the family's connections with other families, organizations, and institutions. It is a tool that enables the worker to see pictorially where the bonds, tensions, supports, and a host of other relationship issues, present themselves to and within a family. It helps

a worker create a visual picture of the family's resources both emotionally and financially.

The ecomap is part of the strategy of networking designed to bring as many people together as possible for therapeutic support and to foster change. Finding out who would be appropriate for such a task is the purpose of the map. There are many people in a client's life who are willing to actively support the family but are never contacted. Also, the professionals in these people's lives are often willing to confer with each other but never meet. The Stantons (1984) point out that each system interacting with the family tends to push it in its own favored direction. This puts sometimes conflicting pressures on the family. When this idea is introduced to the family, even if acceptable, it appears to be an overwhelming task.

The mapping of family networks identifies others who are emotionally significant for the client or who are significant because of their detachment. The therapist can determine the closeness of members emotionally and physically because of the descriptive nature of the map and the concurrent interviewing that goes on. The relationships among members can be examined, even if it is emotionally difficult for the client or if there is a lack of information. It is more than just a listing of pertinent individuals.

When the family understands that the worker is aware of the intricacies and uniqueness of their system, they are more likely to feel comfortable about sharing information.

Diagramming the ecomap creates the opportunity for the therapist to join with the family while working on a shared project, which Atteneave (1976) refers to as a "retribalization process."

Procedure
The data can be collected from the identified client or as a common family project. Together they discuss the different family relationships and support systems available. Original information is obtained by general questions, such as:

"Do you have much family?"
"Do you work?"
"Are people helpful in your neighborhood?"

Slowly, more specific questions can be introduced:

"Are you close to your family?"
"How do you like your work?"
"From whom can you ask for help?"
"Who and where are the members of your extended family?"
"How frequently do you see them or hear from them?"

"Are you an active member of a church?"
"Are you in contact with school officials?"
"What other agencies are you working with?"
"Do you have a family physician?"
"Do you have personal friends?"
"What is expected of you by friends, relations, your boss?"

The information is organized and then plotted on a chart or map. Relationships are ordered in terms of intimacy and significance. People who live in the household are grouped closer than people who don't. Positive and negative relational attitudes are noted (in the context of the identified client). All people who are acquainted are connected by lines. As patterns emerge they are analyzed for substructures. For example, focal individuals are known as nexus and a cluster of such people forms a plexus. Isolates and cliques (open and closed) are identified (Atteneave, 1976). Sex, occupation, family and nonfamily memberships are examined.

The mapping process draws on the symbols and methods used in the genogram and sociogram. (See the descriptions of the genogram and sociogram in this chapter.)

Typical symbols are shown on the next page.

Example
This example is an ecomap of the case of a single-parent family with mother and two daughters (see Figure 5). It consists of mother, Roberta (divorced from father, Joe), and two children, Sally and Kim. Other pertinent institutions, friends, and extended family are included. Kim is the identified client. She is acting out at school, at home, and with friends.

Kim clowns with the other children in school and gets into trouble with her teacher. The principal and school psychologist talk with her and call in Roberta. She has two friends on the block whom she prefers and plays with occasionally.

Sally is a good student, gets along well in school, and has a circle of friends. She is becoming interested in boys. She often scolds Kim and bosses her. The girls enjoy being with Joe's family.

Roberta is a nurse. She enjoys work and is satisfied with the income that she receives. This relationship is translated into a positive connection in two directions with the hospital. Although Kim is the identified client, it is clear that Roberta is the one in greatest need of support and engaged in the most conflict. She feels lonely and isolated.

The example illustrates how the process of "ecomapping" encourages one joint effort between the worker and the clients in collecting information. Engaging in this collaborative activity provided an opportunity for Roberta, the children, and the therapist to begin to develop a relationship based on mutual concerns and trust.

Male = □

Female = ○

Other systems = △

Strong relationships = ————————

Tenuous or weak relationships = – – – – – – – –

Stressful relationships = ~~~~~~~~~~

Cutoff relationship by person on the right = ———⟨——

Cutoff relationship by person on the left = —⟩———

Cutoff relationship by both persons = ———⟩⟨———

Divorce = ——//——

Custodial parent in a divorce = □—//—○ Mother / Children

Flow of energy, resources = – – – – →

Direction of movement = —▶

Person deceased = ⊠

Roberta's presenting problem was a feeling of frustration. She sensed a lack of control in dealing with her daughters.

As can be seen from Figure 5, Roberta is the mother of two girls. The younger, Kim, has behavior problems in school. The school personnel call Roberta often to take Kim home from school. Though this is done with concern, Roberta is angry at the school and feels overwhelmed by the demands she perceives are made by the school. School personnel actively try to find appropriate ways to deal with Kim. Note that the school is drawn as supportive of Kim, and that Roberta experiences the relationship as stressful.

Roberta has been separated from Joe for four years. The relationship is diagrammed as stressful, since Roberta is disgusted with Joe's lack of

Figure 5.   Ecomap of Single-Parent Family*

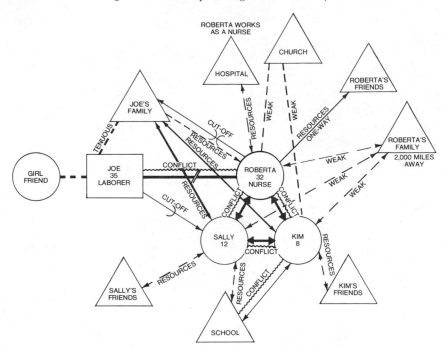

*When the symbols are known it is not necessary to write in the words for the symbols. They are included in this example to help the reader use the map.

responsibility in terms of child support. Joe's parents are close with the children and attempt to help Roberta with child care and support for the children. Roberta resents Joe's family and finds it difficult to accept their help. She says she is unresponsive to their overtures, and this is shown in the diagram by the arrows reaching toward Roberta from Joe's family but no arrows drawn from Roberta to them.

Though Roberta was involved with the church as a young woman, she no longer feels a strong connection. Roberta's family lives 2,000 miles away from her and she has little contact with them. Both these relationships are shown by the dotted line indicating lack of a strong connection.

Roberta has few friends and senses that she helps those she does have with various favors (e.g., babysitting, shopping) but feels uncomfortable about asking for help in return. This is depicted on the ecomap by the arrows that point to a flow of energy from Roberta to her friends.

Roberta was very much involved in studying the visual description of her family and its relationship to the people and institutions around her. The ecomap helped her see that she wasn't fully utilizing the support systems available to her. The therapist and Roberta discussed ways that Roberta could feel more comfortable in asking her friends for help. They also explored the possibility of Roberta being more accepting of Joe's family and appreciating and welcoming their concern and aid for the children. This would help the children maintain contact with Joe's family. It would also aid Roberta with the responsibilities of rearing the two girls.

Uses

Participation in the process of "ecomapping" and studying the finished diagram enhances discussions that follow in terms of planning how a family can draw on resources that it requires for improved functioning and identifying the sources of competing pressures. This approach may provide entry into a closed family and may help the family connect with untapped or underused resources. Workers in many different settings may find the ecomap a useful way of learning about a family's connections with the systems in its environment and psychosocial stressors involved in the family's interactions with many community agencies. It is especially true of the multiproblem family. Each institution also makes demands on the family, some of which may be contradictory or competing. It is also important to identify those forces as well as possible available resources.

The family sometimes provides information for the ecomap that they might otherwise overlook or resist mentioning. The ecomap shows each person's place in the family and in the community. Isolates, stars, and alliances are evident.

Once the map is drawn, it can open the way to calling a family network meeting (Speck and Atteneave, 1973) or creating a surrogate family group (Lifton and Tavantzis, 1979). See "The Surrogate Family Group" in Chapter 7.

RESOURCES

Atteneave, C. Social networks as the unit of intervention. In P. J. Guerin (ed.), *Family therapy theory and practice*. New York: Gardner Press, 1976.

Hartman, A. *Finding families an ecological approach to family assessment in adoption*. Beverly Hills, CA: Sage, 1979.

Lifton, H. and Tavantzis, T. The disappearing family: The role of counselors in creating surrogate families. *Personnel and Guidance Journal*, April 1979, *58*, 161–165.

Speck, R. and Atteneave, C. *Family networks*. New York: Pantheon, 1973.

Stanton, J. L. and Stanton, M. D. "Pick-A-Dali Circus." Workshop
    presented at the National Convention of the American Association
    of Marriage and Family Therapists, San Francisco, October 20,
    1984.

23 | THE STRAW TOWER

Rationale

The straw tower is an early interactive group exercise adapted from group
work for use in family therapy by Peckman (1984). The client group is
asked to take a box of straws and masking tape and together build a straw
tower. Other materials such as building blocks could equally well be used.
This technique permits the therapist to observe directly how family members behave in a situation that requires cooperation.

The members take on their usual roles to accomplish the task. As with
other sociometric devices, it reveals leadership, assertiveness, blocking,
supporting, alliances, isolates, boundaries, and other social dynamics in
the family system.

Through the enacting of the task, the therapist is able to observe how
the family operates rather than merely having them relate it.

Procedure

A packet of about 100 straws plus a roll of masking tape for each group
building a straw tower is needed. The following instructions are given
after the family has agreed to undertake the task:

"I would like you as a group to take these straws and build a straw
tower. In constructing your tower, I would like you to strive toward these
goals. Your tower should be original in design, beautiful, well engineered
(able to stand independently), and durable and portable. You will have
a time limit (10–15 minutes is recommended) which you must observe."

It is further recommended that the first five minutes of the exercise
be done nonverbally. This may add to the frustration and exhibit a different level of observable interactions that will bypass some of their
defenses.

After observing for 8–15 minutes, the therapist can also intervene and
coach the family, ally herself with a subsystem to modify the structure
of the family, question the members in order to help them see what they
are doing, interpret to them what is going on, or describe back what she
is observing so that they can observe it too.

The family and therapist discuss the exercise so that the family can
examine their perceived positions in the family and share perceptions
with other family members. This technique lends itself to inventive variations depending on what aspects of the family's interactions the therapist

wishes to observe, or what structural changes she chooses to make in the family. (See "Uses" section below.) It will of course be necessary to formulate a working hypothesis to establish how best to use it.

Example

The following example is provided by Peckman (1984).

The exercise was assigned to a family of four during their third session. The identified client was David, a 15-year-old, tenth-grade student who had been referred for truancy. David's mother, Lorraine, complained that David never listened to her and tried to come and go as he pleased. Harold, David's father, worked two jobs and was very resistant to coming to therapy. He seemed to relate little to either David or David's sister Susan (aged 13). The family resisted talking about anything other than David's problem.

The therapist asked the family to do the exercise and gave them instructions.

Harold: We don't pay you to come and play with straws.

Therapist: I didn't ask you to play. I asked you to build a tower together. I would like to see how you work together as a family.

Susan: Can we start now?

David: Dad's right! This is dumb.

Therapist: I don't suppose I can force you to do it, but I wouldn't ask you to do it if I didn't feel it could be worthwhile. Why not just do it instead of spending time arguing? I'll tell you what — if you don't think it was worthwile, I'll give you an extra 15 minutes to make up for the time lost. Here are the straws and tape.

The exercise started with David blowing a straw wrapper at Susan. Mom grabbed the straw from his mouth and then started working with Susan on connecting straws into a square. David started shoving ends of straws one into another. When the length was about six feet, Mom looked at David and began shaking her head. She showed David the boxes that she and Susan had made. David went on connecting straws. Mom went on working with Susan. She would occasionally look up at David and shake her head. All during this silent period Harold sat and stared at David. When it was announced that they could begin to communicate verbally, Lorraine began shouting at David.

Lorraine: David, what are you doing? You're not helping at all. You never do anything I ask.

David: But I'm making . . .

Harold: Stop talking back to your mother and do as she asks.

David: Damn!!

Harold grabbed David's length of straws and ripped it apart. Susan picked up the pieces and began to make boxes. Harold then began helping Lorraine connect the boxes to make the tower. (The tower never quite stood on its own.) When the time was up, we began to talk.

Therapist: So, what happened?
Lorraine: As usual, David wouldn't cooperate with me.
David: It would have stood if you did it my way.
Lorraine: You see what I mean. He's so stubborn!
Therapist: Harold — what role did you play in this effort?
Harold: I had to put David back in line and help out Lorraine.

The therapist got a picture of how the family interacts with each other to maintain David as the identified client. Harold tended to be removed from the family. The only time Harold became involved with his wife and the family was to deal with David. He thinks his job is to help Lorraine if she is in trouble. David served to keep his dad involved with the family. Susan's job is to be very good and the firm ally of mother. Mom's job is to get things done in the family. She is the initiator and wants things done her way. Harold and David rebel against her. Harold by withdrawing and David by being overtly oppositional.

The therapist discussed what happened with the family, asking what they observed and what they thought might help the situation. She reflects back on the role each took in the task and the results of their behavior. They can be asked to try again to build the tower, this time using the benefit of their discussion and some coaching by the therapist to help them cooperate.

Uses
There are many ways in which this technique can be used with other techniques. In some variations, the family may be divided into subgroups, each one making a tower. This may be used to emphasize or change structural boundaries or deal with triangles. For example, the therapist could ask Harold and Lorraine to build towers and Susan and David to build separate towers to emphasize the parent–child boundary. One could empower a particular parent by pairing the identified client with the parent and directing the involvement as a coaching technique. An example of a paradoxical intervention might be to allow a five-year-old child the power to design or direct the construction of the tower to allow parents to see the kind of power and control they give up to the child.

The material chosen for the task can be something more closely related to the family symptom such as preparing a meal together, if food is the symbol of love. Building blocks, puzzles, and racing games are among the many other materials that can be selected.

If the therapist wants to observe or emphasize competition, the task can be set up as a competitive game.

After the family completes the discussion of the experience, the therapist can encourage them to do it again, interacting in a more satisfactory way this time.

Sometimes the therapist gets stuck or becomes enmeshed with the family. The Straw Tower technique is a good way to change the pace of the therapy.

RESOURCES

Peckman, L. *The use of interactive group exercises in family therapy.* Unpublished manuscript, 1984.

Pfeiffer, J. W. and Jones, J. E. *Handbook of structured experiences for human relations training.* San Diego: University Associates, 1973.

Rowe, J., Pasch, M., and Hamilton, W. *The new model me.* New York: Teacher's College Press, 1983.

24 | THE FAMILY FLOOR PLAN

Rationale

The family floor plan is an expressive tool that provides important information about family systems and can be used as an intervention. Clients are requested to draw a picture of their home showing all the rooms. The technique was originally developed for use in the training of family therapists. Coppersmith's (1980) view was that learning about one's family of origin and sharing that information with others would assist trainees to acquire the necessary skills for professional competence. Later on the family floor plan was modified to be used with clients in therapy.

Territoriality is an important part of personal and family identity. It is emotionally and operationally associated with belonging and exclusion, comfort and tension, pleasure and pain, closeness and distance, boundaries and enmeshment, power and weakness. Is space used to work in, play in, vegetate in, or fight about? How space is used reveals much about family dynamics.

Procedure

The following procedures and example are taken almost verbatim from an article by Coppersmith (1980). Parents are given a large sheet of newsprint and felt-tipped pens or crayons. They are directed to draw a floor plan of the house they lived in with their family of origin, while the children watch and listen. If the parents lived in more than one house they are asked to choose one which especially stands out in their minds. As the parents are drawing, the therapist slowly interjects the following directions and questions:

1.   As you draw, note the mood of each room for you.
2.   Let yourself recall the smells, sounds, colors, and people in the house.
3.   Is there a particular room where people gather?
4.   When the members of your extended family visit, where do they go?
5.   Are there rooms you could not enter?
6.   Do you have a special place in the house?
7.   Let yourself be aware of how issues of closeness and distance, privacy or the lack of it are experienced in this house?
8.   What is the place of this house in the neighborhood in which it stands? Does it fit or not?
9.   Let yourself recall a typical event that occurred in this house.
10. Let yourself hear typical words that were spoken by family members.

There are several ways in which the family floor plan can be used. The therapist may instruct the parents to draw the floor plan of their families of origin as the children watch. Another version of the technique is to instruct the children to draw the current floor plan as the parents observe. A third approach is for each member of the family to draw the current family floor plan.

The questions raised by the therapist are designed to bring forth memories that are indicative of the family's implicit rules. Also, memories are examined to indicate relationships within the family. Information gathered in this way might be helpful in identifying alliances and cutoffs.

Example
Ronnie complains that his wife constantly rejects him and he can't stand it anymore. Susan fumes that Ronnie is always attacking her and the kids and he doesn't respect her independence, property, or time.

The therapist asked the couple to examine their respective floor plans and to be aware of how issues of closeness and distance, privacy or the lack of privacy were experienced in each house.

Wife's response. "A premium was put on privacy. Mom and Dad had their own room. Sister and I shared a room but there were clear boundaries. She played on her side and I on mine. Everyone in the family respected closed doors. That was really emphasized. I guess what it boiled down to was that each one of us wanted his or her own space. In fact now that I think of it we each had a designated seat at the kitchen table."

Husband's response. "I remember always sharing my bedroom with one or more brothers—sometimes up to three. Privacy, I guess, was something of a luxury we could ill afford since three bedrooms had to accommodate up to 11 people."

The couple discovered that their areas of conflict were related to expectations generated in their family of origin. After participating in the exercise Susan realized that her husband had a very different experience with space in the house of his family of origin compared to her experience. She had not understood that before. She reported that the activity helped them both appreciate their differences without fear of confrontation.

Their respective floor plans became metaphors to explain Susan's need for a rigid, clearly defined structure for living and Ronnie's highly flexible need to use, share, and be involved in most of what is going on or is available. In one another's eyes she's too tight, rejecting, and selfish; he's too loose and intrusive. The technique allows the couple to clarify and negotiate their differences based upon their experiences in their families of origin. The children, observing this process, may become aware of how they are caught up in the conflict, perhaps even taking sides. They may realize how they express similar confusions and demands among themselves and with their parents.

Uses

Much of the following is described by Coppersmith (1980). The family floor plan is an expressive technique, which, when used in family therapy sessions, helps to assess family interaction patterns and to intervene by negotiating ways of using space together and individually. This technique can provide powerful shared experiences for families.

The technique relies heavily on the nonverbal and paralinguistic levels that are vital in family therapy. The technique can be used to elicit material regarding roles and myths in one's family or origin, implicit rules of interaction in one's current family, and the delineation of goals to be accomplished in the treatment.

When this technique is used as indicated above with parents drawing their floor plan while the children watch and listen, the use of this modality allows for the delineation of generational boundaries and subsystems. It involves the parents in an activity together which acknowledges their unique place in the family's constellation, while the children are implicitly demarcated as learners. The family history that emerges when the parents describe their experience of their family of origin can contribute to a sense of legacy and help in the development of empathy and mutuality among family members. Additionally, current issues may be illuminated as spouses discover that areas of conflict may relate to expectations generated in their families of origin. Thus, it can be used to help spouses appreciate their differences.

A second variation involves each family member drawing a floor plan of his present dwelling. Here the therapist tailors the questions listed above to current family life. When the floor plan is used this way it allows the family to discover its own implicit rules along with giving the therapist a view of the family's ways of organizing around issues of closeness and distance, alliances and splits between members, and current sources of stress and support. A shared experience connecting family members in a useful way is provided when disengagement is a family issue. For families with a diffuse boundary to the outside world, this activity seems to delineate the family unit with it's own unique space and ways of operating. This technique is an effective means to promote differentiation and reduce enmeshment because the floor plan allows individuals' differing views of the family's process to come into focus safely.

A third method involves the children drawing the current floor plan while the parents listen and watch. Here the floor plan can be used to differentiate children as a sibling subsystem, while it highlights generational boundaries and respects the children's unique views of family interaction.

In addition, the floor plan can be used in family group therapy and parent groups, focusing either on present family living or family of origin, depending on the goals of the group.

The technique can be used with individuals who are mature enough to remember, comprehend instructions, and communicate. Thus it would appear inappropriate for use with very young children. The technique serves the purpose of providing the therapist with information that might be difficult to obtain through typical interview questions.

The floor plan cuts across many models of practice. It enables the therapist access to information often difficult to obtain in a verbal manner and presents the family with an experience that allows both interpersonal involvement and differentiation, which are so vital to good family functioning.

RESOURCES
Boszormenyi-Nagy, I. and Spark, G. *Invisible loyalties.* New York: Harper & Row, 1973.
Bowen, M. Theory in the practice of psychotherapy. In Guerin, P. J., Jr. (ed.), *Family therapy: Theory and practice.* New York: Gardner Press, 1976.
Coppersmith, E. (Imber-Black) The family floor plan: A tool for training — Assessment and intervention in family therapy. *Journal of Marital and Family Therapy*, 1980, *6*, 141–145.
Haley, J. *Problem-solving therapy.* New York: Basic Books, 1976.

Watzlawick, P., Weakland, J., and Fisch, R. *Change: Principles of problem formation and problem solving*. New York: Norton, 1974.

25 | THE FAMILY SOCIOGRAM

Rationale

The sociogram is a method for chartering relationships within a group based upon the stated preferences of the members. It is adapted here for use in family therapy by Robert Sherman. Members are asked questions about with whom in the group they would either most like to do a particular thing or actually do it. It has been a popular educational tool to assess friendships and interactions in the classroom group. It can reveal alliances, leaders, loners, and who occupies what role in the group. It can serve similar purposes in family therapy. The answers to each question are plotted on a chart so all can visually experience the way the family organizes itself. Both the actual and the ideal connections are obtainable.

The sociogram is a self-report technique. Each participant responds to the same questions posed by the therapist orally or in writing. Like all self-report techniques, it is based on the willingness and honesty of the respondents. The answers are then plotted on a chart which is the actual sociogram.

The assumption is that by making choices about each other, people reveal their beliefs, feelings, actions, and the systemic structure of the family. They engage in active lives of movement in relation to each other in a variety of roles in different circumstances. The connections, therefore, would shift according to the circumstances. One series of sociograms can be constructed around the symptomatic behavior and others to see how the family functions in other situations.

Procedure

The therapist indicates that she would like to get a better idea of how this family functions and requests that each member answers the same questions. She invents a list of questions appropriate to the case for the members to complete. The questions are added to the following two stems:

With whom in your family do you usually. . . . ?
With whom in your family would you most like to. . . . ?

Some examples that can be added to the stems are:

go to the movies
talk about personal things
go to a party
plan a project

do homework
get angry
give a hug
talk intellectually
work together
stay away from
tell jokes or stories
have a fight
play a game
tell a lie
not tell
watch T.V.
play a sport
read a poem
go shopping
run away
go to the beach (country, city, mountains)
learn from
clean the house
feel protected
feel good
feel bad
feel excited
feel sad
feel tired

The answer to each question used is quickly charted.

The therapist carefully formulates a limited series of questions so the process is cost-effective in terms of time devoted to it. Some are directly related to the symptom and others to elicit patterns in other areas of the family's life.

The charts are discussed with the family to indicate how they interact with whom and how they would like it to be. For example, the F. family was asked to answer the question, "With whom in your family do you most like to go shopping?" The chart of their answers is on the next page.

From the chart we can conclude that there is an alliance between mother and Suzie (the two women) and between father and Eric (the two men) with regard to shopping. We might guess that Joan and mother are having some friction. When the answers to all the questions are observed, some definite patterns are likely to emerge.

A variation is for the therapist to use the data to set up a physical sculpture with the family members portraying their relationships (see the techniques on sculpting in this chapter).

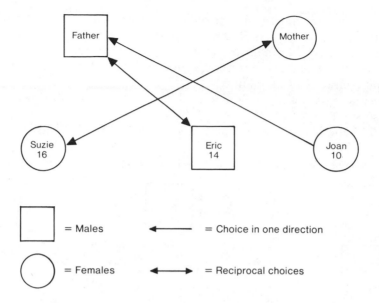

A second variation is the Guess Who? game—Who in the family is. . . . ? Examples are: creating most of the plans; the boss; the biggest grouch; the loneliest; the most angry; the smartest; the funniest; the warmest; the easiest to talk to; the strongest; the best athlete; the best cook; the best mechanic; the best sport; the softie; the kindest; the most generous; the most down in mood; the most optimistic; the most pessimistic; the most enthusiastic.

A third variation to further refine alliances and cutoffs is to ask each person to make both first and second choices in answer to each question. They can be drawn as if both choices are equally important or first choices are plotted on the graph in one color and second choices in another color.

A fourth variation is to include extended family members among the possible choices.

A hypothesis is that the more differentiated the family the greater the spread of choices will be when comparing answers among the different questions presented. Whom I choose to shop with is not necessarily the same person who takes the most initiative or the best mechanic in the family.

Example

Ralph and Mary come in for therapy complaining about the constant fighting among their four children. The eldest has difficulty with peers who tease him. The second child also is lying, stealing, and falling down in school performance. She is the identified patient. This is a remarried family. Mother brings a 15-year-old son, 13-year-old adopted daughter (the identified patient), and 12-year-old daughter. The husband has an 11-year-old daughter in the custody of her mother, unmarried, but with a boyfriend. The daughter visits regularly. The wife's former husband has no contact with the family.

The therapist asked the family the following questions during the second session.

1.   A.   Who in the family *is* your favorite companion? Please give two choices.
     B.   Who *do you most want to be* your favorite companion?

_____ Solid lines are the way it is. Both   ----------- Broken lines are the way they
           choices to question #1 are plotted   would like it to be
           as equal in weight

It is evident that Toni, the identified patient, is largely isolated in this family. No one chooses her. Only mother chooses the stepfather, who is also isolated from his stepchildren. He and his natural daughter Audrey choose each other, thus constituting a separate alliance. In spite of the divorce, Audrey still strongly desires her biological family unit. Mother is closely aligned with her natural children, but favors her natural daughter. Ideally, Jack and Toni would like to get closer to mother, and Meryl would like to get closer to Toni. Neither Jack nor Meryl choose their natural father. Toni verbally expresses curiosity about her biological mother in session but does not choose her. Audrey's mother was not present in the session. Husband and wife seek one another to form a proper parent subsystem but the stepfather prefers his child to his stepchildren.

2. A. Who in the family makes most of the important decisions?

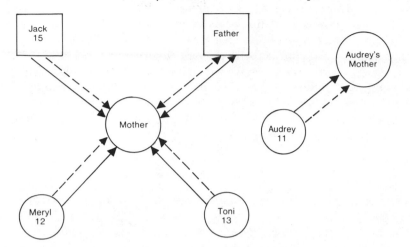

In the chart above we see that mother is presently and ideally the boss. All the family members turn to her. She perceives her husband as making the important decisions and ideally expects him to, but the rest of the family does not agree, including his natural daughter, who turns to her natural mother. Female strength in decision making is a rule of this family. In discussion, father complains that his wife infuriates him by making decisions concerning his activities. When asked if he wants full consultation on decisions, he backs off.

Although married for three years, neither has this stepfather been integrated into the previously existing family, nor have he and his wife organized a new family unit. Stepfather, his daughter, the son, and the adopted daughter are still outside the center of this family. And Toni is loneliest of all. Additional data were obtained from the use of two more questions, but the above illustrates the quality of data obtainable through a sociogram. The entire process took one half hour and led to subsequent fruitful discussions, insights, and movement.

Uses

A sociogram is used to get beyond the complaining mode of talk to a structural picture of the family. It identifies each person's interaction around the symptom, but also the other possibilities and pathways that exist in the family relationships, and suggests those that need to be created or strengthened. The members are sometimes surprised to learn how they are viewed by others in the system and by what their place in the system turns out to be. The method identifies enmeshments, yet also encourages the process of individuation and differentiation among the members as they think about each person separately. The actual centers of power emerge both around the symptom and beyond it. Alliances and cutoffs are revealed in different areas of functioning.

The technique is a method of assessing family roles as they are and role expectations. The difference between the two indicates areas of existing or potential conflict or disappointment.

The technique is most effective with a large family including all children old enough to understand the questions. Others can answer in terms of what younger children actually do in relation to each question relevant to them. It is useful in assessing stepfamilies, especially those built upon a succession of broken marriages.

RESOURCES

Downing, L. N. *Guidance and counseling services*. New York: McGraw-Hill, 1968.

Moreno, J. L. *Sociometry, experimental method and the science of society*. New York: Beacon House, 1951.

The sociometry reader. Glencoe, IL: The Free Press, 1959.

Traxler, A. E. and North, R. D. *Techniques of guidance*, 3rd ed. New York: Harper and Row, 1966.

4

Structural Moves

INTRODUCTION

Structural moves are techniques designed to make changes in the organizational structure of the family system. Relative position, power, role, loyalty, and boundaries among subsystems are subject to these changes. So are the nuclear family constellation and the place of the multigenerational family constellation and the place of the multigenerational family in the larger community.

Historically, recommending a change of environment, job, or school, and placing a child in a foster home or institution are familiar structural moves long predating family therapy as a separate discipline.

In the early part of the twentieth century Adler, coming from a holistic point of view, rejected the dichotomy between structuralism and functionalism. He was very interested in the family constellation. He and his followers examined birth order history, values, and multigenerational guiding lines. Guiding lines are continuing patterns such as maleness and femaleness, vocational interests (entrepreneurial, serving, artistic, etc.), decision-making processes, childrearing methods, and similar traditional ways of being in a particular family over generations. Place psychology was important in terms of how clients subjectively perceived their place in both the system and world and how they then functionally behaved toward others in relation to that perception (Sherman and Dink-meyer, in press). An important part of therapy was to examine that sense of place and its significance.

Place affects and is affected by many interacting influences:

1.   McGoldrick and colleagues (1982) stress the importance of cultural, ethnic, racial, geographic and other socioeconomic factors.
2.   The ordinal position of birth within the family provides a unique perspective of the world and one's position in it (Ansbacher and Ansbacher, 1956; Toman, 1976) and the generation one is born into within the family (Minuchin, 1974).
3.   One's sense of loyalty to members of the family and/or the family of origin (Boszormenyi-Nagy and Spark, 1973), degree of individuation and differentiation among the members (Bowen, 1978), and the creative life style of each of the interacting members (Mosak, 1977) will assert themselves in the way that members organize and maintain the system.
4.   Other major elements in the organization are the distribution of power and how decisions are made (Sherman, 1983); the roles within the system (peacemaker, protector, initiator, humorist, helpless one, etc.); the alliances and collusions among the members and triangulations among them which interfere with dyadic relationships; and the degree of physical and emotional closeness and distance among the members (Hoffman, 1981).

If one takes a holistic approach, then, a change in any one of the foregoing factors will effect a change in the entire system. This is an assumption of most family therapy theories and the major rationale for structural moves.

A second major assumption is that behavior is purposive or instrumental and that therefore the place and role assumed by each person serves a useful function for the system. The nature of this usefulness needs to be understood by the therapist in selecting techniques for change.

Each theory has its own principles and assumptions about the nature of the family organization. For example, is the whole the sum of its parts (learning theory), greater than the sum of its parts (Gestalt), or a hierarchical structure with its parts functionally subordinated to and integrated within the whole (biological developmental theories)? Is the purpose of the behavior to achieve a future final goal (Adlerian), a homeostatic balance (structural and strategic), a reaction to a prior cause or stimulus (psychoanalytic and S-R learning theory)?

Such differences in conception will lead the therapist to formulate her ideas about which technique to use, when, and how.

Structural therapists such as Minuchin (1967, 1974, 1981, 1984),

Aponte (1976, 1980, 1981), and Stanton and Todd (1979) primarily emphasize the use of structural moves as most befitting to their theoretical orientation. Others such as Haley (1976, 1980, 1984), Madanes (1981, 1984), and Papp (1983) use structural moves extensively within their strategic models.

Patterns of organization and place can be observed by the therapist verbally and nonverbally as she works with the family. For example, who sits next to whom, how far from whom, looking at whom, leaning toward or away from whom? Who wanders about, when, and how do the others react to it? Who withdraws attention from whom and when? The therapist can intervene and change the observed patterns that appear to maintain the symptom.

Structural techniques are very important in the beginning stages of therapy. A major move on the part of every therapist is to somehow join with the clients without being absorbed into their system. Whether it is called rapport, joining and accommodating, or transference, the therapist has to find a place with the clients. Essentially this creates a new system — the therapeutic one. It includes structuring the therapy (the rules of this new game), empathy, and agreement about what the work of this new group, including the therapist, will be. The therapist lets the clients know that they are heard, understood, and valued in their own context.

The objective of structural techniques designed to bring about change is to reorganize the system by getting members to move from one place to another, from one role to another, and to establish and reinforce appropriate boundaries between places in the system, thus causing the system to reorganize itself.

Advantages and Uses
Structural techniques can be used for many purposes.

1. Create movement. Clients typically feel stuck in their present positions and don't know how to get out of them. A structural move immediately triggers a shift. This may encourage clients toward further movement. Disengaging a child from a parental role may produce the space for a less adequate parent to move toward more competence and to undertake the job of parenting.

2. Change perspectives. Having clients assume a new place or position with its attendant new roles and rules stimulates clients to observe things differently and apply different meanings to the same facts.

3. Shift distribution of power. By allying with various subsystems the therapist can increase the weight of one relative to the others to overcome inequities or break oppositional deadlocks. Backing up the parents in their role as rule setters for the family and backing up the children in their need for respect and more responsibility are examples of such alliances. Detriangulating the wife's mother by establishing a boundary between the couple and the next generation leaves the couple as equal partners in their disagreement.

4. Disrupt coalitions. Sometimes two or more people combine in opposition to a third. Often a parent and child will combine against the other parent. The child is removed as an ally and stopped from interfering in the interaction between the parents.

5. Form new alliances. People can be helped to combine their efforts by cooperating and working together. For example, the parents can be coached to agree on parenting matters and implement their agreements.

6. Clarify boundaries between and among the subsystems. Who is included how, when, and in what functions; who is responsible for what; recognition of the differences among generations; and reducing too rigid boundaries to allow more sharing and cooperation are the kinds of issues attended to.

7. Discover new aspects of selves. By changing places people have the opportunity to try out new behaviors and to discover new dimensions of their own being. For example, role reversals may put the serious, rigid partner in charge of family fun and the more flighty partner in charge of organizing the work.

8. Normalize the experience of being in a particular place. People will sometimes view themselves as bad, unworthy, or powerless because they occupy a certain place in the system. The therapist can say something like, "If I were in your shoes I would be depressed too"; or "People in a position like yours generally will do or feel similar things"; or "What are the advantages in this position?"

9. Reframe the meaning of being in a particular place. One client complained of the burdens of being the eldest child. The therapist replied, "Yes, that's true. That's what happens to most eldest children. But it also trains them for leadership in the world and others look up to them."

10. Change the family system while working with one individual. If the assumption is correct that when one person changes position the system has to reorganize, then the therapist can encourage and support one client to assume a new role in the organization, forcing the others to adapt.

This chapter samples the variety of techniques available to produce structural changes: tracking, supporting generational boundaries, allying with a subsystem, strategic alliances, the family ritual, the vacation, role reversal, and the complementarity challenge.

RESOURCES

Ansbacher, H. and Ansbacher, R. (eds.), *The individual psychology of Alfred Adler*. New York: Harper & Row, 1956.

Aponte, H. J. Underorganization in the poor family. In P. J. Guerin, Jr. (ed.), *Family therapy: Theory and practice*. New York: Gardner Press, 1976.

Aponte, H. J. Family therapy and the community. In M. Gibbs, J. R. Lachenmeyer, and J. Sigel (eds.), *Community psychology*. New York: Gardner Press, 1980.

Aponte, H. J. and Van Deusen, J. M. Structural family therapy. In A. S. Gurman and D. P. Kniskern (eds.), *Handbook of family therapy*. New York: Brunner/Mazel, 1981.

Borszomenyi-Nagy, I. and Spark, G. *Invisible loyalties: Reciprocity in intergenerational family therapy*. New York: Harper and Row, 1973; Brunner/Mazel, 1984.

Bowen, M. *Family therapy in clinical practice*. New York: Jason Aronson, 1978.

Haley, J. *Problem solving therapy*. San Francisco: Jossey-Bass, 1976.

Haley, J. *Leaving home*. New York: McGraw Hill, 1980.

Haley, J. *Ordeal therapy*. San Francisco: Jossey-Bass, 1984.

Hoffman, L. *Foundations of family therapy*. New York: Basic Books, 1981.

Madanes, C. *Strategic family therapy*. San Francisco: Jossey-Bass, 1981.

Madanes, C. *Behind the one-way mirror*. San Francisco: Jossey-Bass, 1984.

McGoldrick, M., Pearce, J. K., and Giordano, J. *Ethnicity and family therapy*. New York: Guilford Press, 1982.

Minuchin, S. *Families and family therapy*. Cambridge, MA: Harvard University Press, 1974.

Minuchin, S. *Family kaleidoscope*. Cambridge, MA: Harvard University Press, 1984.

Minuchin, S., et al. *Families of the slums*. New York: Basic Books, 1967.

Minuchin, S. and Fishman, C. *Family therapy techniques*. Cambridge, MA: Harvard University Press, 1981.

Mosak, H. *On purpose*. Chicago: Alfred Adler Institute, 1977.

Sherman, R. The power dimension in the family. *American Journal of Family Therapy*, 1983, *11*(3), 43–53.

Sherman, R. and Dinkmeyer, D. *Adlerian family therapy: An integrative theory*. New York: Brunner/Mazel, in press.

Stanton, M. D. and Todd, T. Structural family therapy with drug addicts. In E. Kaufman and P. Kaufman (eds.), *The family therapy of drug and alcohol abuse*. New York: Gardner Press, 1979.

Toman, W. *Family constellation: Its effects on personality and social behavior* (3rd edition). New York: Springer, 1976.

26 | TRACKING

Rationale

The purpose of tracking is to discover explicitly and in detail a specific pattern of behavior, thought, or feeling in its systemic context. We want to learn exactly what happens from the beginning to the end of a sequence. It is possible to track such things a symptom, an action, a communication, an interest, a family theme, or a nonverbal metaphor. Clients are asked to show or describe specifically details about the sequence of their experience through their own symbols and metaphors.

Most schools of therapy utilize the tracking technique. For example, psychoanalysts will track the resistance, Adlerians the internal logic, and other cognitive therapists the irrational belief system. Strategic therapists seek to elicit the pattern of the positive feedback loop in which the family is stuck. Structural therapists use it as a way of joining with the culture and language of the family system in order to later change the system. This last group probably has written most about the technique from a systems point of view.

Aponte and Van Deusen (1981) indicate that "the language, life themes, history, values of the family, all come to represent aspects of the family's identity" (p. 330) and these symbols are found in the content of their communications. The therapist communicates with the family, using their own symbols and thereby building a relationship with the members.

Minuchin and Fishman (1981, pp. 34–39) describe tracking as an essential element in the process of joining with a family and gently directing them toward new behavior. It is a major element in their overall therapeutic strategy. Through structuralization, enactment, and task setting, clients and therapist set up transactions. The therapist joins with the clients in these transactions, helping them tell their story and tuning in to their process. The therapist also notes the pressures exerted on her by the family to organize her behavior in particular ways within the family transactions. She first listens to the story and then moves the level of transaction from content to interpersonal process, focusing on the same issue and leading the clients to explorations of new behavior.

Procedure

Minuchin (1974) advises that:

> The therapist follows the content of the family's communications and behavior and encourages them to continue. He is like a needle tracking grooves in a record. In its simplest form, tracking means to ask clarifying questions, to make approving comments, or to elicit amplifications of a point. The therapist does not challenge what is being said. He positions himself as an interested party. Tracking operations are typical of the nonintrusive therapist. The parsimonious "um hum," the statement prompting continued talk, the repetition of what a person has said, the

rewarding of a statement by showing interest, and the question asking for expanded content are time honored ways by which dynamic and non-directive therapists control the direction and flow of communication. (pp. 127–128)

The systems therapist may ask, "Who is the first to do something in this situation?" "Then what does the other one(s) do?" "Then what does the first one do?" "Then what does the other one do?" "What are other family members doing while this is going on?" The therapist continues until the entire sequence of events related to the symptomatic behavior or complaint is laid out, the final outcome is identified, and the sequence begins again. The sequence constitutes a self-reinforcing feedback loop. The therapist now can observe how each member behaves to maintain the repetitive pattern which the family complains about as the symptom. The questions are presented in a nonjudgmental way by the therapist, who is very interested in what the family does. As the therapist learns the family's language the questions are increasingly couched in terms of the family's own metaphors.

The therapist may also ask the clients to enact a specific event. To the parents: "Could you sit down and join your children in playing with the puppets."

The therapist uses the data to make her own hypotheses, but also to give some form of feedback. "So it's your job to make peace between your parents? How long do you think they will need you to be the peacemaker?"

The feedback is usually reframed in positive terms in order to validate each person and the system and create a friendly, cooperative atmosphere. The feedback also encourages the members to look at what they are doing and gently encourages them to change.

Example
The following is abstracted from a case described by Minuchin and Fishman (1981, pp. 35–38):
The identified patient is a depressed husband, who among other things complains that the house is messy.

Minuchin (to mother): Do you think your house is too much of a mess?
Mother: My house is not much of a mess, but it could be better.
Minuchin: When your husband thinks the house is a mess, does he think that you are not a good manager? . . .
Mother: Yes.
Father: Yes.
Minuchin (to mother): And can he tell you that or does he need to swallow it? . . .
Mother: It varies . . . it depends on whether he can cope with my being upset . . .
Father: I think when something like that irritates me it builds up and I

> hold it until some little thing will trigger it, and then I'll be very, very
> critical and get angry. . . . When I'm harsh I feel guilty about it.
> Minuchin: So, sometimes the family feels like a trap.
> Father: It's not the family so much; it's just (indicates wife). . . .
> Minuchin: Kit? (Minuchin and Fishman, 1981, pp. 35–36)

The tracking goes on throughout the interview. The therapist tracks the identified client's complaint that the house is messy to the process by which the family maintains him in a frustrating bind — a "trap" — which reinforces his depressed feelings and role. If he is angry he will upset his wife. The interview continues and quickly reveals that the wife is also afraid to be direct with her husband for fear of upsetting him.

By mirroring back in a direct, explicit way what the behavior is, the therapist simultaneously joins with the family members and challenges the system. The couple is led to see that not being direct and not wanting to upset one's partner creates a trap. This leads to discussion of their ability to argue and criticize one another as a means of his being less depressed and her need to cry less frequently.

By alternately joining first with one and then the other, the therapist is able to validate each person's position and need while at the same time challenging and questioning the effects of the behavior. The unspoken question appears to be "Do you really want to stay in this position that you now see you are in?"

Uses
Tracking encourages the clients to describe or enact their experiences in concrete terms rather than through vague generalizations. It gets past the family's mythology surrounding the symptom and allows them to see how the situation really is. It allows the therapist to observe the actual sequence of events, how each contributes to the sequence, and who will fight hardest to maintain it.

The technique can be employed in verbal interview format, or the family can show it in enactment of an event, in play, and in games. People of all ages can be involved through judicious communication by the therapist. For example, what happens when she links fingers with an infant?

RESOURCES
Aponte, H. J. Organizing treatment around the family's problems and their structural base. *Psychiatric Quarterly*, 1974, *48*, 8–12.
Aponte, H. J. "Under-organization in the poor family." In P. J. Guerin (ed.), *Family therapy: Theory and practice*, New York: Gardner Press, 1976.
Aponte, H. J. Family therapy and the community. In M. Gibbs, J. R.

Lachenmeyer, and J. Sigel (eds.), *Community psychology: Theoretical and empirical approaches*. New York: Gardner Press, 1980.

Aponte, H. J. and Van Deusen, J. M. Structural family therapy. In A. Gurman and D. Kniskern (eds.), *Handbook of Family Therapy*. New York: Brunner/Mazel, 1981.

Minuchin, S. *Families and family therapy*. Cambridge, MA: Harvard University Press, 1974.

Minuchin, S. and Fishman, C. *Family therapy techniques*. Cambridge, MA: Harvard University Press, 1981.

Papp, P. *Family therapy*. New York: Gardner Press, 1977, p. 146.

Stanton, M. D. and Todd, T. Engaging resistant families in treatment: Principles and techniques in recruitment. *Family Process*, 1981, *20*(3), 261–293.

Weeks, G. R. and L'Abate, L. *Paradoxical psychotherapy*. New York: Brunner/Mazel, 1982, pp. 82–83, 87–89.

27 | SUPPORTING GENERATIONAL BOUNDARIES

Rationale

Many techniques are available to help distinguish the subsystems of the family from one another. Most Western-oriented theories of family therapy note the importance of maintaining generational boundaries between grandparents, parents, and children. Structural therapists particularly emphasize this factor. They believe that a family functions most effectively if there are appropriate, distinct boundaries regarding rules, roles, responsibilities, and interactions for the parents and children. The formation of alliances or triangles across generational boundaries is seen as interfering with peer dyadic relationships between the parents or between the children. Allowing one child to assume a pseudo-parental role equal to the parents or even parenting a parent is defined as a dysfunctional pattern of family organization. Other examples include covert alliances in which one parent secretly supports the acting-out behavior of a child; a child acts out to demonstrate to one parent how he should handle the other parent; or a grandparent undercuts the disciplinary behavior of the parent with a child and treats the parent as another child in the family on the same level as the grandchildren. In each case the structure of the family is regarded as being out of line. The major assumption is that the family is a hierarchical organization.

It becomes important for the therapist to move in such a way as to protect the hierarchy by strengthening the generational boundaries which separate parents from children. Many structural moves have been developed for this purpose. Some are listed below under Procedure.

Procedure
The therapist observes that there is either a blurring or violation of the hierarchical boundaries in the family and the behavior which supports it. She then invents structural moves that will shift the members around in order to create and reinforce appropriate subsystems so that the parent subsystem and the child subsystem are properly separated with the parents in charge.

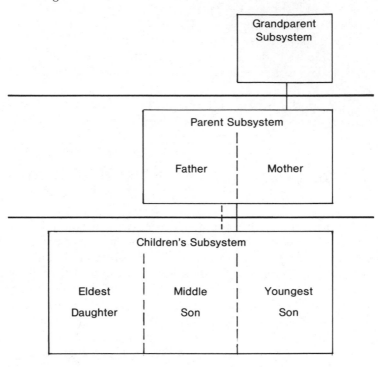

These include the following:
1. Changing seating arrangements to place parents together and children together.
2. Changing tasks to emphasize the difference between the parents' jobs and the children's jobs.
3. Meeting with the parents (without the children) in executive session to deal with their parenting issues so that they decide together on their parenting roles.
4. Asking parental permission to do something with the children.
5. Reinforcing the need for privacy and each person's own territory in the home, with closed doors, where possible, for both parents' and children's rooms. Territory can include agreement on exactly who is responsible for which family tasks and which tasks are personal.

6. Reinforcing time alone for both parents and children to pursue their own activities.
7. Reinforcing the "weight" of parents in disciplining their children.
8. Encouraging parents to consult with their peers or experts concerning their problems rather than involving the children.
9. Encouraging parents to act on an adult level with their children rather than regressing in frustration to childish behavior.
10. Encouraging parents to allow children to act and be their own age.
11. Helping parents to structure for and with the children responsibilities and consequences of behavior appropriate to each child's age and to disengage from a constant "watchdog" role of super-involvement with the children.

Other moves include sculpting (see Chapter 3), role playing (Chapter 2), and game playing (Chapter 5).

Example

The P. family was recommended for family therapy by their daughter's school counselor. She contends that their daughter Lee, 12, has very poor attendance, uses profanity, and is receiving mediocre grades despite her abilities. The school counselor had a conference with the family and she began to assume that there were serious problems in the operation of the family as a group.

The family is comprised of Timothy, 14 years old, Lydia, 16 years old, the client, Lee, Mr. P., 42 years old, and Mrs. P., 39 years old.

Prior sessions had revealed that the initial implicit marital contract of this couple indicated that the husband was expected to help the wife, accompany her, pay close attention to her, and express profound interest in her. This behavior makes her happy. She is required to be assisted with problems. In turn, she must be pleasant and agreeable, express her admiration for her husband, and allow him to be the leader. It is apparent that infringement of this contract can cause emotional pain.

In the interviews Lee would repeatedly misbehave, perhaps by throwing a gum wrapper on the floor. Mrs. P. would reprimand her and tell her to stop. Lee would answer back, Mr. P. would smile, and Mrs. P. would become very quiet. The other two children, Timothy and Lydia, would alienate themselves from the session. This process was repeated several times during the initial segment of the interview. Consequently, the therapist considered this misbehavior as an example of the adolescent being used as a conflict weapon between the parents. She decided to strengthen the intergenerational boundary by giving the wife more support and corroboration to increase the closeness between them.

Lee continuously chews gum and throws the wrappers on the floor. The mother in a soft voice says, "Lee stop that. You are being rude."

Lee answers, furiously, "Stop bugging me." The father remains silent, making no contribution (no support). The therapist says to the wife, "You look like you need help presently, but you are not requesting it from your husband." The therapist is recommending that the wife and husband work together. This was part of the original contract. The mother begins to cry. The therapist inquires about her crying. She replies that her crying doesn't signify anything. The therapist interprets: "You are afraid he won't help." He makes a confirming statement. The mother seems to answer yes, by nodding. The therapist then says, "Let's find out."

The therapist says to the husband, "Do you want to help?" Here the therapist is supporting the wife's effort. The husband, who is intellectualizing, responds, "I always make an effort to be accessible to her, when I am able, but my position as an office manager requires an excessive amount of time in the office." The therapist asks, "You are far away?" She is placing emphasis on this issue. The husband answers, "Yes." She asks him, "Are you at a great distance now?" The husband responds, "No." This signifies that the husband is willing to assist his wife. The therapist says, "It's unfortunate that you are sitting far away from her when you do not feel far away." The therapist is illustrating the inconsistency. Beginning to become disconcerted, the husband replies, "I am not always sure she wants me." He also seems to exhibit sentiments of consternation. The therapist states, "When she looked at you, you were not certain what she meant." "I am not always certain," the husband answers. The therapist asserts that he should ask her if she wants him at a distance. Generally, the therapist is insinuating that he should investigate this. The husband asks, "Do you?" The wife quickly replies, "No."

Then the therapist suggests that the husband should sit close to the wife. He changes his seating arrangement and holds his wife's hand. Reinforcing the generational boundary, the therapist inquires, "Does that feel better?" The wife smiles. The therapist asks the husband if he feels restful and he responds positively. The therapist indicates that their sitting together is an amelioration and a fulfillment of the original marriage contract. She contends that it seemed perplexing when they sat apart. She also asks, "Do you sit together much at home?" The husband replies, "No." The therapist is supporting the generational boundary. The therapist informs the couple that they should attempt to work on this issue and adhere to their initial contract. Thus the therapist has created a stage adherence to a contract and a task assignment.

This session indicated to the therapist that both parents were interested in ameliorating their relationship and following the rules of the initial marital contract. She also recommended that the parents spend a minimum of two hours each week participating in activities without their children. This task assignment further supported the boundary that had been set.

With the parents united as a subsystem, the therapist can now coach them to discipline Lee, who will no longer be rewarded by father for acting out against mother.

The violation of boundaries in the case stems from the breakdown in dyadic communication between the parents and the observance or renegotiation of their unspoken marital contract.

Uses
Supporting generational boundaries is used to help the family members assume their appropriate places in the system. It disengages alliances and collusions that support dysfunctional behavior. It frees children of entanglement and overinvolvement with their parents, and parents with their children. It promotes parental unity and greater consistency in parenting. It may also help expose and repair pseudo-mutuality between parents when they pretend to agree on the surface in order to avoid the threatening condition of disagreement. The disagreement is then acted out by the child.

It is important to consider cultural values when observing generational boundaries. Different cultures may choose to advocate somewhat different boundaries.

RESOURCES
Gurman, A. S. and Kniskern, D. P. (eds.) *Handbook of family therapy*. New York: Brunner/Mazel, 1981.
Minuchin, S. and Fishman, H. C. *Family therapy techniques*. Cambridge, MA: Harvard University Press, 1981.
Nicols, M. *Family therapy*. New York: Gardner Press, 1984.

28 | ALLYING WITH A SUBSYSTEM

Rationale
Allying with a subsystem is a technique emphasized most in structural family therapy. It is employed to help develop appropriate boundaries within a family to upset existing dysfunctional organization of power and distance/closeness relationships. Examples are dealing with families in which: the members are too tightly involved or triangulated; a child or grandparent is more dominant than the parent; or one spouse appears to dominate the other. By entering into a temporary alliance with one subsystem (parents or children), the therapist adds her power, prestige, and authority to that person or group. She can later shift her alliance to another subsystem to strengthen the second group in a new way after obtaining a shift in the family's pattern of organization through her first move.

The underlying premise is that the family is a hierarchical structure with parents constituting a subsystem in charge of the executive function providing authority and leadership for their children. Children are excluded from this leadership role. The parents ideally retain a position of equality with one another as partners and as parents. Children are each part of a second subsystem allied with one another as children. The sick, disturbed, or misbehaving child is assuming an inappropriate leadership role. The use and distribution of power are recognized as a central issue in all conflicts and all organizations, and therefore need to be a focal point in therapy. Power is expressed through alliances and collusions. If these cross proper subsystem boundaries, they will be a source of difficulty. The degree to which subsystems are too close and overlap one another (a lack of boundaries) or are too distant and unconnected are further sources of problems in the structure. Therapists who perceive their role to be neutral or nondirective would not utilize this technique.

Procedure

The first step is to identify which subsystem needs to be further empowered. For example, parents who are ineffective in carrying out their executive function in disciplining acting-out children may be the subject of the therapist's first alliance. By joining with the parents, the therapist coaches and strengthens their leadership. Similarly, if one spouse is ineffectively dominant over another, the therapist may join with the resisting one to stop the domineering efforts of the first one and strive to create a more equal relationship between them. This is consistent with the theory that members of a given subsystem are equals. Allying with a subsystem unbalances the existing system and can be used to push that subsystem to be effective in its appropriate function. When the therapist allies with one subsystem, the bonds between the members of that subsystem are strengthened, and by aiding them in opposition of another subsystem, the therapist strengthens the boundary between them.

Some methods for creating such alliances and empowering a subsystem are:

1. Sit with the members of a subsystem and act with them. This move also identifies subsystem boundaries.
2. Listen carefully to the members of a subsystem and make sure that they are heard and acknowledged by other family members.
3. Interpret to the other subsystems how they are using their power inappropriately and getting the opposite effect of what they say they want (e.g., the misbehaving child claims to want mother off his back, but continuously engages her instead. The domineering wife continues to nag and demand, even though the effect is that her husband becomes increasingly passive rather than more active. Parents

demand that the schizophrenic adult child "grow up," while they treat him as a baby.)

4. Coach parents in appropriate parental behaviors and have them implement those behaviors immediately with the child. The therapist does not take over for the parents because that undercuts their authority.
5. Help subsystem members clearly identify their position and their needs and then make these known in a clear, direct, assertive manner. The therapist then directs the other subsystems to react directly and constructively to those needs and begin a negotiation process.
6. Define roles and tasks to clearly differentiate boundaries. Who will make child-rearing policy? Who will discipline? What are the jobs of each child? What are the jobs of the grandparents, child care workers, each spouse? Who is in charge of fun, socializing, initiating intimacy? As an ally, the therapist helps to establish appropriate boundaries.
7. Remove a child from a pseudo-parental or parent peer role by seating him with the other children. The child is stopped whenever he begins to act as if he were on the same level or above his parents. The parents are asked to do whatever the child was about to do.
8. Remind each subsystem of its appropriate place in the family and help family members define the rights, privileges, and obligations of each subsystem.

The therapist may switch alliances as shifts occur in the couple or family patterns of organization. She may have to continue unbalancing the system for a number of sessions in order to cause sufficient stress for the family to undergo a transformation that will enable the system to find new alternatives to resolve conflict.

Example

Mary and her six-year-old son, John, have lived with Mary's parents since her divorce one year ago. All four members have entered family therapy. The presenting problem is John's temper tantrums. In the initial interview the therapist becomes aware of the ineffectiveness of Mary in exerting control over John. Her parents have taken over much of her parenting role. The boundary between Mary and John has become inappropriately enmeshed. Their relationship is more like that between siblings close in age.

The therapist asks the grandparents to sit together to one side of Mary while John sits on her other side. This seating arrangement defines the three subsystems in the family while emphasizing the primary importance of Mary in issues relating to John. The therapist sits close to and facing Mary. Throughout the session she listens carefully to Mary, crediting her insight into the problem and validating her efforts to deal with it. She asks Mary to turn to each of the other two subsystems and explain what changes she would like in the family. In the second and later sessions the therapist encourages Mary to assume executive control over her child. She will join with Mary to take on the resistance offered by the grandparents and John.

The therapist, sitting next to Mary, inquires of the grandparents whose child this is and who is responsible for him. The grandparents say Mary is responsible and they wish she would take over, but Mary asked them for help. The therapist points out that it is not a case of all or nothing. If help is needed and they are willing to give it, it does not mean taking over completely. It means assisting Mary with her primary responsibility. The therapist then allies with them and praises them for their efforts in raising their own children and being willing to help out now in Mary's emergency.

The therapist then encourages Mary to be very specific about the kind of help she would like from her parents and the support she desires for her disciplinary policies with John. Mary is given specific recommendations for dealing with John in session and at home.

The therapist says to John that of course he wants to be a good boy and to do the right things. She asks John what he could do better to be a good boy and make the most of his time with mother and his grandparents. She solicits the boy's cooperation with the rules of the parent. Each time he behaves appropriately the therapist indicates that that is a way to be a good boy. She also allies with the boy to obtain constructive time and attention from a working, harried mother still dealing with the effects of her divorce. The therapist reminds mother that the boy misses his father who is largely absent since the divorce, which is difficult for him to understand and accept.

The result of six sessions is less conflict among the three subsystems, clearer rules and expectations, more order in the house, less anxiety for mother and child, more friendly relationships, and better lines of communication for the child in getting what he wants. Mother and child spend more relaxed time together.

The shifting alliances of the therapist empowered and rewarded each subsystem in order to reorganize the entire family.

Uses

Allying with a subsystem is a procedure to help the therapist redistribute power in the system, detriangulate members who are interfering with couple relationships, and establish proper boundaries among subsystems. It gives the therapist great flexibility to maneuver within the system. This reduces the chances of getting caught in one particular place and being incorporated into maintaining the problem in the system. It recognizes that the family comes to the therapist as an expert and a person of power to bring about change. It models for the family the importance of flexibility and change in coping with life or the need for rules to maintain order.

The technique is used primarily in structural and strategic family therapy when working with an ineffective subsystem. By creating imbalance in the family system it forces the family to assume new positions vis-à-vis one another and to search for new solutions to its conflicts.

Therapists need to be aware of the subtle differences between "allying with a subsystem" and "taking sides." Allying with a subsystem is a conscious effort to redistribute power, loosen interference, and establish boundaries. It presents a possibility for new solutions. Taking sides is a subconscious act in which the therapist identifies with one or more of the clients *against* the other(s). When the therapist allies with the subsystem, there is a danger that she may be seen as taking sides. A far greater danger exists if this appearance is reality. (See also the technique "Strategic Alliances" which follows.)

RESOURCES
Minuchin, S. *Families and family therapy*. Cambridge, MA: Harvard University Press, 1974.
Minuchin, S. *Psychosomatic families*. Cambridge, MA: Harvard University Press, 1978.
Minuchin, S. and Fishman, C. *Family therapy techniques*. Cambridge, MA: Harvard University Press, 1981.

29 | STRATEGIC ALLIANCES

Rationale
The strategic alliance technique is a method for meeting with one member of a family or couple in order to support that person in making changes that will alter the entire system. The technique is used primarily by strategic therapists and is described by Watzlawick and Coyne (1980), and Watzlawick, Weakland, and Fisch (1974). The material presented here is primarily taken from Breit, Im, and Wilner (1983).

The object of this technique is to create a special relationship with one member, meeting with that person alone. A prescription is given to that person to behave in a new way which will position that person differently in the system, thus creating a new situation to which the other members must now react. The result is a change in the system that will modify the symptomatic behavior. The prescription is carefully planned, based on an understanding of the meaning of the symptomatic behavior and of the origin of the resistance to change. It may be a straightforward task or a paradoxical intervention.

Procedure

In forming a strategic alliance the therapist chooses to meet with one member of the family to share information or make a suggestion without other members of the family knowing what has been said. This one member is brought into a special relationship with the therapist in order to effect desired changes in the family system.

Individual meetings with members of a couple or family are not uncommon in more traditional forms of marriage and family therapy. In traditional therapy, a therapist might choose to meet with each member individually to gather information, to learn about family secrets, or to be supportive to a member who appears to be in great distress or have the greatest degree of pathology. This differs from a strategic alliance in which the therapist uses the alliance to make a specific intervention.

Strategic alliances may be effective when they are made with the healthiest member, the most powerful one, or the one who is suffering the most. Alliances can be made with several members of the family consecutively, each one being given differing but dovetailing instructions which together help the family achieve its goal. Forming an alliance increases the probability that the directive will be carried out since motivation is enhanced by virtue of the therapist's having placed the individual in a special, privileged position. The impact of the action taken is also more effective because the change appears to be coming from the individual and not from the therapist. What appears to be unplanned is, in reality, carefully planned. In making strategic alliances with a member of the family the therapist is actually teaching that member to become a strategist.

Example

Breit and colleagues (1983) presented the case of a family in which a strategic alliance was formed consisting of a father, a stepmother, and a 15-year-old daughter. The daughter had come to live with her father and stepmother for a one-year period against her wishes. She therefore ignored them, refused to talk, and attempted to punish them by showing her unhappiness in refusing to make friends or to enjoy herself. The stepmother made several attempts to win her affection. Despite Herculean efforts, the girl rebuffed and rejected her. The father blamed his daughter's unhappiness primarily on his wife, claiming she did not know how to handle children and was too strict and harsh. At the time they entered therapy the wife was experiencing severe anxiety and rage. She felt victimized by her stepdaughter's belligerent and discourteous behavior and by her husband's attitude of holding her responsible for the girl's behavior.

The therapist felt that the father incorrectly interpreted the girl's abusive behavior as stemming from the poor relationship that existed between his wife and his daughter. Because he saw some justification in his daughter's resentment of his wife, he was unable to take the appropriate corrective measures. The therapist decided to form a strategic alliance with the stepmother to effect a change in the father–daughter relationship. Meeting with her alone, the therapist confided her fear that the daughter was having a damaging effect on the marriage. She was told that in order to preserve her marriage, she would need greatly to reduce contact with her stepdaughter. She was not to try to win her affection, nor was she to advise her husband how to deal with his daughter. By extricating herself from the relationship, she not only would save her marriage but would also spare herself the pain of rejection from her stepdaughter and criticism from her husband. She was relieved to hear this suggestion and eagerly carried it out. The intervention had the desired effect.

Uses
The strategic alliance technique can overcome the circular, self-reinforcing pattern of dysfunctional behavior by extricating one key person from the pattern. The person is allied to the therapist in a new set of behaviors instead of the old pattern. It is a method for overcoming resistance to change by inserting a new alliance into the system, upsetting the old balance of power. It enables the therapist to inject some new options for organizing the system. The prescription, given in private, usually has an element of surprise when implemented, thus catching the reciprocal members off guard and freeing them to respond in a new way. Since the prescription can be either straightforward or paradoxical, the technique can be used with a compliant or oppositional member. Making an alliance does not mean assigning guilt to one of the partners. This means that the therapist must be very conscious of what she is doing by reinforcing one partner, always aware of the possibility of subconscious transference.

RESOURCES
Breit, M. M., Won-Gi Im, and Wilner, S. Strategic approaches with resistant families. *American Journal of Family Therapy*, 1983, *11*, 51–58.
Watzlawick, P. and Coyne, J. C. Depression following stroke: Brief, problem-focused family treatment. *Family Process*, 1980, *19*, 13–18.
Watzlawick, P., Weakland, J. H., and Fisch, R. *Change: Principles of problem formations and problem resolution.* New York: Norton, 1974.

30 | THE FAMILY RITUAL

Rationale
The Family Ritual is a technique designed to change the rules of the existing family game by changing the family structure and sequences of behavior. As described here, it was developed by the Milan group (Selvini Palazzoli, Boscolo, Cecchin, and Prata, 1977, 1978) and is typically used within the framework of strategic family therapy. Other therapists also use variations of this method.

A social ritual is an action or actions carried out collectively by the members of a group in which all the behaviors are sequentially defined. Rituals are a major source of group cohesion and group rules. They serve a normative function in which the behavior of all is directed toward a common goal. Burial and mourning customs, birthdays, weddings, and celebrations of special holidays are overt examples of powerful cultural and family rituals. A repetitive symptomatic pattern of interaction also typically functions as a ritual form of behavior.

The Family Ritual technique is a ritual created by the therapist and prescribed to the family without explanation in order to rely on the analogic level of functioning. The emphasis is on the prescribed actions including time, sequence, details of place, and who should carry out the activities in what specific manner. It is difficult for the therapist to invent an appropriate ritual to be inserted into the family structure as a substitute for the present dysfunctional one. She must first thoroughly understand the system.

It is assumed that the symptoms are related to a very critical family myth necessary for the maintenance and survival of the family. If that survival is threatened, then rigid rituals are created by the family in the service of the myth to preserve the family. Therefore, the therapist needs to explore the family system multigenerationally in order to discover the myth and the meaning of the symptomatic behavior. When these are understood, a new ritual can be developed to change the existing structure by inserting new communal norms into the system as part of the prescribed ritual. If the family agrees to enact the ritual, they are enacting the new norms, thus changing the system.

Procedure
While developing a good relationship with the family, the therapist observes carefully the specific interaction that is in need of change as well as the family dynamics, rules, and myths and how the symptom serves the system. A ritual that meets the needs of this family can then be developed. The ritual is designed to include the context in which the interaction takes place. The design of the ritual is very specific concerning how long it will be utilized (e.g., only once or repeated at specific inter-

vals), when it is to take place, which members are to participate, what environmental factors need to be manipulated (doors locked, telephone disconnected), what topics are to be discussed, what to do if a member chooses to be silent. Goals related to the use of the family ritual may include the definition of boundaries, increasing differentiation of members, improved communication patterns, and improved alliances (intragenerational).

The therapist stresses the importance of adhering to the original myth and obtains a firm commitment from the family to carry out faithfully the prescription about to be given. The prescription is then given in detail. It may also be written out for each member. A part of the ritual may be for one family member to read the prescription to the rest of the group on a fixed occasion at home. By maintaining staunch adherence to the family myth, the ritual has a paradoxical effect. The ritual can be simple: "John will worry every evening from 7 to 8 in his room and no one is to disturb him. He is to worry about the welfare of every member of the family and his own. He is to write down carefully everything he thinks about, but not share it with anybody." The object is to make overt John's role as the protector of the family and to disengage the others from this activity instead of reinforcing it by their existing behaviors.

The ritual can be complex, incorporating behaviors relative to the extended family, community, and the nuclear family as in the example below adapted from Selvini Palazzoli and colleagues (1978).

Example

As an example Selvini Palazzoli et al. (1978, pp. 445–453) describe a family that consisted of a 15-year-old daughter who was 5 feet 9 inches tall and weighed 70 pounds. Her behavior was psychotic and she was very attracted to a female cousin who was her rival. Another daughter was 22 years old, enrolled in college, and emotionally distant from her younger sister. The mother was overinvolved and took care of everyone in the large extended family. The father clung to the extended family myth of "one for all and all for one," as did all other members of the family in handling their interactions. Anger, criticism, and competition were forbidden and denied. The person who expressed anger was pressured to conform by the others. After an attempted suicide by the younger daughter the following ritual was given:

Every other night after dinner the family was to lock and bolt the front door. The four members of the family were to sit around the dining room table cleared of all objects except an alarm clock in the center. Each member of the family, starting with the oldest, would have 15 minutes to talk, expressing his own feelings, impressions, and observations regarding the behavior of the other members of the clan. Whoever had nothing to say would have to remain silent for the assigned 15 minutes while the rest of the family would remain silent and attentive. It was absolutely forbidden to continue these discussions outside the scheduled hour. All such discussion was limited to the scheduled evening meetings, which were ritually structured. As for relations with members of the clan, a doubling of courtesy and helpfulness was prescribed.

The Selvini Palazzoli team described the objectives as follows:

1. To define the nuclear family as a unit distinct from the clan, substituting for the prohibition, the obligation of speaking clearly about the tabu subjects, while . . . imposing secrecy. (The locked door.)
2. To give back to Nora her position as a full-right member of the nuclear family.
3. To encourage the newborn intragenerational alliance between the two sisters.
4. To establish . . . the right of each member to express his own perception without being contradicted or disqualified.
5. To expose any eventual reticent member to the anxiety of silence.
6. To prevent, through the prohibition of discussion outside of the evening meetings, the persistence of secret coalitions.

The family was much improved within two weeks as each recounted their understanding and complaints about other members of the clan. The rule that anyone who "speaks badly of his relatives is bad" was broken, leading to rejection of the old myth and rapid changes within the family. Further stressing the importance of superloyalty to the clan had the paradoxical effect of rebellion against that myth.

Uses
The family ritual technique highlights the existing behavior pattern and family myths in a very dramatic way, exposing them to all the members. It uses the very rigidity of the family structure to produce change. It provides new built-in constructive behaviors and norms as substitutes for the dysfunctional patterns. The ritual functions at the level of meta or analogical communication and therefore arouses less resistance than a direct interpretation or explanation of the symptom might elicit. It tends to go with the family and turns it around rather than going against it. The technique is particularly effective with rigid, enmeshed families and those with pathological members.

Rituals also may be prescribed in a straightforward way for underorganized families. In this case, the objective is to provide structure, common goals, and narrative behaviors to achieve those goals resulting in family cohesiveness. An example is arranging a fixed time for the entire family to gather for dinner. Criticism, complaints, and discussion of family problems are not allowed during dinner. The family is to discuss events of the day, politics, individual dreams, things they've read or been thinking about, play word games, tell stories. It is to be a pleasant and relaxed time. Another example is to prescribe that the family take note of each member's birthday and arrange an important celebration in that person's honor. The development of new customs and traditions in the form of rituals is particularly helpful for recently created stepfamilies.

RESOURCES
Selvini Palazzoli, M., Boscolo, L., Cecchin, G., and Prata, G. Family rituals: A powerful tool on family therapy. *Family Process*, 1977, *16*, 445–453.
Selvini Palazzoli, M., Boscolo, L., Cecchin, G., and Prata, G. *Paradox and counterparadox*. New York: Jason Aronson, 1978.

31 | THE VACATION

Rationale
Sending a member of the family on vacation is a structural move. The therapist's goal is to help the family develop appropriate boundaries between members by having dominant or overactive members step back and disengage from an enmeshed interaction process that both results in a power play and helps maintain the symptom (Minuchin and Fishman, 1981). It is used more literally by Selvini Palazzoli and her colleagues in strategic therapy (Selvini Palazzoli, 1981) to have the parents leave home and go away for a weekend or longer. This forces the symptomatic child to shift for himself and work out his place with siblings while the parents are away having a good time. The child and symptom are removed as the center of attention. The child is no longer physically between the parents. The parents are relating together in a more relaxed atmosphere without interruption from the children and have a structured opportunity to review their life as a couple.

In more technical terms, when an enmeshed member is sent on vacation the boundary between that person and others is strengthened, while a rigid boundary between two other subsystems can be opened up more by the increased contact among the members of the remaining subsystems. In the example just given the boundary or separateness between parents and children is strengthened. But more interaction is opened up between the parental couple on the one hand and among the children themselves on the other hand.

Procedure
The therapist might express concern for the dominant enmeshed member, focusing on the demands placed on him and the great personal effort and sacrifice he extends (in the symptomatic activity). She then suggests that

the person needs and deserves a long-overdue rest and prescribes either that he take a vacation from the task or take a physical vacation from the family. Among the typical symptomatic behaviors are nagging others to do things, protecting other family members, doing for others and serving them, disciplining the children, working continuously to provide for the family but being uninvolved with the members. Another direction would be an example of enmeshment with an outside factor that distances the person from the family. Here the therapist might encourage the person who overworks to take more time from his work and vacation with his family.

Next, the therapist might ask the family what they could do to help. Can they manage to assume that person's responsibilities for a specified time period? They then discuss how this can be arranged, enlisting the help of all. The therapist predicts that it may be difficult. She predicts that the member on "vacation" will probably try to interfere and that they will be tempted to interrupt the vacation to get the person back on the same routine as before. However, the therapist stresses the importance of the vacation and how essential it is for all to combine forces to allow it to happen.

A second version, in the case of a symptomatic child, is to see the parents alone. The parents are given a prescription to go away from home for a weekend without telling the children in advance. A note is left telling the children that the parents are on vacation but not where they are going. Of course, supervision would need to be arranged for young children. The technique is more effective with older or adult children living at home and left unsupervised.

Example

Susan is enmeshed with her six-year-old son, Robert. Her boyfriend, Greg, has lived with them for one year and Susan is planning to marry him very soon. However, Greg and Robert have very little contact. Robert has not seen his father since he was an infant and Susan has always assumed full responsibility for him. Robert's disruptive behavior in school was the presenting problem. Greg reports that Robert constantly demands his mother's attention by misbehaving. Susan reports that she is constantly fighting with Robert over every detail. "He just won't cooperate."

Therapist: Yes, Susan, you look very tired tonight, as though you've been working very hard with Robert. Has it been a difficult week?

Susan: Oh, yes. It seems like Robert must fight with me over everything. And then I know Greg gets annoyed by the whole thing. I just don't know what else I can do.

Therapist: I really don't think you can possibly do any more than you're already doing. You have devoted yourself to the boy and you're wearing yourself out. You do everything possible to be a good mom. It's a great personal sacrifice. (Turns to Greg) I'm worried about Susan. She has been living under a good deal of stress and I'm not sure how much longer she can go on like this. I wonder if we could find some way to help her out.

Robert: I'll try to be good.

Therapist: Robert, that could help a lot. But there are times when you need adult help too and you should have it, only Mommy is so tired.

Greg: I think I could help out.

Therapist: (to Susan) What do you think? How could Greg help?

Susan: Well, after dinner is the worst. I'm just so tired and Robert is cranky by then and there's still homework to finish and a bath and bedtime to be gotten through.

Greg: How about if I supervise the homework and bath every night?

Susan: Gee, I don't know. Robert's used . . .

Therapist: Robert, what do you think? Can we let Mom have a rest each evening?

Robert: Yes.

Therapist: What exactly could you do to help.

Robert: I could do my homework, get undressed and take a bath. I guess it's okay as long as Mom kisses me goodnight.

Therapist: Well then, it seems like everyone is willing to give it a try this week. But you know, it won't be easy, Susan, when you hear Robert and Greg struggling you'll want to pitch in, but it's very important for everyone that you remain on your vacation. Although it may be too difficult for you. Any idea of how you'll spend the vacation time?

Susan: I think I'll take a bubble bath and read.

Therapist: Sounds good. But you know, Robert and Greg, it's going to be really tough managing without Susan for a while every night. It might be too much to manage. Even so, Greg, do you think you could manage one more thing—to invite Susan out some evenings so she could have some fun? Perhaps Robert will allow someone to babysit one night this week. What do you two men think of that?

Greg: Sure.

Robert: Sure.

Therapist: Okay, we'll have a lot to discuss next time.

By removing Susan for a brief time each evening, the therapist is helping the family to build a stronger boundary and more distance between Mom and Robert. The task is set up so Robert will become more independent and differentiated in his own right. He will turn to Greg when necessary, weakening the rigid boundary that now separates them and bringing them closer. The therapist involves the entire system in the task and predicts the possibility of failure. In spite of the power play, there seems to be a desire for cooperation when the identified patient is switched from Robert to mother. Identifying Robert and Greg together as the two men with a task initiates a new alliance in the family.

Uses
This technique can be used in structural or strategic therapy with any family having at least one inappropriately enmeshed boundary. It is an effective method of aiding members change their positions vis-à-vis each other and creating the possibility of new solutions to their conflicts. It is also a technique for detriangulating one member who gets between two others, as Robert does in the above example. It disengages the power play between two enmeshed members or subsystems. It substitutes fun for fighting.

RESOURCES
Minuchin, S. *Families and family therapy*. Cambridge, MA: Harvard University Press, 1974.
Minuchin, S. *Psychosomatic families*. Cambridge, MA: Harvard University Press, 1978.
Minuchin, S. and Fishman, C. *Family therapy techniques*. Cambridge, MA: Harvard University Press, 1981.
Selvini Palazzoli, M., Boscolo, L., Cecchin, G., and Prata, G. *Paradox and counterparadox*, New York: Jason Aronson, 1978.

32 | ROLE REVERSAL

Rationale
Role reversal is both a sociometric structural move and a dramatic technique to help assess the client's willingness or ability to see through the eyes of another person and experience emotionally and physically the role of the other. The way the client enacts the role suggests how he views himself and the other person. It helps the client observe different aspects of behavior and gives him another viewpoint. In addition, it enables the client to think, feel, and act out interactions instead of just talking about them.

The role reversal technique is among the many developed by Moreno (1940, 1946, 1951) and his colleagues in psychodrama and sociodrama. It is here adapted for work with couples and families. The assumption is that the world and the family relationships will look and be experienced in a different way if the members exchange places. The results are greater empathy and understanding of both the other person and how one's own behavior and position are affecting that other person.

It is recognized that people create reciprocal roles in relationship: leader-follower, pursuer-distancer, rescuer-scapegoat, overadequate one-inadequate one, etc. In a repetitive conflict each tries harder in the role already occupied and becomes stuck in that pattern. Having the couple enact in session and/or as a homework assignment an exchange of roles may help break the existing pattern. For example, in a case in which one partner is constantly the doer and worrier and the other is accused of being irresponsible, the therapist might reframe the roles (see Chapter 6) and relabel them as the one in charge of work and the other in charge of fun. Then she asks the couple to reverse roles. The doer is put in charge of organizing the family fun and the irresponsible one is put in charge of organizing the family tasks. The purposes are to: (a) disengage them from their usual pattern; (b) practice new behaviors that are part of the new role; (c) attend to an area that each needs to strengthen; (d) reduce conflict between them; (e) create a new challenge in the relationship; and (f) experience the world in the shoes of the other person. It also has a paradoxical effect when the overadequate person becomes less responsible, steps back and leaves a vacuum that forces the less adequate one to move in and take over. The same is true for most reciprocal roles since both sides are necessary to complete the whole.

Procedure
When the clients are insensitive to one another or to one's effect on others, or are at an impasse over an issue, role reversal may be an effective tool.

The therapist might say to selected participants; "Let's see if we can find a way to overcome this problem. Would you be kind enough to look carefully at the other person and think of what it must be like to be that person in this situation we're talking about. (Silence). Really feel yourself into it. Become that person. (Silence). Now exchange places, please. (They change seats.) Please be that person and talk to each other as that other person."

The therapist serves as a guide, encouraging the clients to speak in turn and holding them to the new roles. She observes the verbal and nonverbal content, reflects back, questions, probes, asks for clarification, and makes interpretations. She may ask other family members to assist the role players or serve as alter egos. She asks questions such as: "What do you think when the other person does that?" "What do you really want to do right now?" "Do you feel heard and understood?" "What would you like the other person to do differently?" "What do you think you could do differently?"

After the role playing, the therapist asks what each learned, what they felt about each other, and what changes they would like to make. The agreed-upon changes are then prescribed as homework assignments.

A variation is for the therapist to suggest that it might be a good idea for the participants to exchange jobs and take a vacation from their usual responsibilities. She then prescribes that each assume the positively re-framed version of the other's critical role related to the symptom. The participants are asked to enact a scene on the spot or to assume the new roles at home until the next meeting. Each may be asked to keep a log of what he does, what he thinks and feels about it, and how he would like it to be.

Example

John and Mary are the parents of Greg (15), Amy (13), and Jean (11). Greg is the identified client. He is not doing his homework, cuts classes, and doesn't help at home. The mother and Greg start shouting at each other over his failure to do his homework.

Therapist: Would you mind reversing roles to see how it feels being the other person? Let's start with switching chairs and sitting like you see the other person sits. (The mother sits slumpy. Greg exaggerates his mother's uptight posture.)

Greg (as the mother):   It makes me angry the way you sit, you should sit straight up.

Mother (as Greg):   What do you care?

Greg: I care; you are irresponsible; you want things to be done by themselves.

Mother: And you nag me all the time to do this and this and this. You think you are the only one who cares? (Both mother and son start laughing.)

Therapist: Now be yourself. What did you learn from the experience?

Greg: I learned that I could let her know that I care.

Mother: I should get off his back about doing things.

From the above example the family members could see their behavior and how they implicitly cooperated to maintain their behavior. By becoming and acting the other person they were enabled to experience the events and feelings through a different perspective. The "game" became apparent to them; they laughed and realized some changes were in order.

Uses

Role reversal can be used in order to resolve a particular issue. It can involve each member of the family who is capable of taking over another person's role. It gives information about thoughts, feelings, and actions that are relevant to the issue in focus. It indicates how well family members pay attention and understand one another as compared with projecting one's own feelings and beliefs onto others. It also reveals a willingness or unwillingness to believe that what the other person says and does is the truth or a conscious or unconscious defensive maneuver. It permits the clients to experiment with other roles and other ways of being in the world. By guiding the role playing, the therapist can lead the participants to new insights and actions.

RESOURCES

Minuchin, S. and Fishman, H. C. *Family therapy techniques*. Cambridge, MA: Harvard University Press, 1981.

Moreno, J. L. Psychodramatic treatment of marriage problems. *Sociometry*, 1940, *3*, 20.

Moreno, J. L. *Psychodrama*. New York: Beacon House, 1946.

Moreno. J. L. *Sociometry, experimental method and the science of society: An approach to a new political orientation*. New York: Beacon House, 1951.

33 | THE COMPLEMENTARITY CHALLENGE

Rationale

The theoretical foundation of the structural model of family therapy rests on the belief that "the whole and the parts can be properly explained only in terms of the relations that exist between the parts" (Lane, 1970). One of the therapeutic goals in structural and Adlerian family therapy is to help family members experience their belonging to an entity that is larger than the individual self. In individual therapy, the focus is on the individual as a whole. But when the individual becomes a part of a whole (the family), the other parts of that whole are seen as affecting the behavior and experience of all the parts. All members of a family contribute to maintaining the appropriate style of life that feels harmonious for that particular family. The technique as described here is taken primarily from the work of Minuchin (1974; Minuchin and Fishman, 1981).

The concept of complementarity describes the balanced, reciprocal nature of interpersonal behavior. There cannot be a leader without a follower, a rescuer without a victim, or a pursuer without a distancer. Each must cooperate in the performance of their reciprocal roles. One who ceases to be a victim no longer has need of a rescuer.

Complementarity as a technique aims at changing the hierarchical relationship among family members by challenging the existing hierarchy.

First, the therapist challenges the problem — the family's certainty that there is one identified patient. Second, the therapist challenges the linear notion that one family member is controlling the system, rather than each member serving as a context of the other. Third, the therapist challenges the family's punctuation of events, introducing an expanded time frame which teaches family members to see their behavior as part of a larger whole. (Minuchin and Fishman, 1981, p. 194)

Procedure

The following procedures are described by Minuchin and Fishman (1981).

1. Challenging the problem. The therapist challenges the certainty of an identified client. She observes how people act and are activated in the system. Sometimes the therapist, who occupies the hierarchical position of the expert, may make a simple statement such as "I see other things going on in the family that contradict your opinion that you are the client." Sometimes she will challenge by expanding the problem to more than one person: "This family has a problem in the way you relate." A client may be described as the family healer, since the family's concentration on him serves to distract them from problems between other family members (Minuchin and Fishman, 1981, pp. 194–195).

2. Challenging linear control.

The therapist challenges the notion that one member can control the family system. . . . The therapist describes the behavior of one family member and assigns the responsibility for that behavior to another. The therapist may say to an adolescent, "You are acting like a four-year-old," and then turn to the parents and ask, "How do you manage to keep him that young?" . . . The therapist is, in effect, affiliating with the person he seems to attack. The family member whose behavior is described as dysfunctional doesn't resist the description because the responsibility is placed on another. (Minuchin and Fishman, pp. 196–197)

The same technique can be used in signaling improvement. "Now you are acting your age," the therapist may say to the child, and then shake hands with the parents, saying, "Clearly you did something that allowed John to grow up. Can you describe it?" . . . By pushing the family to own the change of one of its members, the therapist encourages the system as a whole to accept the notion of the reciprocity of each of its parts. . . . (Minuchin and Fishman, 1981, p. 197)

3. Challenging the punctuation of events. "The therapist challenges the family's epistemology by introducing the concept of expanded time, framing individual behavior as part of a larger whole" (p. 197). To get this point across the therapist must be able to expand the family members' focus of attention. She teaches them to see the whole pattern of movement among the members rather than an individual action.

The techniques of introducing an expanded framework are generally of a cognitive nature. The therapist may point out to family members that their transactions . . . obey rules which transcend the individual member.

> . . . For example, in an enmeshed family a youngster sneezes; the mother hands the father a handkerchief for him. . . . The therapist says, "My goodness, look how one sneeze activates everybody. This is a family that makes helpful people. (p. 198)

This statement broadens the context and reveals how the family's behavior transcends each individual member.

Example

Minuchin and Fishman (1981, pp. 198–206) use the following example (abridged) to illustrate the process.

> The Abbotts are a couple in their thirties who have been separated for one month, the husband having left his wife and two very young children and moved into an apartment to find himself. . . .

Gregory [Abbott]:   . . . What's happening with me right now with regard to my relationship with my wife is that I'm feeling less depressed having left the house. . . .

Therapist: Are you saying that Pat [his wife] depresses you? . . .

Gregory: I don't give her that responsibility, you know . . . I don't lay that on her. I feel depressed and I felt really depressed for some time in the situation.

Therapist: Hold it! You said you were depressed at home, you left home, and you are less depressed. You are saying that Pat depresses you.

Gregory: No, I really take responsibility for being depressed. I can't put it on her.

Therapist: For a moment, follow me. You are depressed, and your wife does not help you with your depression.

Gregory: Right.

Therapist: Why doesn't she help you?

Gregory: I guess I feel that a lot of my needs weren't being met. I felt very frustrated. . . .

Therapist: Can you be more concrete? I don't know in what way your wife isn't helping you.

Gregory: We had planned a vacation in Florida in December, and we had a lot of problems dealing with getting away on vacation or arranging for babysitters.

Therapist: You wanted to have a vacation with your wife alone, without the children?

Gregory: Yes. . . .

Therapist: (to Pat) How did you see that enterprise?

Pat: . . . It's very painful for me to leave the kids at this age, . . . but I was willing to go because he wanted to go and it had been an issue for such a long time. It was just very hard to leave them. . . .

Therapist: So, you're depressed also?

Pat: I'm very depressed now. I've been very depressed since he left.

Therapist: What does your husband do to depress you?

Pat: He talks about leaving frequently. And I feel that he doesn't want me for me.

Therapist: I want to force both of you to think concretely. What does he do to you that makes you feel like you want to kick him?

(to Gregory):   What does she do to you that makes you feel like you want to leave? Talk with each other about that. (pp. 198–201)

The therapist has challenged the idea of a single client by pointing out that each partner is depressed. Interventions related to individual dynamics are avoided that by instructing each spouse to think about the other as a context for their own feelings and eventually their own changing.

The initiated transaction between the spouses will show each partner that they eventually must help the other to change by changing themselves in how they relate to their partner.

Uses

The complementarity challenge process can be used in any interpersonal system to help the members identify their own part in the interaction and to accept responsibility for changing themselves and assisting others to change by behaving differently themselves. It can defuse both the scapegoating process and the power play between a couple or in a family. It also cuts through the righteousness of being "right" and making the other "wrong" with all the attendant feelings of moral privileges and entitlements that come with being "right." Further, it permits the therapist to ally with each subsystem and to upset the existing balance of power in order to properly readjust the hierarchical structure of the system.

RESOURCES

Gurman, A. S. and Kniskern, D. P. (eds.) *Handbook of family therapy*. New York: Brunner/Mazel, 1981.

Lane, M. *Introduction to structuralism*. New York: Basic Books, 1970.

Minuchin, S. *Families and family therapy*. Cambridge, MA: Harvard University Press, 1974.

Minuchin, S. and Fishman, H. C. *Family therapy techniques*. Cambridge, MA: Harvard University Press, 1981.

Nicols, M. *Family therapy*. New York: Gardner Press, 1984.

5

Behavioral Tasks

INTRODUCTION

Every therapeutic technique is in some sense behavioral. For purposes of this chapter behavioral techniques are defined as those that deal cognitively with such matters as (a) problem definition, goal clarification, values clarification, boundaries clarification; (b) problem solving, planning, identification and negotiation of differences; (c) therapeutic contracts, formation and implementation of agreements, and assignments of concrete tasks and; (d) commitment to and evaluation of the process.

Therapist and clients are dealing directly with the problems at hand rather than striving for change through meta communication of one kind or another, as they do with imagery or paradox. The techniques focus on a conscious level of logical thinking and action and the relationship between thinking and acting. Behavioral techniques are action oriented; clients must "do" something.

The techniques emerge from several different theoretical orientations:

1. Behaviorism and its underlying classical conditioning, operant conditioning, and social learning theories.
2. Cognitive psychology theories with their emphasis on thinking and reasoning;

147

3.   Social exchange theories in which persons do things for each other for mutual gain;
4.   Communication theories emphasizing speaking, listening, negotiating and nonverbal forms of relating;
5.   Problem-solving theories such as those in education and the fields of business management, which focus on step-by-step analysis, brainstorming, planning, and evaluation.

Fundamental assumptions underlying many of these techniques are:

1.   Behavior is learned and new behavior can be learned;
2.   Clients are intellectually and emotionally capable of identifying their needs and expectations, defining their problems in logical ways, thinking through their problems, discovering new solutions, applying those solutions in action, evaluating the results, and refining their solutions;
3.   As observers of their own thoughts and actions clients will be able to discover illogical or irrational thoughts and behavior and substitute the newly developed ones;
4.   Undesirable client behaviors can be extinguished or desensitized and new ones elicited, learned, and reinforced;
5.   Clients are normal people with problems to be solved;
6.   The therapist is an active leader, consultant, facilitator, or resource person.

Two major aspects of the techniques included are that they provide opportunity for the participants to brainstorm and exchange ideas and to safely practice and reinforce new behaviors.

Of course, each theorist can adapt a given technique for her own system whenever the circumstances warrant. In that case it will probably be conceptualized and utilized within the framework of that particular theory.

There are many advantages of behavioral techniques for couple and family counseling.

1.   They are carefully organized and structured step by step, thus reducing the risk of failure in accomplishing the tasks. Success in turn builds positive feelings and greater self-confidence. The organization reduces chaos and provides the model of a workable structure.
2.   They emphasize wellness, health, competence, and the power to do. This encourages a sense of being "OK" and capable.
3.   They are overt, not mysterious. Couched in lay vocabulary they are readily teachable and learnable.
4.   They break the negative cycle of being upset, complaining, getting more upset, and complaining more. A positive cycle is installed in

its place by the very nature of the technique. Clients begin a series of prescribed constructive actions.

5. They produce rapid movement in connection with the task over a delimited time. Clients see the progress and feel encouraged.
6. They teach the clients one or more aspects of problem-solving methodology, in which difficulties are resolved through the cooperation of the participants. This serves as a model for coping with future problems and disagreements that will inevitably develop as the changes in the normal life cycle unfold.

Behavioral techniques discussed in this chapter include the Couple Conference and Family Council — formal meetings to improve communication and intimacy; Structured Communication Training — specific training in speaking and listening; Symbolism and Gift Giving — a nonverbal means of communicating awareness of others and expressing good feelings; Caring Days — small steps to please one another; Positive Exchanges — identifying each person's wants, stating them in direct, positive ways, and committing oneself to positively provide for the other's wants in surprising ways; Within-Session Structured Tasks — to vividly and concretely engage families in working constructively together on a task while the therapist either diagnostically observes the process or intervenes by coaching the participants; the Marriage Contract Game — a board game played by the couple to learn how to negotiate problems; Reading Aloud Together — bibliotherapy to improve communication among the members; and Choice Awareness.

Most of the techniques represent methods for reducing conflicts and prompting mutually reinforcing interactions through assigned in-session or homework tasks designed by the therapist.

Behavioral techniques engage the clients directly in positive structured activities designed by the therapist to provide immediate change in the dysfunctional way they are doing things. New behaviors are thus taught or modeled by the therapist. Change does not have to await analyses and deep understanding of former behaviors, even though acquisition of insight is considered by cognitive theorists to be highly desirable. The therapist can creatively invent any kind of task that will help the couple or family behave more constructively. In-session tasks permit the therapist to observe the interactions and to coach the members toward possible changes in process. This is also a form of behavioral rehearsal so that the members can acquire skills to be used at home. Homework tasks are used to establish new patterns of behavior and a more positive emotional climate in the home. Becoming more aware of one's own needs and feelings and those of the other members, improving communication and negotiating skills, changing roles and place in the system, and substituting new patterns for old ones are major outcomes for the family. Another possible use is to teach democratic methods and help the couple or family attain a system of greater equality, ultimately leading to a more egalitarian society. Equality, of course, does not mean sameness; nor does it remove the generational boundary. It does recognize that each individual is equally important, occupies a different place, and contributes significantly, but uniquely, to the whole.

Behavioral techniques can also be used to help family members engage if they are too distant or disengage if they are too enmeshed or fused. The techniques can assist in forming generational boundaries.

Such methods are appropriate for any families that are able to follow directions. Less verbal families may especially appreciate the concrete, action-oriented approaches.

RESOURCES

Bandura, A. Behavior theory and the models. *American Psychologist*, 1974, *29*(12), 859–869.

Bandura, A. Self-efficacy: Toward a unifying theory of behavioral change. *Psychology Review*, 1977, *84*, 191–215.

Beck, A. T., Rush, A. J., Emery, G., and Shaw, B. *Cognitive therapy of depression.* New York: Guilford Press, 1979.

Dreikurs, R. *Children the challenge.* New York: Hawthorne, 1946.

Dreikurs, R. *The challenge of marriage.* New York: Hawthorne, 1946.

Ellis, A. *How to stubbornly refuse to be ashamed of anything.* Cassette recording, New York: Institute for Rational Living, 1973.

Ellis, A. *Sex and the liberated man.* New York: Lyle Stuart, 1976.

Ellis, A., Grieger, R., with contributors. *RET handbook of rational-emotive therapy.* New York: Springer, 1977.

Gottman, J., Markman, H., and Notarius, C. The typography of marital conflict: A sequential analysis of verbal and non-verbal behavior. *Journal of Marriage and the Family*, 1977, *39*, 461–479.

Jacobson, N. S. Behavioral marital therapy. In A. S. Gurman and D. P. Kniskern (eds.), *Handbook of family therapy.* New York: Brunner/Mazel, 1981.

Lazarus, A. *The practice of multimodal therapy.* New York: Brunner/Mazel, 1976.

Schwartz, L., Sherman, R., and Norris, H. The action counseling workshop. *Counselor Education and Supervision*, 1975, *15*(2), 144–148.

Sherman, R., Norris, H., and Schwartz, L. Applying action counseling to institutional change. Paper and demonstration presented to the annual convention of the American Personnel and Guidance Association, New York, 1974.

Sherman, R., Norris, H., and Schwartz, L. Principles of action counseling. Paper and demonstration presented to the national convention of the American Personnel and Guidance Association, New York, 1975.

Stuart, R. B. *Helping couples change*. New York: Guilford Press, 1980.

34 | THE COUPLE CONFERENCE AND FAMILY COUNCIL

Rationale

The couple conference and family council are formal meetings held on a regular basis by the couple or the family. They are methods designed to increase and improve communication. The technique is particularly prescribed by Adlerian family therapists and follows the principles of that theory. The meetings operate on the basis of democratic methods by providing all with equal opportunity to participate. Dreikurs and his associates popularized the idea (Dreikurs, 1948; Dreikurs et al., 1959; Dreikurs and Soltz, 1964; Dreikurs, Gould, and Corsini, 1974; Corsini and Rigney, 1970; Dinkmeyer, Pew, and Dinkmeyer, 1979; Manaster and Corsini, 1982).

Most couples or families caught up in a power contest around a symptomatic conflict tend to engage in little other communication. Each experiences not being heard, understood, or acknowledged by the other(s). In a typical interaction, one speaks, the other interrupts and takes off on one point and adds his own agenda. The first picks up on one point and goes off in another direction. Instead, during the conference, each is instructed to pay strict, uninterrupted attention to the other(s). Just being heard all the way through has a powerful effect on those so engaged.

According to Manaster and Corsini, there are four purposes to conducting a family council:

1. To allow free communication among family members.
2. To avoid emotional showdowns and violence in the family.
3. To teach children and parents democratic means of settling differences.
4. To operate an orderly and peaceful home. (1982, p. 231)

The family council is based on the philosophy that democratic methods introduced into family life will encourage respect among all members, increase cooperation because all have a voice in appropriate decision making, increase interest in and feeling for one another because all are involved, and help develop a sense of group identity while clearly recognizing each person's individuality, contribution, and value.

The therapist prescribes the conference and/or council as a homework task. She carefully instructs the members in detail about the rules for conducting it at home or another designated place. It becomes a particular couple and family ritual. Adlerian couple and family educators regularly prescribe it as a developmental enrichment process as well as a remediation technique.

The Couple or Marriage Conference Procedure
Once the therapist has ascertained that there is a need for improvement in communication between the couple, she suggests that it might be a good idea for the couple to schedule a regular fixed time, place, and frequency per week to meet together. During that time they are to be totally and exclusively there for one another without external interruption. Once the idea is accepted, the couple then discuss and agree upon a mutually convenient time when they are willing and able to be at their best with one another, rather than when they are totally depleted. They also agree to abide by the established rules, which are written down and handed to the couple. These can be varied by the therapist to suit the couple's specific needs. Typical rules are:

1. They will meet at the agreed on fixed times and place between now and the next therapy session and will not allow external interruptions. (A minimum of one such meeting a week.)
2. One spouse will begin and have a fixed time, usually half an hour, to speak or be silent, having 100 percent of the partner's attention for the entire half hour. She can communicate feelings, dreams, plans, hurts, desires, needs — anything she wants. The partner is not to interrupt. During the half hour, the partner is to pay close attention, listening and watching carefully. He is not to smoke, move about, or do anything to distract from the process. Exactly at the end of the time, the spouse stops.
3. The partner then briefly (three minutes) indicates what he has heard his spouse say and mean and acknowledges her position without attacking it.
4. He now begins his half hour with the spouse carefully attending to him. He can communicate anything he wants.
5. The spouse now has three minutes to acknowledge that she heard and understood her partner.
6. The discussion is to end exactly on time.
7. The items discussed are not to be introduced again until the next conference.
8. The couple comes back to the next session and reports on what happened. The therapist uses the material in the session, reinforces the rules, and repeats the prescription.

It should be emphasized that the couple conference is not a problem-solving technique. Its purpose is to open up communication, increase constructive intimacy, and at least partially defuse the power play.

The Family Council Procedure

Once the therapist has concluded that the family council will be a useful way for this family to improve their communication and their decision-making capability she introduces the idea to the parents or to the family as a group. She anticipates with them that it will be difficult to implement since it is different from their usual manner of discussing issues and solving problems, but that it provides them with some new options for improving their family life style. She may choose to encourage them by pointing out that up to now the family has demonstrated excellent skills in cooperation by agreeing to fight together and these same skills can be applied to learning to agree together.

The therapist next describes the rules of the council.

1. Set a definite regular time and place for the meeting so there are no interferences or interruptions.
2. The council is to include the entire family, but no one is forced to attend. An absentee must agree to abide by the decisions arrived at. Every effort is made for everyone to be present at every meeting.
3. Decisions made during the meeting cannot be unilaterally broken or ignored. They can be renegotiated at a subsequent meeting.
4. Everyone can propose agenda items. Some families keep a sign-up sheet in a high-traffic place like the refrigerator door, so that agenda items can be written down immediately when they come to mind.
5. The agenda is anything that concerns the welfare of the children, family outings, decisions that effect the family as a unit. Parents do not invite a six-year-old to help decide whether they should invest in real estate or a money market account or whether or not he chooses to go to school. The parents may seek certain agreements from the children such as cooperation in taking care of family chores, rules about being home at a certain hour, behavior with visiting friends. The children may have issues concerning privacy, more independence, more flexibility around chores, and television viewing time. The children may seek assistance in resolving disputes among themselves. Some items may have to do with sharing feelings, hopes, achievements, experiences, and they may require no decisions. The chairmanship of the meeting is rotated among the family members who are capable of leading. This person exerts whatever leadership and authority are required. The parents do not sit as *The* authorities. The usual rules for conducting any democratic meeting are followed. However, it is better to achieve a unanimous, negotiated consensus than a majority vote.
6. All must participate in carrying out the decisions agreed upon, both in spirit and word. Hairsplitting is not acceptable.
7. Both parents and children need to feel that they have a genuine voice and what they express will be heard, accepted, and seriously con-

sidered. A certain degree of good humor and ability to laugh at human foibles rather than at people is a helpful addition.

8.   The meeting is held to overcome problems, not to attack people.

The family is cautioned that the meetings may not be productive until everyone learns how to use the council as an effective vehicle for their concerns.

The family returns for the following sessions and reports their experiences. These are discussed. The material generated is used by the therapist in the session. She then reinforces the rules, helps the family work out some of the problems in execution, and encourages them to continue with the meetings.

Uses

These procedures provide the therapist with the opportunity to teach democratic techniques and social and negotiating skills which will be practiced at home. They convert the agreement to fight together into an agreement to negotiate and share together. They generate agenda items for the next therapy session with a clear notion of where the members are stuck, the disputants all wanting their own way. The therapist is able to point out that disputing someone else's way is just a difference of opinion and not a rejection of another person — or a hateful act. By encouraging more equality within families, we may be able to achieve greater equality in society at large.

RESOURCES

Corsini, R. J. The marriage conference. *Marriage Counseling Quarterly*, 1970, *5*, 21–29.

Corsini, R. J. and Rigney, K. *The family council*. Chicago: Rudolf Dreikurs Unit of Family Education Association, 1970.

Deutsch, D. A step toward successful marriages. *Journal of Individual Psychology*, 1956, *12*, 78–83.

Dinkmeyer, D. C., Pew, W. L., and Dinkmeyer, D. C., Jr. *Adlerian counseling and psychotherapy*. Monterey, CA: Brooks/Cole, 1979.

Dreikurs, R. *The challenge of parenthood*. New York: Meredith, 1948.

Dreikurs, R., Corsini, R. J., Lowe, R., and Sonstegard, M. *Adlerian family counseling*. Eugene, OR: University of Oregon Press, 1959.

Dreikurs, R., Gould, S., and Corsini, R. J. *Family council*. Chicago: Henry Regnery, 1974.

Dreikurs, R. and Soltz, V. *Children: The challenge*. New York: Hawthorne, 1964.

Manaster, G. J. and Corsini, R. J. *Individual psychology*. Itaska, IL: Peacock, 1982.

35 | THE MARRIAGE CONTRACT GAME

Rationale
The marriage contract game is a board game described by Blechman and Rabin (1980). It is played by one couple with the therapist out of the room. This game is designed to help couples negotiate problems in an explicit, rational manner. It is a method of training couples in problem solving in such a way that it permits replication, studying, and dismantling of the treatment process. This game elicits successful, explicit negotiation of real relationship problems each time it is played.

A couple will play just to write a contract that will resolve a serious problem, or play to rehearse a strategy they can apply to future conflicts of interest. Should the game succeed in accomplishing those purposes, replication and dismantling will be easy, since the couple's negotiations are completely guided by the game's instructions. The game provides the players with a clear set of rules to govern their negotiations and with a set of specific examples of what players do when they follow the rules. Empirical data suggest that the game promotes effective problem solving and pleasant, effective behavior. The marriage contract game is conceptually related to the social psychology of bargaining and social exchange theory. It is assumed that there is a quality of self-interest in social interactions that involve "getting" to reinforce willingness to give. By setting up a negotiating process, automatic recognition is given to each participant's need to give something as well as to get something. "To obtain what I want I also have to be interested in what you want."

The technique as presented here is taken primarily from the article by Blechman and Rabin (1980).

Procedure
The game begins with the couple being shown a set of written rules in the game box. The therapist is responsible for introducing the game to the couple. She is to provide them with the rationale, answer their questions, and review agreements written by the couple to encourage successful implementation. She is to use empirical data to make decisions about the desirable length of treatment and the need for additional treatment procedures. The therapist also implements a practice game and when that is finished she leaves the room and sets the time for 20 minutes.

The game equipment includes general rules, an issue card sort, a game board with 20-minute instruction squares to be read aloud by players as they move their tokens around the board; minute timers near some game board squares; seven card decks labeled Trust, Real Issues, Sample Goals, Risk, Bonus, Sample Compromises, and Blank Compromise Cards; and a contract form.

The issue card sort is presented to each partner before the game starts.

Common marital complaints are printed on the cards. Each spouse sorts the cards into five categories to indicate the amount of work needed on the problem (1 = very little work needed; 5 = a lot of work needed). Issues rated as needing much work are randomly distributed to the real issues deck (for resolution during future games), or to probes (unstructured discussions), which will test for generalization from the game. Ten-minute unstructured discussions probe for generalization of the game's effects; the probes are collected periodically before, during, and after intervention. To ensure sufficient issues for game-guided negotiation and for probes, couples are asked to put eight issues into category five during the first presentation of the issue card sort. The card sort is readministered without forced categorization. This use of the card sort provides a repeated measure of the couple's subjective ratings of a pool of issues. Some of the issues will have been discussed during the games, others during probes; some issues will be targeted for change in current contracts, other issues will not yet have been discussed.

Bonus and risk cards are the same for all players. They are drawn to reward agreement and penalize disagreement. Bonus cards instruct players to make positive statements. Risk cards require players to do and say silly things. Sample goals, trust cards, and sample compromise cards are standard for all players. Blank compromise cards are filled in by players as they negotiate their own agreements. Couples begin by rolling the dice. The high roller gets a blue marker and becomes the complainant, the one who chooses a real issue for negotiation. The low roller is green, the target of the complaint and of a request for new behavior. Once an issue has been selected, the board directs the players through 20 squares. Throughout the game board, instructions promote nonverbal and verbal behaviors that are likely to enhance problem solving. Although the game is designed to promote resolution of specific issues, the game also encourages actions likely to enhance the bond between a couple. Throughout the game, players are prompted to express feelings about proposals and to paraphrase the partner's feeling statements; bonus and risk cards prompt laughter and touching.

Example
Blechman (1980) discusses the following case.

Mr. and Mrs. A. decided they needed brief training in marital problem solving. They disagreed about many things and fought often. During their first appointment, the A.'s described the issues they wanted to discuss. Criticism was a theme common to all these issues.

During the first session the couple played the marriage contract game. Mr. A. chose the issue "expression of feelings with words" and quickly requested, as a compromise, that his wife compliment him three times a day or more. Mrs. A. had difficulty deciding how to cooperate with the proposal. First, she made such vague requests as "you should take more responsibility around the house." But game instructions prompted her to make a first-person request.

During her turn, Mrs. A. chose the issue "money management." Her vagueness caused problems. Because of vaguely stated requests, she kept losing money and drawing risk cards. Eventually she said, "I would like my husband not to criticize me about my management of money more than once a week." Although game instructions require a request for more of a desired behavior, Mrs. A. made a big step when she converted her vague displeasure into a specific request.

Mrs. A. was pleased that she did not have to justify her request. In the past, the couple had justified at length every request to each other. Since Mr. A. was more skilled at stating his case, Mrs. A. would give up and avoid conversation. *The discovery that problem solving required classification and specificity, not justification, put the couple on more equal ground.*

During the intervening week, the couple was asked to have a few informal discussions (probes) during which they were to practice the communication approach they used when they played the game. They had three productive discussions and an enjoyable week. They were also asked to carry out the agreements they wrote during the first session. They did not follow through on their contracts because they were so absorbed in game play that they did not take the terms of the contracts seriously when they agreed to them.

During the second session, the couple played the game twice with no help from the trainer and with careful attention to the content of the negotiation. Mrs. A. made clear, focused requests.

The game demands that when one partner disagrees with a solution proposed by the other partner, the first partner must make a counterproposal. For the A.'s this procedure circumvented lengthy explanations and allowed Mrs. A. to become an equal and creative partner in the discussion. The couple reported that they carried out the contract they wrote during the second session and that the contract helped resolve the issues. They volunteered that they now were able to communicate without conflict.

Uses

This game is used only with a couple and both must be present. They must be willing to learn how to work out the differences between them and to comply with both the therapist's instructions and the rules of the game. Compliance with the rules places limits on how disagreements are acted out and defuses much of the anxiety and anger in the interaction. This is a pleasant way to teach couples how to communicate and negotiate resolution of conflicts.

The rules also create a position of equality for both members. One cannot be above the other, for they have equal chances and power in the game and cooperative behavior is rewarded. Finally, it forces the couple to identify concrete, operational problems and concrete solutions, taking them one at a time, step by step. This helps them get past the feeling that their problems are overwhelming and insoluble. (See also "Positive Exchanges" on pp. 164–168.)

RESOURCES

Azrin, N. H., Naster, B. E., and Jones, R. Reciprocity counseling: A rapid procedure for marital counselling. *Behaviour Research and Therapy*, 1973, *11*, 365–382.

Blechman, E. A. Family problem-solving training. *American Journal of Family Therapy*, 1980, *8*, 3–22.

36 | CARING DAYS

Rationale

Couples may enter therapy feeling burnt out from conflict and are typically more attuned to negative exchanges with one another, thus losing sight of "what works well" between them. The positive approach of "caring days" rekindles a more balanced dynamic in the relationship.

Caring days is a technique devised by Stuart (1980) within the model of social learning and behavioral therapy which has the aim of promoting positive change in a relationship early in treatment. Couples are essentially taught to elicit frequent, small, specific positive behaviors from one another by acting "as if" they care on these caring days. With measurable, successful, and immediate change in a couple's experience of one another, it is theorized that they are more likely to commit themselves to therapy with its positive, long-range effects, and also work toward building a sense of commitment to their relationship. Behaviorists assume that the quality of the relationship is determined by the balance of positive and negative exchanges; thus, a symptomatic partner is one who suffers a low rate of positive reinforcement. Trust is built from a continual flow of positives, and learning to like one another is essentially learning to anticipate rewards from the other person (Lott and Lott, 1968). The advantages of using this technique are that it is ideal for beginning treatment, based on positive behavior in the first session. It trains the couple in using a change-oriented language and demonstrates that change in feeling is possible through structured behavior change. The treatment situation provides practice in a specific kind of negotiating skill.

Procedure

The following procedure is abstracted primarily from Stuart (1980, pp. 197–202).

Couples are asked to begin the process of change by acting as if they do in fact care for one another and are told that they will not immediately experience those feelings until they have changed their behaviors. The therapist urges the couple to recognize that there are specific legitimate conflicts the couple can resolve. She communicates to the pair that change is an orderly process and the first step begins with the development of request-and-acknowledgment skills which she will help them to learn. The therapist emphasizes that the initiation of change depends on both of them. Each must make investment in change independently of the other and act to make changes first without waiting for the other. At present, each is probably caught in the nonproductive game of waiting for the other to change. The term "caring," and not "love" is used, avoiding mythical associations and expectations of the outcome of treatment.

Each partner is asked to answer the question: "Exactly what would you like your partner to do as a way of showing that he (she) cares for you?" Requests to be considered acceptable for making agreements must be: (a) positive; (b) specific; (c) small, so that they may be emitted at least once daily; and (d) must not be the subject of current conflict. Such positive requests aim for an increase in constructive behaviors, not a decrease in unwanted responses, so that "Please ask me how I spent my day" is acceptable, but "Don't ignore me so much" is unacceptable. "Be home for dinner at 6 p.m." is specific but "Show more consideration for the family" is too vague to be included in the list.

The therapist aids the couple in setting up a list of at least 18 items, including both partners' requests. They are encouraged to add several items each week to build sufficient coverage of both partners' needs. The partner making the request must state precisely what, when, or how she (he) would like the other to respond, and both partners are to completely understand the requests and communicate what they each want from one another. Each partner must emit five of the items on the caring-days list daily and each one records on the chart the date on which she (he) benefited from the positive gesture of the other. It is recommended that the therapist telephone the couple two or three days after the first session to review with the clients any new items they have added and to remind them of the five daily requests. This also impresses upon the couple the importance of following through with this method of gradual small steps toward larger changes.

Example

John and Mary, ages 37 and 35 respectively, have been married for 11 years. John agreed to come for therapy only after Mary threatened to leave him. Their presenting complaint was lack of communication and Mary felt that John was too caught up in his career, ignoring her and treating her like a "second class citizen." John felt that Mary was not supportive of his work.

The therapist decided that she needed to quickly engage the two so that they would make a commitment toward therapy and demonstrate that change can take place quickly to revitalize the marriage.

After Stuart (1980, p. 200) the following is part of the caring-days list for John and Mary.

John Dates Performed	Agreements	Mary Dates Performed
	Ask how I feel when I come home.	
	Put dirty clothes in the hamper.	
	Listen when I tell you my business problems.	
	Bring me a small surprise gift occasionally.	
	Give me a message.	
	Hold me sometimes during the day.	
	Accept it if I call and say I'll be an hour late.	
	Tell me you appreciate that I work hard and provide for the family.	
	Let's go easy for a weekend without the children.	
	Talk to me during dinner and during the evening.	
	Let me watch one sports event without interruption during the weekend.	
	Let's meet for lunch once a week.	

Mary succeeded in getting more attention and more conformity with her "rules of the house." John got more personal attention and recognition of his needs. The couple learned how to frame clear, direct positive requests of one another instead of complaining about the other's shortcomings. They experienced the partner's performance of the behaviors and, in recording them on a chart, in effect acknowledged the performance to self and partner. Getting more of what they each wanted injected a sense of optimism that change was possible, that they had the power to change, and that the partner cared enough to change, too.

By adding new requests daily, they were soon solving many of the conflicts between them.

Uses

The caring-days technique is designed to function as a low-risk way of initiating a much larger commitment to the process of relationship change: Couples are asked to offer one another apparent, small caring behaviors analogous to a "foot-in-the-door" procedure for therapeutic- and relationship-building process. The written record serves as a visual reminder of the amount of change taking place, in spite of initial conflict or pessimism about the partners' relationship with its surplus of negative interactions.

The caring-days technique is effective for the beginning of treatment, as it builds positive behavior quickly and is especially impactful for those entering in conflict. For those couples who have been able to maintain reasonable rates of positive exchange but nevertheless are coming for help, this technique is useful for reinforcing existing relationship strengths, learning to make positive requests, and learning the power of small, specific behavior changes as a means toward making changes in larger areas. It teaches respect for one another's needs and point of view. It gives each the sense that "I count in this relationship" and it encourages saying "Yes" to one's partner more often than "No."

See also Positive Exchanges in this chapter.

RESOURCES

Lott, A. J., and Lott, B. E. A learning theory approach to interpersonal attitudes. In A. G. Greenwald, T. C. Brocke, and T. M. Ostrom (eds.), *Psychological foundation of attitudes*. New York: Academic Press, 1968.

Stuart, R. B. *Helping couples change*. New York: Guilford Press, 1980.

37 | WITHIN-SESSION STRUCTURED TASKS

Rationale

Within-session tasks may serve as an educative or diagnostic tool or as an intervention technique. Working within the session rather than assigning tasks for between sessions offers the therapist opportunities to (*a*) engage resistant family members; (*b*) engage those who may not be verbally oriented; (*c*) introduce the unexpected; and (*d*) bring to life concretely and vividly those issues for which a family seeks help.

Most schools of therapy employ tasks of some kind within the session. Freudians use free association and reporting of dreams. Behaviorists favor tasks that involve identification of goals, planning, and behavior rehearsal of actions to accomplish a particular goal. Gestalt therapists invite clients to create experiments in living.

The tasks referred to in this section are highly structured by the family therapist, who uses them to observe and assess a family in action and to join with the family to redirect the flow of the action in order to produce behavior change. Typically, the family is asked to solve a problem, make choices, or make something together. Structural therapists in particular formulate such tasks (Minuchin et al., 1967). Communication patterns, executive functioning, role assignments, and affective relations among members can be quantitatively and qualitatively assessed both clinically and by using group dynamics instrumentally. The latter requires the presence of a skilled observer; the therapist may step out and become the observer during the course of the task.

Strategic therapists are more inclined to structure an in-session task that links the thematic hypothesis already formulated about the family functioning with a specific desired behavior change related specifically to the problem presented.

In-session tasks may be differentiated from homework tasks. Homework is usually designed to practice something which has evolved from the session or paradoxically to rebel and do the opposite.

A multitude of tasks can be assigned. We illustrate ten of them. Whatever the task, every member is asked to participate.

Procedures
This procedure is described by Watzlawick (1966).

The following ten tasks are designed as in-session diagnostic tools to be observed by the therapist. The therapist instructs the family to perform the task or set of tasks or has them operate a tape recorder which allows them to listen to instructions. She then leaves the room to observe through a one-way-vision mirror.

Typical tasks may be to:

1. Plan a meal together. The family is told that there must be one meat, two vegetables, one drink, and one dessert, and they may talk but must end up agreeing on one meal everyone will enjoy.
2. Talk together about who in the family is the most bossy, the biggest troublemaker, the biggest crybaby, the one who gets away with the most things.

3. Talk over and agree on how they would decide to spend X amount of money.
4. Remember a past argument, who started it, who was in it, who wasn't, what went on, and how it turned out.
5. Offer ideas about what pleases or makes each member feel good about what each other member does in the family.
6. Build or make something together. A model is provided for the family to copy or the therapist furnishes a picture or example of what is to be made. Any kind of art materials or commercial toy building blocks can be used to make the copy. (See "The Straw Tower" in Chapter 3.)
7. Choose and play with puppets that are made available. (See "Family Puppet Interview" in Chapter 2.)
8. Select only one of three gifts that are offered to the family:
   a) a group game;
   b) a gift that can be used by only one person;
   c) a gift suited only to an older or younger child.
9. Divide refreshments that are offered as a test of nurturance. One cookie or one drink less than the number of people is provided to observe interactions in relation to cooperation and competition.
10. Have the parents, separately from the children, define the meaning of a proverb such as "A rolling stone gathers no moss." After they have worked it out the children are brought in. Then the parents are to teach the proverb to their children.

Responses are observed and scored. Information is gathered on such factors as leadership (who directs, makes summary decisions, misleads); request for leadership; behavior control (who controls whom); guidance in performing the task; supportive remarks; suggestions; agreement; aggression; affection; and indirect control.

Again, styles of communication, parent–child coalitions, and family rules emerge in the process.

Example

Use of an object-sorting task with a single-parent family in which the "executive function" is weak and oldest child is showing signs of becoming a parental child. In this example, the therapist's role is one of observer, assessor, and intervener. The therapist preselects various household or office objects and randomly places them on a surface and keeps them out of view until instructions are given to the family.

The children are instructed to take 20 minutes to classify the objects into several categories according to a specific feature which makes them alike (e.g., all red objects, all objects that can be eaten, all writing tools). At the end of the 20 minutes they will report on the different categories and how they were chosen. The mother is instructed to supervise. While the children are working on the task, the therapist takes note of the following: (*a*) leadership styles (who takes charge, who instructs, delegates); (*b*) capacity for cooperation and competition; (*c*) who yields to whom; (*d*) individual cognitive styles and levels of development; (*e*) how the mother supervises (dictating, encouraging, taking over); and (*f*) the degree of task completion.

In addition to observing these patterns, the therapist may coach the children, differentially reinforce each child for his part, and remove the parental child from his maladaptive role. The mother is reinforced and directed to "parent" her children.

Uses
This technique can be used with couples and families and is especially useful with action-oriented people for whom verbal intervention may not be effective. Used for assessment, this technique can highlight communication patterns, rules, and organization of the family system. As an intervention it engages the family or couple immediately, and it can educate them in new productive ways of interacting. By utilizing group dynamics tests to score the observations, family behavior patterns can be assessed in more objective terms.

RESOURCES
Minuchin, S., Montalvo, B, Guerney, B. G., Rosman, B. L., and
    Schumer, F. *Families of the slums*. New York: Basic Books, 1967.
Watzlawick, P. A. Structured family interview. *Family Process*, 1966, *5*,
    256–271.

38 | POSITIVE EXCHANGES

Rationale
Most couples in marital therapy are engaged in blaming or complaining or feigning helplessness. One goal of behavioral therapy is to change this process around so that the couple is practicing positive, cooperative behaviors with one another, thus forming a constructive, collaborative set based on positive exchanges. Positive exchanges are rewarding, reinforcing activities related to the maintenance of the marriage and to the satisfaction of the couple. Three steps are recommended:

1. Identify clearly and specifically what each person wants.
2. State these wants in a direct, positive way rather than stating what is not wanted.
3. Surprise the spouse regularly with positive behaviors.

Members of a couple hold longstanding assumptions about each other and anticipate both negative behavior and negative results from each other. They behave defensively even when they are offensive. In terms of social exchange theory each will act to match the other's rewards and deficits in the relationship.

Of course, for any conflict to continue a couple must cooperate to maintain the fight. The object is to help them to learn to cooperate in positive interchanges, respect their differences, and learn to negotiate those differences. They learn to overcome problems rather than one another (Dreikurs, 1946).

The therapist therefore prescribes the identification and practice of positive exchanges and sets goals with the couple for how the tasks will be carried out at home. Properly implemented, the technique changes the direction of behavior from the negative to the positive and from vagueness to specificity, changes the climate from hostile to collaborative, and changes the expectations from pessimistic to optimistic. It also shifts responsibility for change onto each individual rather than each waiting for the partner to change first. It replaces blaming with pleasing. It replaces self-interest with interest in the partner. The technique can be used with families as well as with couples.

Procedure

The following procedure is explained by Jacobson and Margolin (1979).

The therapist asks each partner to list three activities the other partner could perform to please him. The activities are to be very specific. They are to be stated in positive terms, what each wants done rather than what each typically complains about.

Each partner is then encouraged to agree to perform at least three tasks prior to the next session that will please the spouse. These can be agreed on during the session. A variation is for the therapist to suggest that they be surprises which the spouse must try to identify and relate during the next session. In either case the therapist follows up carefully during the next session to discover what each has done to please the other to conform with the agreement.

Another variation occurs when the couple is competitive and reluctant to follow the prescription. The therapist can use their competitiveness as an effective energizer. The idea is to set up the task as a competition:

Who can please the other more and prove the more loving, cooperative spouse?

The therapist suggests: "I wonder if either of you knows how to please the other. Let's find out if you can. Would each of you keep a satisfaction rating. Each time you do something to please your partner give yourself a check. Each time your partner does something to please you give him a check. Let's see if either of you gets any check marks from yourself or your spouse. At our next session we'll compare notes."

In order to be right, to impress each other and the therapist, and to overcome the partner, the couple enters the competition and engages in positive, pleasing behaviors.

The foregoing activities can be introduced at any point in the therapy when a switch from negative to positive interactions seems appropriate.

If the couple, or one of them, resists the exercise, the therapist can acknowledge that they have a right to disagree. She then requests that as an act of faith, since what they are doing is not satisfactory to them, they try the therapist's prescription, assume she is right, and see how it works out.

Example

John and Jane come to therapy complaining that they do not get along. Jane is bitter that her husband pays little attention to her and is never available to help around the house. John is upset with his wife's constantly criticizing him. He says he's ready to leave. The following occurs during the later part of the first session:

Therapist: Jane, what three things could John do to make you feel better?

Jane: He could get his head out of the TV and give me a hand.

Therapist: Could you say what you would like him to do?

Jane: It would be nice if John cleaned the yard, helped with the kids, and called home when he is going to be late.

Therapist: Jane, you say these things would be nice; exactly what does that mean for you?

Jane: It would make me feel good that John is helping out.

Therapist: Could you be more specific about the kids? Just what can John do with the kids that would please you?

Jane: When I'm doing the dishes he could bathe them.

Therapist: John, what could Jane do that would please you?

John: Stop nagging me, have dinner on time, and stop asking me for money.

Therapist: Just what is nagging, what is it Jane should stop doing?

John: Stop telling me what clothes to wear and to quit asking me for money.

Therapist: You've said that the three things you want Jane to do to
please you is to stop telling you what clothes to wear, stop asking
you for money, and to have dinner ready on time. What would you
like her to do instead of telling you what clothes to wear and asking you for money?

John: I would like her to tell me sometimes that I look good. And . . .
(long pause) I want her to tell me that she appreciates that I work
so hard and bring home the bacon, so to speak.

Therapist: OK. Jane, are you now aware that what John would like
from you is that you will have dinner ready on time, tell him that
he looks good, and that you appreciate that he works hard and supports the family?

Jane: Yes.

Therapist: John, and you are now aware that Jane would like it if you
would bathe the children, clean the yard, and call home when you're
going to be late.

John: Yes.

Up to this point the therapist has helped the couple to put their wishes
and expectations into clear operational terms and for each to acknowledge
being aware of what the other one wants. The intervention stopped the
process of blaming and encouraged each to tune in to the other's needs.

Therapist: Jane, are there some things you would be willing to do this
week to please John in the three areas he has listed for you.

Jane: Yes, if he is willing to do some of the things that I want.

Therapist: Without qualification. Just because you take responsibility
for doing it.

Jane: Okay.

Therapist: What will you do this week?

Jane: When he brings home his paycheck, I'll tell him how much I appreciate it that he works so hard. I know he does and I do appreciate
it.

Therapist: Good. That's one.

Jane: I'll tell him he's handsome and looks good. But I wish he would
change his clothes when he gets home.

Therapist: Could you put a period at the end of the first sentence and
stop there? What else will you do?

The process continues until both partners have committed to several
things that they will do for each other during the week. The therapist
then indicates that she expects them to live up to their agreements and
to go over the assignments in the following session.

The couple are now actively engaged in the process of committing to please one another rather than attacking one another. They are learning and employing specific skills for creating positive exchanges. They are eager to complain and attack, but the therapist keeps them on a more constructive course. She addresses herself first to Jane in each major segment because Jane is more frequently the initiator in the relationship.

Uses
The technique is used to teach skills in relating positively to one another. It is a means to stop the power play and redirect the behavior into more constructive channels. It forces the participants to at least pay attention to one another's needs and wishes and acknowledge them. It encourages the couple to define and to do very specific things for one another and to eliminate vagueness in communication, which can itself fuel conflict. By establishing a positive, cooperative set, the couple is better enabled to attack the various problems and issues which they face instead of attacking one another. The technique can be used with both couples and families.

RESOURCES
Dreikurs, R. *The challenge of marriage*. New York: Hawthorne, 1946.
Gurman, A. and Kniskern, D. (eds.) *The handbook of family therapy*. New York: Brunner/Mazel, 1981.
Jacobson, N. S. and Margolin, G. *Marital therapy*. New York: Brunner/Mazel, 1979.

39 | READING ALOUD AS AN INITIAL ASSIGNMENT IN MARITAL THERAPY

Rationale
Reading aloud is a behavioral/communications technique elaborated by Hamburg (1983).

The couple who seek therapy because of marital problems generally have a problem with verbal communication. The communication between the couple has either broken down or been reduced to arguing, avoidance, and repetitive rehashing of past arguments. The couple are directed to read aloud to each other in a structured way between sessions from books that directly address marital relations. This is given as an initial assignment and can be used with couples of average or better intelligence.

Reading aloud helps the couple to focus on listening to each other. The task also requires that they spend time together on an activity that is directed toward repairing the marriage. It requires them to negotiate an agreement on when they will do the reading, thus fostering at least some degree of positive cooperation. The content of the reading assignment chosen by the therapist universalizes and normalizes marital conflict. The clients identify in the readings not only the spouse's maladaptive behavior, but also their own. Seeing that other couples can solve similar problems stimulates an optimistic attitude about their own ability to improve their relationship and their patterns of communication.

If the couple were to go on a short trip or to a restaurant, the focus would be diluted. The couple is directed to read a specific book and is also told to limit the discussion very sharply. The reason for this instruction is to avoid the type of communication in which the couple has been engaged. When the couple discovers that they are able to communicate in this manner, they are likely to feel that they have begun a course of marital therapy that is going to be successful.

Procedure
The procedure is described by Hamburg (1983). After the couple has presented enough information about themselves for the therapist to form a preliminary hypothesis about the nature of the conflict, the therapist begins her instructions for the technique. The need to improve communications and learn new techniques is stressed to the couple when making the assignment. The need to read aloud together will ensure some form of cooperation and the couple is instructed to read aloud five times a week for at least a half hour following the initial interview. A book for the couple to read *aloud* together on marital conflict is selected. Among the scores of possible suggestions are:

Bach, G. R. and Wyden, P. *The intimate enemy — How to fight fair in love and marriage*. New York: Avon, 1970.
Dreikurs, R. *The challenge of marriage*. New York: Hawthorne, 1964.
Rogers, C. R. *Becoming partners: Marriage and its alternatives*. New York: Dell, 1972.

The couple are then requested to negotiate without help from the therapist the uninterrupted time they will need to arrange to read together between sessions. The couple are also requested to discuss who will be responsible for obtaining the book, and a time factor is built into this part of the assignment. The responsibility for time keeping (i.e., who will be the one to remind the other spouse of the assignment) is assigned by the therapist to the "non-nagging spouse" (Hamburg, 1983). The couple are then asked that while doing the task of reading aloud they prepare themselves to discuss issues or recommendations they approve or disapprove of in the book.

Ten minutes are usually allowed in the first session for those negotiations to take place. Then the therapist requests a report of the discussion and intervenes for renegotiation, if necessary. This time, she provides coaching to assist them in the task. After the renegotiation process is completed, feedback is requested from the couple on how the renegotiation was different from the first effort without the therapist.

During the second session the therapist checks whether the task has been completed in the agreed manner. The couple then have the opportunity to share their experiences regarding the task. The therapist will reassess any conflict related to the original agreement while using the content provided by the discussion of the book.

Example
This example follows the procedure that Hamburg (1983) describes; it illustrates a couple's negotiation of the task in their first session.

Therapist: I would like the two of you to agree on five half-hour periods when you can read together during the week.
Joe: It might be difficult this week. I have a lot of late meetings at work.
Mary: Couldn't we do it in the morning?
Joe: Well, maybe. But we'd need to get the book.
Mary: I can do that tomorrow after I drop the kids off.
Joe: Well, I guess we could try, then.
(Silence.)
Therapist: You've agreed then? You'll read in the mornings. Have you set a specific time or decided which five days it will be?
Joe: I guess it'll have to be before the kids get up — say 6:30 or 7:00. What do you think Mary?
Mary: Sounds okay. Should we do it Monday through Friday?
Joe: Yeah, I guess so.
Therapist: Well, that was pretty easy. Are your negotiations at home as successful as that?
Mary: Not really.
Joe: No way.
Therapist: What was different this time?
Mary: I think it was because you were watching. At home I often feel we've agreed to disagree. I felt I was trying really hard to make it work and at first I thought Joe wouldn't go along. But then he did and I felt that we were both on the same side for a change.
Joe: At first I was unwilling. What is reading together going to do for us? And it's inconvenient. Then I saw how important it was to Mary, so I tried.
Therapist: Yes, I felt the two of you were working together, too. You know, Joe, I think it would be a big help in carrying out the task if one of you was responsible for seeing that the schedule is followed

and remind the other partner in case things get hectic and the task might otherwise be forgotten. Could you be in charge of that?

Joe: I guess so.

The task promoted in session a sample of Mary and Joe's ability to negotiate. In this situation Mary took the initiative. Joe resisted at first, then reluctantly agreed, and finally took an active part in the planning. The couple were able to plan adequately with very little assistance from the therapist. It was hypothesized that Mary was the pursuer in this relationship while Joe was the distancer. Their ability to negotiate on the initial task was a good sign for the outcome of the therapy. The therapist praised them and set the couple to thinking about how this successful effort differed from their other experiences in negotiating. Finally, the therapist enlisted the help of the more resistant spouse by requesting his aid as "time keeper."

Uses

The technique can be used with couples of average intelligence or better, including couples with a depressed spouse or a history of physical violence (Hamburg, 1983). The task has several uses:

1. It generates useful information for the therapist.
2. It provides for the couple an immediate example of their communication problem and the therapist's expertise.
3. It engages the couple in an immediate experiential learning situation while serving as a prototype for the rest of the therapy.
4. It maximizes the likelihood that the couple will complete their first task successfully, thus creating an optimistic attitude about participating in and succeeding with the therapy.
5. It expands the couple's knowledge base and the availability of additional options through the content of the prescribed readings.

RESOURCES

Haley, J. *Problem-solving therapy*. San Francisco: Jossey-Bass, 1976.

Hamburg, S. R. Reading aloud as an initial assignment in marital therapy. *Journal of Marital and Family Therapy*, 1983, *9*(1), 81–87.

Nikelly, A. *Techniques for behavior change*. Springfield, IL: Charles C Thomas, 1971.

Patterson, G. R. and Hops, H. Coercion, a game for two: Intervention techniques for marital conflict. In R. E. Ulrich and P. Mountjoy (eds.), *Experimental analysis of social behavior*. New York: Appleton-Century-Crofts, 1972.

Stuart, R. B. *Helping couples change: A social learning approach to marital therapy*. New York: Guilford Press, 1980.

Weiss, R. L., The conceptualization of marriage from a behavioral perspective. In T. J. Paolino, Jr. & B. S. McCrady (eds.), *Marriage and marital therapy: Psychoanalytic, behavioral and systems theory perspectives*. New York: Brunner/Mazel, 1978.

40 | TEACHING CHOICE AWARENESS

Rationale

Teaching choice awareness is a cognitive procedure. It is based on the theory that human beings have the ability to make some choices in nearly all situations. The idea that humans are thinking creatures who can use the decision-making process in a rational manner is a cornerstone of the process. Nelson (1976, 1980) describes the technique for couple counseling, and most of what is presented here is based on Nelson's work. Couples who complain about boredom or lack of direction in their relationship can be taught to use it as a means of enriching their lives together. The couple is helped to understand that what they say and what they do is based on choice. They are taught that since they can think, they can control what they say and do.

The understanding that *even nonaction is a form of choice* is another important concept. If the couple can realize that excuses such as "Well, that's the way I always do things," or "That's part of my personality," are choices for nonchange, the couple can begin to make strategic changes in the relationship. If the awareness that we make choices in all that we say and do is accepted by the couple, they can enrich their interaction and develop a better understanding of each other.

Nelson (1976, 1980) makes five classifications of choice awareness: caring, ruling, enjoying, sorrowing, and thinking. These ideas form the acronym CREST. Since any given situation affects the behavior, a specific choice sometimes overlaps categories or falls into different categories. For example, a kiss may sometimes be used to show caring, extend a greeting, or express sexual enjoyment of the other person.

Nelson labels the choices "OK" or "OD." When a choice acts toward building a positive balance in the relationship it is labeled OK. An OK choice that can occur daily is greeting the spouse upon entering the home, making a comment about the pleasant aroma of dinner, and the like. A major OK choice would involve a very positive action or comment.

A negative comment or action is called an OD (overdraft) choice. A minor OD choice would be slamming a door, interrupting without apologizing, and so on. A major OD choice would be a physically aggressive act, a direct insult, or a strongly negative comment. The couple learns that in order to effect a balance that there must be enough OK choices enacted to offset the OD choices.

Procedure

The procedure for choice awareness is described by Nelson (1976).

The therapist begins with a brief introduction informing the clients that they are in charge of their behavior and the behavior is based on the choices each one makes about what to do. A short demonstration can be given; for example, they may be asked to pinch their own hands. Discussion reveals that they thought about whether or not to do it, how hard to pinch, and so forth, illustrating that one thinks about an action and makes choices about how to act. The therapist then describes the difference between positive (OK) and negative (OD) choices. She asks the couple to give one or two examples of each in their marriage. Once the couple understands the concepts, work is begun on the problems expressed with the intention of helping the couple identify the process of making choices and increasing the number and percentage of OK choices.

After some work has been done, the level of awareness of choicemaking is deepened by teaching the couple the CREST classification system. They then begin to identify more clearly the purpose of the choice as a desire to care, overcome, sympathize, and the like.

The following example occurs after the preliminary teaching about choicemaking has already been done.

Example

Much of the following case is adapted from Nelson (1980).

A couple visits the therapist and present their difficulty. She complains of being bored by her husband and he of being bothered by his wife.

Therapist: Would you tell me what happened yesterday that had made you feel the way you do?
Wife: He walked into the house and got washed up and sat down to read the newspaper.
Husband: I don't know why that should bother her. I always walk in, wash up, and sit down and read the newspaper.
Therapist: You have been doing this since you got married?
Husband: I guess so, I never thought about it. And I really don't know what's wrong with my doing that. Most of the guys I know read the paper when they get home.
Wife: It's not the reading of the paper that's bothering me. It's just that the same thing happens day after day.
Therapist: You would like something to be different.
Wife: Yes.
Therapist: What changes would you like?

Wife: He used to say something when he came in. Now, it's as if I'm not even alive until he finishes the damn paper!

Therapist: After he reads the paper, you begin to talk to each other. Are you saying you would like him to talk to you before he reads the paper?

Wife: I guess so.

Therapist: Would you be able to talk to her before you read the paper? Is this a choice that you would be able to make?

Husband: Not really. After working all day I really like to sit by myself and read the paper. I'm not ready to talk until after I've finished reading. I know that she's around, I just don't feel like getting into any big discussions for a while.

Therapist: There seems to be different needs that each of you have at that particular time of day. Your choice is that your husband talk to you and his choice is to read.

Wife: I don't need to have a whole conversation. I'd just like to know that he knows I'm alive.

Therapist: How do you want him to do this? Perhaps you can go outside and enter the room and show him what you would like. Are you both willing to try this?

Wife: Yes.

Husband: Yes.

Therapist: Well, you go outside and enter the room and make a choice that would be OK for you.

(Wife leaves the room and reenters.)

Wife: Hello honey. I'm home. Is everything all right?

Husband: What am I supposed to say?

Therapist: Just say whatever comes to your mind that you now feel would be her response. Then let's carry it a little further with each of you taking the other's part.

Husband: OK—that's funny—I guess I'm beginning to see I can make an OK choice. I'd like to try to come in and say something. I'd like to work it out that way.

Therapist: Fine. Mr. H., you may go outside and come in as if it's 7 p.m.

(Husband goes outside and reenters the room.)

Husband: Hello honey. I'm home. (Walks over and gives her a hug.) Is everything all right?

Wife: That felt good!

Husband: I'm glad—I'm going to wash up and read the paper.

Wife: We have fish for supper.

Husband: That's OK. (to therapist) Is that OK?

Therapist: Why don't you ask her?

Husband: Is that what you meant?

Wife: Yes. I think that the evening would start off much better. I don't
even think I'd get bored with a hug every day. (They both laugh.)

The session continued with the couple learning to make OK choices.
Under the tutelage of the therapist, the couple learned that each chose
certain behaviors based on his or her own need. They became more aware
of both their own and the other's needs. They appreciated that each was
willing to think up and practice some new behaviors that have a positive
affect and effect. It increased their sense of personal potency and enriched
the relationship. They discovered that in being positive one did not lose
one's independence or personal integrity, that making a positive choice
was much more powerful than merely giving in to the partner. Each
began to believe that "my partner cares about me."

Use
This technique can be used at any stage in the therapy. The couple may
try a dialogue with or without active role play. The therapy is more effective if the couple also practice OD choices. OD, or overdraft, are
choices that are generally negative or overdemanding. The couple can
even be encouraged to use the expression OK or OD to indicate to the
partner what pleases or displeases him or her. This is an added form of
communication in the marriage.

Most important, it encourages the couple to be aware of the choices
being made and their purpose. It also signals that they are both intelligent,
thinking people who can control and are responsible for their own behavior.

The technique is helpful in defusing a power play. It distinguishes between differences in needs and wishes and lack of love or appreciation
for one another.

RESOURCES
Nelson, R. C. Choice awareness: An unlimited horizon. *Personnel and
Guidance Journal*, 1976, *54*, 462–467.
Nelson, R. C. and Friest, W. P. Marriage enrichment through choice
awareness. *Journal of Marital and Family Therapy*, 1980, *6*(4), 399–407.

41 | SYMBOLISM AND GIFT GIVING

Rationale
Gift giving is an important kind of symbolic communication. It can be
used to help the therapist in family assessment and to enhance a family's ability to communicate. It can involve the analysis of gifts presented

by the family to the therapist. It may be used as an intervention technique to encourage family members to become more aware of one another's needs and feelings and to express their own feelings to one another. The extent of the family dysfunction is generally proportionate to the degree of communication impairment. When there is difficulty in verbal communication, feelings can be expressed metaphorically through the giving of objects such as a gift.

Individuals and cultures perceive a symbol in different ways. The meaning of the symbol can become personalized. Individuals often attach significant meanings to objects that are connected with some past events that have subjective meaning for them in the present. For example, a wedding ring can have different meanings to different individuals depending upon the past experience connected with the ring and the marriage; or a phonograph record containing a particular song may arouse certain feelings.

Gift giving is a very complex process. It can carry multiple messages. Symbols may serve as vehicles for unconscious as well as conscious ideas and feelings.

Among nonverbal gifts are jewelry, food, greeting cards, and doing things for another. Even criticism and demands may be considered by the giver to be a gift.

Gift giving is also related to power used positively or negatively in human relations. It can be a form of reaching out, an attempt to influence or bribe, a way of establishing superiority ("Now you owe me one," "I am nobler than thou,"), or an altruistic expression of love and caring. It can be an example of moral responsibility or righteousness as in charitable giving. It can be patronizing or used to establish a greater equality (as in sexually seducing the therapist) or moving from a constantly taking mode to an "I can give too" mode. It can be a sincere token of appreciation.

There are many times when clients and/or families feel the need to give gifts. There are feelings that they want to express that are beyond words. Some families are embarrassed to express how they feel.

Therapists' responses to accepting gifts from families vary, depending upon the therapist's experience, attitudes, and interpretations of gift giving and acceptance. There is a point when ethics would be in question, such as when the gift is obviously too expensive. Most ethical therapists would graciously decline an overly expensive gift. However, expensive gifts are not usually the case. Gift giving can be utilized by the therapist for assessment, evaluation, and therapeutic purposes.

The therapist can also prescribe gift giving among family members as a therapeutic intervention to improve positive forms of communication and to enhance the emotional climate of the family.

Procedure

A. *Receiving a gift from the family.* Gift giving is family-initiated. The family may offer a gift at specific points during the course of the therapy. The time usually is significant. The therapist engages in the following steps:

1. Assess whether or not it is appropriate to accept the gift. Accept if appropriate.
2. Graciously acknowledge thoughts and feelings symbolized by the gift, e.g., "That is very thoughtful of you." This will enhance rapport by communicating that the thought and feelings behind the gift are important to the therapist, thus increasing the family's self-esteem.
3. Look for deeper, perhaps unconscious meaning symbolized by the gift. What are the feelings, needs, and expectations implied by this gift for the family and for the therapy?

B. *Prescription of gift giving within the family.*

1. The therapist suggests that one or each person think of between one and three gifts that he or she can give to the family or a particular member between now and the next session.
2. The gift should be one that the person will be pleased to give and which the recipient will enjoy getting. It is not to be something he thinks the recipient "ought" to want.
3. The gift can be an action (performance of a desired chore, an invitation to a pleasurable outing, a hug, a warm greeting on arrival); or an object (an article of clothing, a game, flowers, a book, a favorite dish).
4. The gift does not have to be expensive, only thoughtful and timely.
5. It is best if the giving is reciprocal, but not an automatic exchange of gifts at the same time as at Christmas or anniversaries. Each gives and receives at different times so that there is some spontaneity to the process and it is not perceived as a quid pro quo: "I give you and you have to give me."
6. Whoever receives a gift is to verbally express thanks and appreciation.
7. The following session the therapist inquires how well the assignment was carried out, whether it was pleasing, and what effect the process produced.

A variation on the theme is the surprise gift. In most instances of dysfunctional communication the members are observing carefully to catch one another being "wrong." Therefore, the prescription is to give the gift of *positive actions* rather than objects. The person is not to inform the others when the gift is being given. The others are assigned the task of discovering the surprise gifts. This programs them to look for positive rather than negative actions in other family members.

Example: Gift Giving to the Therapist

An extended, three-generational, enmeshed C. family of ten comes for therapy. A 63-year-old mother and her four adult children all live with the eldest daughter, her husband, and two young children. One of the adult children, a 30-year-old diagnosed schizophrenic, is the identified client.

During the third family session, Mrs. C. brought a freshly cooked (it was still warm) Philippine delicacy. It was a dessert made of "sticky" rice cooked with coconut milk and brown sugar, wrapped in several layers of aluminum foil intended to retain its warmth.

Mrs. C.: I cooked this "biko" today and I brought some for you. I hope that it is still warm.

Therapist: (Interprets to herself what the gift could symbolize: The importance placed on the "warmth" could symbolize the family's feelings of comfort with the therapist; the family has accepted the therapist as someone who understood them [the therapist is of the same culture and the family brought a cultural dish]). This is very thoughtful of you and I appreciate this very much. I would like you to know though that it is not necessary for you to do this.

Mrs. C.: I know, but I was cooking it for the family and I thought of you. We always do this in the Philippines, don't we? (It is a common Philippine practice to send a neighbor or friend a dish, if one cooks something special.)

Therapist: You cooked this yourself and this should stay warm for quite a while, considering the way you wrapped it. You know, I don't even remember now how this is made.

Mrs. C.: (Goes into some detail about the procedure. All effort was on her part with no assistance from her family.)

Therapist: If this is a sample of your cooking, I can see how much you care for your family by seeing that your family is well fed. You all would surely not have to miss these native foods in this country. You seem to put a lot of effort in cooking, Mrs. C.

Nina (identified client): My mother likes to do the cooking. She also prepares the family breakfast and lunch which my brothers and sisters take to work. She washes and irons the family clothes, too.

Therapist: Is that right!

Lisa (oldest daughter): My mother likes to stay busy.

Martin (oldest son): She has always liked to stay busy — even in the Philippines.

Assessment value. Increased therapist's understanding of the family dynamics.

1) Mother keeps the children (who are all adults) dependent on her.
2) The mother's resistance to give up the "doer" role and allow the children more independence is apparent. In later sessions, although the mother agreed to let Nina take responsibility for the family dinner, she often undercut this agreement, saying that Nina was "too tired and too cold, so I cooked."
3) The family is stuck together, especially to the mother, and needs to be less enmeshed.
4) Nina is resentful of her dependence on mother, but has difficulty in becoming independent.
5) Other siblings manifested a "patronizing" attitude toward the mother's need to be a doer. Annoyance was evident later on.
6) Some clues to the family rules, values, and tendencies toward cultural practices become evident.

Therapeutic value.

1) Acknowledgment of the thoughts behind the gift raised family self-esteem, especially that of Mrs. C. This was done in very general terms.
2) Acknowledgment of the dish being warm and continuing to stay warm because of efforts at special wrapping indirectly recognized the feeling of warmth and comfort (unconscious at this point) being expressed. The family, though very polite and concerned about each other, are unable to say positive things to each other. For example, Mrs. C. shows her caring and love through her hard work and services to the family. The latter symbolized her love, which unfortunately the children do not perceive as love but (as the son later pointed out) as "being a martyr." The effect of this "martyrdom" on the children is annoyance and anger mingled with guilt.
3) Reframing Mrs. C.'s overfunctioning (hard work and service) as an expression of her love for the family helped to clarify the meaning of her actions. It changed the children's perception of mother constantly doing for all, keeping them in a dependent position. "Doing for" and warmth are defined as positive values. This intervention also made Mrs. C. feel good and loving. It sets the stage to differentiate being loving from being overadequate. The goal is to lessen her overfunctioning, so that the children will do more and be more responsible for themselves.
4) Encouraging exploration and participation of the children through comments that mother "likes to stay busy" and Nina's remark about mother doing so many other chores for the family gives the therapist

an opportunity to help mother to recognize how she has the children dependent on her—yet, it positively acknowledges her efforts.

At session 13, the oldest sister Lisa handed the therapist a small package of freshly baked cookies. The package again was carefully wrapped in layers of aluminum foil to keep it warm.

Lisa: *We* brought you some cookies which Nina baked.
Therapist: Oh, the package is still warm. (Opens the package.) How did you manage to bake these delicious-looking cookies and be here on time for our session! (Nina leaves day treatment program at this mental hospital at 3 p.m., goes home, and comes back at 7 p.m. for the family session.)
Nina: I baked them very early this morning before I left home and the family had them for breakfast. The mix was brought home by Neal from where he works. I saved some for you and warmed them up just before we came.
Therapist: This looks like a joint effort. Neal supplies the mix. Nina bakes the cookies and Lisa hands this to me. I imagine *everybody* at home enjoyed it. I know *I* will, too. Thank you *very* much.

Assessment value.

1) The family has changed subtly throughout the 13 sessions.
2) The sibling subsystem has become closer and strengthened, symbolized by the joint effort.
3) The mother was significantly absent at this session, symbolizing distancing of the parental system, which allowed the sibling subsystem to move closer together.
4) The warm cookies symbolized the continued comfortable feelings experienced by the family. This time it is not only toward the therapist, but also toward each other.

Therapeutic value.

1) Recognized, reinforced, and therefore made overt the cooperative effort of the siblings.
2) Increased Nina's self-esteem by remarks such as: "How did you manage to bake these delicious looking cookies . . . and be here on time!" "Everybody enjoyed them. I will too!" (Brother and sister acknowledged the cookies were good.)

Uses
This technique can be used with any family. Giving a gift to the therapist is a form of expressive behavior that allows the therapist to gain insight into their framework of meanings. It also permits her to assess how she fits into the family system.

Prescribing gift giving changes the framework and focus of communication from the negative to the positive. It encourages members to be more aware of one another's needs and preferences. It focuses interest in one another as individuals, thereby providing for differentiation within the system. It sets up a functional atmosphere for mutual appreciation. It makes people feel good about themselves and the family.

RESOURCES

Cohen, A. *Symbols and sentiments: Cross-cultural studies in symbolism.* New York: Academic Press, 1977, pp. 117–128.

Dolgin, J. L., Kemnitzer, D. S., and Schneider, D. M. (Eds.). *Symbolic anthropology: A reader in the study of symbols and meanings,* New York: Columbia University Press, 1977, pp. 3–34.

Freedman, A. M., Kaplan, H. I., and Sadock, B. S. *Modern synopsis of comprehensive textbook of psychiatry* (2nd ed.) Baltimore: Williams & Wilkins, 1976, pp. 302–306.

Freud, S. *The interpretation of dreams.* New York: Avon Books, 1968, pp. 380–449.

May, R. Values, myths and symbols. *American Journal of Psychiatry,* 1975, *132* (7-9), 704.

May, R. *Love and will.* New York: Norton, 1975.

Minuchin, S., Montalvo, B., Guerney, B., Rosman, B., & Schumer, F. *Families of the slums.* New York: Basic Books, 1967.

Sherman, R. The power dimension in the family. *American Journal of Family Therapy,* 1983, *11*(3), 43–53.

Sutterly, D. C. and Donnelly, G. F. *Perspectives in human development: Nursing throughout the life cycle.* Philadelphia, Lippincott, 1973, pp. 104–126.

42 | STRUCTURED COMMUNICATION TRAINING

Rationale

The theoretical base of communication training draws from three major sources. The skills taught are based on communication theory and certain Rogerian client-centered principles. Expression and acknowledgment of feelings are a primary focus. Some of the major skills involved are the same as those employed by client-centered therapists. The methods employed to teach these skills are broadly based on operant and social learning theories. The communication principles emphasize the reciprocal nature of good communication. The technology used in the training utilizes modeling, shaping, and positive reinforcement procedures. Three major elements can be identified in the training process:

1. The couple are given clear, concise guidelines to follow in the dialogues they carry out as they are learning communication skills.
2. The trainers coach the couple, during each dialogue, providing immediate and consistent feedback.
3. The subject matter of the dialogue is carefully controlled so that the couple begin with topics that are not emotionally loaded and progress to increasingly difficult topic areas only as their skills build.

Procedure

The material for this version of the technique is adapted from Guerney (1977).

Selecting and preparing couples for communication training begins with the screening interview common to all approaches to marital counseling. In this initial conjoint interview, the couple present their immediate concerns and their reasons for seeking consultation. The emphasis is to begin exploring the various areas of conflict and to give the couple an opportunity to decide that they are both willing to enter counseling. If it appears that a couple would benefit from communication training, the trainer explains the objectives of this training to the couple.

The couple is given explicit descriptions of the speaker and listener modes that will be taught. For example, the Speaker, in communication training, is the individual in the dyad who, at any time, is assuming the expressive mode. The rules which define this mode make it clear that good communication is as much the responsibility of the Speaker as of the Listener. Couples are told that the more the Speaker is able to be openly and honestly expressive of personal feelings, the more accurately the Listener will be able to make empathic responses. Similarly, the more accurate the Listener's responses, the greater is the possibility of open, honest expression by the Speaker.

The partner selected as Speaker chooses the topic to be discussed. This may be broadly defined as any content area or situation about which he has some feelings. In the early dialogues, the Speaker is asked to limit the choice of topics to those that will be easiest for the Listener to hear. While it is explained that personal or I-related topics are more likely to elicit better Listener response than relationship or we-related topics, it is the Speaker's responsibility to make this decision based on immediate knowledge of what topics are "heavy" issues in the relationship.

The Speaker must discuss the topic by expressing his own feelings about it. The Speaker's statements may include some description or content about the topic but must always include a clear expression of feeling. For example, this may take as simple a form as "I feel . . . " followed by a word identifying such primary feelings as "happy," "sad," or "lonely."

The Speaker cannot ask questions. It is pointed out that asking a question of the Listener will result in a shift of mode if the Listener answers the question. There is a specific method for switching modes but, like the modes themselves, switching is clearly defined and structured.

The Speaker cannot make blaming or attacking statements. It is important for the trainer to state this rule separately. Most couples are relieved to hear this rule spelled out so specifically, since it implies that the trainers are fully prepared to help them control a part of their communication process that has resulted in much pain and anxiety for them. This implication is made explicit when couples are told that the trainers will offer the Speaker help in rephrasing statements which are accusatory.

The Speaker's statements should be short and concise. This is spelled out concretely as five to six sentences covering no more than one or two primary feelings about the topic. It is stressed that this will enable the Listener to stay with the Speaker and will allow the Speaker to clarify his feelings fully before moving into further affect and content on the topic.

The partner assumes the responsive mode and is designated the Listener. Following each Speaker statement the Listener makes a response that reflects the Speaker's feelings about the topic area. It is acceptable to use the form "you feel . . . " followed by a "feeling word" in early dialogues. While the Listener's response may appropriately reflect both feeling and content, primary emphasis is placed on the development of comfortable responses to feelings. This requires that the Listener be able to distinguish between the content of the Speaker's statement and the feelings expressed in them.

The Listener must suspend his own judgment or opinion about both the topic and the Speaker's feelings. This is a separate rule which is explained to the couple, and the difficulty this presents to the Listener — especially when the Speaker is discussing an emotionally intense issue — is noted. The trainers must provide assurance that the Listener will be granted the same opportunity to express his feelings.

The Listener, also, is not permitted to ask questions, because to do so would result in the Listener assuming control or direction of the Speaker's topic. Couples can fairly quickly recognize that most questions the Listener is inclined to ask are "curiosity" questions rather than questions that must be answered in order to understand the Speaker's feelings. It is helpful for the trainers to share with the couple one or two "curiosity" questions that may have occurred to them during the initial interview but seemed unrelated to the goal of helping them with their relationship. As training progresses, the couple will find that answers to questions that seem possibly relevant to the topic are usually provided as the Speaker continues the dialogue.

The Listener keeps responses short, usually one or two sentences concisely reflecting the feeling words the Speaker is using. Since the Listener is limited to very short verbal responses which serve primarily as feedback to the Speaker, it is important that the Listener be aware that voice tone, body posture, and facial expression must support the verbal message of concern and caring. Conflicted couples work at being aware of contradictory nonverbal responses.

It is recognized openly with couples that the strict definition of modes will seem artificial as they start the training. At the same time, the trainers should be firm in their conviction that this structure is essential to learning and maintaining the modes that are desired. However, switching modes is both appropriate and necessary at times. This request may be initiated by the Speaker, the Listener, or a trainer.

Thus, with the Speaker and Listener modes, as well as the switching of modes, carefully defined and explained, the couple is now ready to begin dialogues. This may take place in a training group of several couples or in conjoint marital interviews. The trainers now switch to a coaching or guided practice method that will teach skills in a structured, graduated manner, applicable to the immediate experience of the participants. The trainers must ensure that the couple begin with subject areas that they can handle with little difficulty, are immediately rewarded for the successful demonstration of skills, and receive direct and specific feedback on difficulties they are having in either mode.

To identify topics at varying levels of intensity, the couple may be given a homework assignment in which each writes down three topics that would be easy to talk about, three topics that are of moderate difficulty, and three topics that would be intensely difficult. These lists should be retained by the trainers and used to structure not only the beginning dialogues but topics in later sessions.

Two other steps are useful before the couple begin their own dialogues. The first is a "feeling-word exercise" designed to increase the couple's vocabulary of words referring to emotions and to sensitize them to the area of feelings. The exercise consists of the couple and both trainers completing the sentence "I feel . . . " by adding a feeling word. This is done, in round-robin fashion, until 50 words are listed. The couple are given a homework assignment to list 50 more words. (See "Sentence Completion" in Chapter 2.)

After the feeling-word exercise, the trainers give a brief modeling demonstration of a dialogue, assuming the Speaker and Listener roles themselves. In doing this, the Speaker always talks about an issue that is immediate and personal; the modeling dialogue is not role played. After discussion of the trainer-modeled dialogue, the couple begin their own dialogues.

Participants will need a good deal of coaching in the early stages of dialogue, and, most critically, they will need a high amount of reinforcement for successful approximations of either the Speaker or Listener mode. At least 90 percent of the trainer's responses should be positive reinforcement. The trainer takes care to vary her vocabulary or reinforcing words, and, in the late stages of training, gradually reduce the frequency of her reinforcement.

Couples are expected to spend at least one-half hour a week practicing communication skills at home. They should follow the defined rules, alternate as Speaker and Listener, and use topics at the intensity level covered in the previous training session. The couple note any difficulties they experience without the trainer coaching, and these are discussed and worked on in the next training session.

Example
Mr. and Mrs. T., an attractive couple in their late twenties, were finalizing plans to separate and divorce as they entered counseling. They presented a very confused, detailed and rambling marital history during the initial interview and both were highly verbal, though neither focused his conversation well or listened to the other.

They agreed to four sessions of counseling which would concentrate on communication training. Mr. and Mrs. T. were relieved by the imposed rules and apparent control which prevented their usual angry, painful outbursts. At the conclusion of these sessions, both had become good responsive listeners, though each still had difficulty in openly expressing himself.

At this evaluation point, Mr. T. was particularly concerned that they still needed help discussing the crisis that had brought them in — Mrs. T.'s supposed infidelity, which she denied. Three sessions were scheduled for further communication training using this as the topic. With minimal coaching from the trainers they were able to handle this intensely emotional topic well. A follow-up interview, three months later, found that the marked improvement in communication had been maintained; and the couple reported substantial improvement in their overall relationship.

Uses
Communication training is broken down into various levels. The work is gradual and the skilled therapist proceeds one step at a time. The new learned skill is particularly useful since it is not only helpful for the couple in dealing with the presenting problem but can be used in a variety of situations. Once channels of communication are broadened couples are better equipped to deal with new situations.

Structured communication training teaches conflicted marital couples a series of skills that will enhance their ability to express important feelings, thoughts, and beliefs and to respond accurately to such stimuli.

RESOURCES
Ely, A. L., Guerney, B. G., and Stover, L. Efficacy of conjugal therapy. *Psychotherapy: Theory, Research and Practice*, 1973, *10*, 201–207.
Guerney, B. G. *Relationship enhancement.* San Francisco: Jossey-Bass, 1977.
Wachtel, P. L. *Psychoanalysis and behavior therapy: Toward an integration.* New York: Basic Books, 1977.
Wells, R. A., Figurel, J. A., and McNamee, P. Group facilitative training with conflicted marital couples. In A. S. Gurman and D. G. Rice (eds.), *Couples in conflict: New directions in marital therapy.* New York: Jason Aronson, 1975.

43 | THE SQUEEZE TECHNIQUE IN SEX THERAPY

Rationale
The Squeeze Technique developed by Semans (1956) and incorporated into their work by Masters and Johnson (1970) is used in sex therapy, particularly by those who follow behavioral approaches similar to those of Masters and Johnson (1970). The technique is employed when the male has a problem of premature ejaculation. It is designed to help the male reach a state of sexual excitation without ejaculating. For complete resolution of the problem, the male needs some understanding of the origin of distress, a cooperative, involved sex partner, and implementation of this technique. As in most behavior modification methods, the process is broken down into small steps that are rehearsed a number of times. Progress is reinforced by continued use of the methods for six months, even after the problem appears to have been resolved.

   Prior to introduction of the squeeze technique a careful examination is conducted. It is necessary to determine if this is one of the rare cases of organic dysfunction. According to Krohne (1982), treatment is likely to begin first with sex education and helping the couple to understand their sexual functioning, physiology, and the stages of a man's orgasmic experience. Those men who normally are able to control themselves and their lives may be able to take control when they become more aware of their functioning. They can learn to slow down. Psychotherapy is used if there are unresolved conflicts to work out. Sensate training may also be used to help the male slow down. It is at this point that Krohne recommends the use of the squeeze technique by a therapist who understands sexual functioning.

Procedure
The procedure as described in this section is adapted or directly quoted from Masters and Johnson (1970, pp. 101–115).

> . . . the wife's back is placed against the headboard of the bed (possibly supported with pillows) with her legs spread, and with the husband resting on his back, his head directed toward the foot of the bed, . . . with his pelvis placed between her legs, his legs over hers so she may have free access to his organs. As soon as full erection is achieved, the Squeeze Technique is employed. (p. 102)

As soon as the male feels he is about to ejaculate, the female places her thumb on the frenulum located under the head of the penis, and her first and second fingers are placed on the surface of the penis. The first finger is placed on the outside of the head and the second finger adjacent. "Pressure is applied by squeezing thumb and the first two fingers for an elapsed time of three to four seconds" (p. 103).

The therapist should have an artificial model to demonstrate how to do it. If the strong pressure required is used, the male will instantly lose his need to ejaculate. He will also lose 10–30% of his erection. The wife resumes her stimulation of the penis about 30 seconds after her partner has controlled his ejaculation. They repeat this procedure at least four or five times during the first session. The woman may be afraid to apply sufficient pressure. The man can tell her how much or guide her fingers with his own.

Successful control helps the couple to reduce their fears and increase their confidence. It is a major step toward improving cooperative communication between them. Three days of this activity usually will result in complete control.

> The next step in progression of ejaculatory control involves nondemanding intromission. The male is encouraged to lie flat on his back and the female to mount in a superior position, her knees place approximately at his nipple line and parallel to his trunk. . . . In this position, leaning over her mate at a 45-degree angle, she is comfortably able to insert the penis and then to move back on, rather than sit down on, the penile shaft. (p. 106)

The wife holds the penis intravaginally without movement or stimulation so that her partner gets used to it. If he becomes too excited anyway, the wife elevates herself, thus removing the penis from the vagina, and immediately employs the squeeze technique to prevent ejaculation. After 30 seconds the penis is reinserted. The activity is repeated until the male is able to control ejaculation regularly.

The next step is for the male to begin to exercise slight pelvic thrusting to maintain erection. As his control improves, the female is encouraged to join in with some pelvic thrusting, always returning to quiescence or to the squeeze technique when control is too threatened. Eventually the couple can enjoy themselves moving freely. This usually takes about two weeks of repeated training sessions.

The couple is told that there are times when control will be difficult and the technique needs to be practiced for at least a year. They are cautioned that there might be a brief period of impotency shortly after termination of the therapy, which will soon pass (p. 111).

The final step is the suggestion that the couple assume a lateral coital position, which gives the female more opportunity to express her needs by pelvic thrusting while making less demand on the male for immediate ejaculation.

Through the use of this technique the males gains control, and the female restores her sexual appetite, thinks more about her sexuality, and learns to give more expression to it. The couple greatly increase their sexual activity and communication from the beginning of treatment.

Uses
Of course, the squeeze technique is designed primarily to improve ejaculatory control. However, it does have additional uses and consequences. It helps the couple improve their pattern of intimate communication verbally and nonverbally. It encourages a high degree of cooperation between them. It is a strong expression of caring for one another so that both may enjoy their relationship. It demonstrates a model for changing complex behaviors one step at a time and the patience required to do so. The woman may become more sexually stimulated as she is more active in the process and finds more possibility for orgasm.

This technique has a very high rate of success and should only be used by therapists who have a great deal of knowledge of the physiological makeup of men and women, and who have the appropriate artificial models needed for demonstration.

RESOURCES
Krohne, E. *Sex therapy handbook: A clinical manual for the treatment of sexual disorders*. New York: Spectrum Publications, 1982.
Masters, W. and Johnson, V. *Human sexual inadequacy*. Boston: Little, Brown, 1970.
Semans, J. H. Premature ejaculation, a new approach. *Southern Medical Journal*, 1956, *49*, 353–357.

6

Paradox

INTRODUCTION

We are confronted by paradox daily in many aspects of our existence. The injunction "Doing your own thing as long as you don't hurt anyone else" is a paradox. If you do your own thing it may indeed be harmful or against the wishes of others, while regard for others may inhibit you from doing what you want. The existential paradox of life is that as long as you are alive you are dying.

Paradox is a contradiction that follows correct deduction from consistent premises. The most famous and the most frequently studied and reported is that class known as the "Be Spontaneous Paradox." A command to be spontaneous creates a no-win situation. The person who refuses to act spontaneously remains unspontaneous. Anything that is initiated is only a reaction to the command and hence not spontaneous. An example is the wife who wishes her husband to change his behavior and persuades him to come into therapy with her. The therapist prescribes specific actions to the husband, which he accepts and performs. The wife then rejects her husband's new behavior because it came from the therapist and not from the husband. The contradiction leaves all the actors in a double bind. The wife cannot be pleased whether the husband changes or not. The husband loses either way. And the therapist fails because no matter what the husband does, the wife will reject it.

Philosophers have been studying the nature of paradox since ancient times. Wittingly or unwittingly, creative people have always used paradoxical techniques to obtain behavior change. Watzlawick and others (1974) give numbers of examples. Parents and teachers long ago discovered the virtues of reverse psychology in dealing with children. Psychotherapists naturally began to develop paradoxical methods to help clients, especially to deal with oppositional and rigid behavior patterns. Morita developed a system of paradoxical therapy in Japan described in 1920 based upon Zen philosophy (*Time*, 1972).

Adler (Dreikurs, 1967) called his techniques the "anti-negative, or spitting in the client's soup." It consisted of recognizing the client's strongly held belief or behavior, accepting it, and exaggerating it. In this way he joined with the client rather than attempting to oppose him. Clients who took a negative position were now forced to become more positive in order to remain negative. By joining with the client's negative position, Adler in effect coopted it. Further, using a reversal technique, he might advise the mother of a child who refused to perform to become more inadequate and helpless than the child, thus stimulating the oppositional child to mobilize himself into greater activity.

Frankl (1975) called his process the "Paradoxical Intention" and encouraged the client to emphasize even more the problematic value, belief, or behavior described as the symptom. The client thus gains control over the symptom by intentionally willing himself to engage in the symptomatic behavior.

At first glance, behavioral theory seems to be opposed to paradox. Guthrie (Hill, 1977), however, presents an approach that is consistent — at least in practice — with some paradoxical techniques. To Guthrie things can be learned in one trial and recency is more important than frequency. Thus the candy store worker who is made to eat candy until he vomits remembers not the many pleasant experiences he had with chocolate, but the final sickening sweetness. Stampfl and Lewis (1967) use this exhaustion technique with phobias. In a technique called Implosion that recalls Aristotle's theory of tragic relief as much as it recalls Guthrie, the therapist repeats a horror story about a sex-mad, cannibalistic giant spider over and over again until (like the Grimms' fairy tales) what remains with the client is not "thoughts about spiders are connected with horrible anxiety" but, rather, "thoughts about spiders are connected with prosaic reality." Such techniques must be carried to their exhaustive conclusion.

Mozdzierz (1983), another Adlerian, sees paradox as behavioral dialectics applied to psychotherapy, viewing behavior in terms of its implied opposites. Thus in the power of passivity there is an element of violence. Similarly, people who have a strong, positive sense of self are committed to sharing with and caring for others as well as comfortable maintaining interpersonal distance. Those who demand and long for the greatest closeness and intimacy will often reject it out of fear of being absorbed as a person.

Mozdzierz (1983) sees people who behave in a rigid pattern as extremists who think in terms of opposites — thesis and antithesis. For example, a person strives for superiority (thesis) in order to overcome feelings of inferiority (antithesis). The need is to create a new synthesis, one of equality, thereby overcoming the dichotomous thinking.

Every negative or symptomatic behavior pattern has inherent within it positive and constructive possibilities. The therapist can reframe the meaning of the behavior by shifting it to the positive side and providing the clients with a new way of looking at it.

Paradoxical techniques are developed by Mozdzierz and colleagues (1976) as a form of encouragement to accomplish several possible objectives:

1. *Neutralize* the clients' attempts to control the therapist and others in their lives.
2. *Tranquilize* the clients relative to the symptom by helping them befriend the symptom (spend more time on it than they choose to and take away pressure and stress by giving clients permission to continue with the symptom when everyone pressures them to get rid of it).
3. *Energize* clients into new action. The clients are placed in a therapeutic double bind in which if they obey the therapist's prescription they cooperate with her and if they recoil from it they cooperate with others. Like Milton Erickson, Mozdzierz uses stories, parables, and jokes to create a communication meta to the symptom. He sees paradox as an encouragement process which also builds self-esteem and interest in others.

Mozdzierz and others briefly describe 12 paradoxical techniques:

1. *Making a neutral response* to inflammatory comments when an angry or defensive response is expected.
2. Giving clients *permission* to maintain the symptom as necessary and probably desirable.
3. Encouraging clients to *postpone their decision*, thus delaying or prolonging the crisis situation.
4. *Forbidding* the clients to do what they are already *not* doing to avoid injury.
5. *Predicting* the return of the symptom.
6. *Exaggerating* the symptoms by taking them even more seriously than clients presented them in their complaints.

7.   *Championing the cause* for retaining the symptom.
8.   *Redefining the symptom* from the negative to the positive.
9.   *Prescribing continuation of negative behavior*, but under the direction, control, and cooperation of the therapist.
10. Encouraging the clients to *practice the symptom more* and work at improving their performance.
11. Treating the symptom as a valuable skill and requesting clients to *teach the symptom to the therapist.*
12. Provoking clients positively by *pairing a negative behavior of the client as the opposite of a behavior or trait about himself of which he is pleased* and proud. How could he do such a thing?

As a group, it is the strategic family therapists, beginning with the double-bind theory of Gregory Bateson (1972), who have devoted the most attention to both the theory of paradox and paradoxical techniques. Among the many who explored and described it recently are Anderson and Russell (1982), Andolfi (1980), Andolfi et al. (1983), De Shazer (1982), Duhl (1983), Haley (1980, 1984), Weeks and L'Abate (1982), L'Abate (1984), Madanes (1981, 1984), Papp (1983), Selvini Palazzoli and others (1978). These are all systems theorists who see the symptom as created in order to maintain balance in the system. Their main contribution in the use of paradox is to link both the symptom and its purpose in serving the system to the paradoxical intervention. They are also greatly refining the creation and delivery of such interventions within systems change models. But there are also variations in the thinking of the different theorists.

For the sake of general illustration, Papp's position (1984) will be briefly summarized. She postulates three assumptions:

1.   The family is a self-regulating system.
2.   The symptom is a mechanism for the self-regulation of the system.
3.   There will be systematic resistance to change because if the symptom is eliminated, that important part of the system will now be unregulated, constituting a threat to the family. The family wants to change the symptom without changing the system which requires it. This is impossible. Therefore, therapy is the process of countering resistance to change.

If the family is cooperative and accepts recommended changes, the therapist helps them with direct linear prescriptions such as "It might be a good idea for the entire family to have dinner together three nights this week." If the family rejects or does not implement direct recommendations or come up with changes of its own, then paradoxical work may be useful. It is utilized primarily to interrupt long-term, rigid, repeating patterns of behavior in which the family is engaged. Families that require increased structure and controls are probably not suitable candidates for paradox.

The objective is to present a series of drastic redefinitions of the family's behavior leading to a perceptual crisis. The family can no longer see itself the same way or continue to regulate itself through the same symptomatic repeating pattern of behavior. They then have to move to something new.

Papp (1984) lists three major steps in paradoxical interventions:

1. Redefining. The problem behavior is relabeled and presented to the family in a different framework of meaning which supports the inner logic of the family. Each member's behavior is described as a positive interaction intended to be in the best interest of the family. The therapist indicates that the symptom is necessary to the family's existence and stability. Anger is relabeled as caring, suffering as self-sacrifice, distancing as a means of reinforcing closeness.

2. Prescribing. The therapist prescribes that the members do more of the same because the family needs the behavior to continue. By overtly and consciously enacting the cycle that produced the system, the family loses its power to produce the symptom. The secret rules are out in the open and the family must take responsibility for their actions. A common example in the authors' case load is that of a child who acts out to involve a distant husband/father in the family circle. The pattern is that the child misbehaves. Mother yells. Her yelling upsets father, who comes in from the other room and joins mother while participating in the fight. Father overreacts, so mother rushes to defend the child, undercutting father and sending him off into the distance again. This upsets the child, who begins the cycle again. The symptom is linked to the system when the child is encouraged to continue his misbehavior because he misses his father and wants to help him join the rest of the family. This also reveals the secret rules underlying the power play.

Papp (1984) enjoins her readers that merely encouraging each member to continue doing what he is doing without linking the behavior to the system will not work. The prescription must capture the exact truth of the family's functioning. When confronted by its own truth, the family is likely to recoil from it and seek another pathway.

3. Restraining. When the family shows signs of changing, the therapist cautions the family against change. She worries about the consequences of change, controls its pace, and anticipates problems. Once she takes a paradoxical position she has to stick with it for maximum effectiveness, accepting change grudgingly. The typical response of the therapist well schooled in learning theory is to praise and positively reinforce the desired behavioral changes when they are exhibited. However, this would act against the paradox and countermand its effect. Paradox depends on the oppositional behavior of the clients rather than their cooperation. Providing praise and encouragement for the new behavior will in turn encourage the clients oppositionally to return to their previous pattern.

There are defiance- and compliance-defiance–based interventions in this model, but both rely on the clients' resistance to change.

A *defiance-based paradox* is a prescription given to an oppositional family in the expectation that it will behave opposite to the prescription.

A *compliance-defiance–based paradox* depends on both cooperative and oppositional family members. Cooperative members are given a paradoxical intervention as a direct recommendation to be delivered in turn to the defiant ones, who it is hoped will recoil and act opposite to the recommendation. For example, a young couple is troubled by the constant advice and intrusion of parents and in-laws who refuse all requests to limit their kindness. The couple is instructed to thank the parents and in-laws for their help and to request that they perform many more needed tasks.

L'Abate (1984) contends that paradox is related to issues of control. One paradox of therapy is that clients regard their own behavior as somehow involuntary, unexplainable, and beyond their responsibility. A second paradox is that therapists need to be in control in order to give it away. Control is necessary for effectiveness. Once achieved, the control is given away to the clients so they can be effective. The therapist first takes charge of herself and then helps clients take charge of themselves. The therapist in contracting with the family in effect asks if they wish to achieve control over the symptom. If they say "no," there is no contract.

L'Abate (1984) suggests several ways to achieve control.

1. *Redefine the symptom in a positive frame.* This puts the therapist in charge of the symptom.
2. *Start the symptom if you want to stop it.* Through reenactment, pretending, role playing, or prescribing the symptom, the clients are told to start the presenting behavior. If they can start it, they may begin to see they have some power and responsibility for it. It is better to prescribe it where and when it most often naturally happens. The paradox is that by prescribing it, it is no longer happening "naturally" but is now under control of the clients.

For maximum control L'Abate (1984) recommends that the prescription include precisely *where* (the usual place or a dramatically new one), exactly *when* (how often, how long, when begin, when end), how *intense* it can be, and *how to be with each other* when carrying out the prescription. This last category enables the therapist to change the existing interactional patterns in the family and go beyond symptom relief to a more effective system.

The issue of control is a principal concern of the critics of paradoxical interventions. They assert that it is a covert, manipulative operation performed without permission of the clients and therefore probably unethical.

The authors believe that it is not covert and certainly not any more manipulative than any other techniques from reflection of feelings to questioning to interpretation of the resistance. The clients have agreed that they want to get rid of the symptom and change their behavior. Just as the psychoanalyst presents an interpretation which is her impression of the truth of the client's behavior, so too the paradox is really a way of visibly confronting the family with an interpretation of the inner truth of their behavior. Having seen it, they have the choice of continuing to behave in the same manner or rejecting it and doing something differently. For this reason proponents of paradoxical methods argue that they diligently respect the clients rather than unduly manipulate them.

Paradoxical techniques present many advantages.

1. They permit the therapist to join fully with the family's pattern of behavior. The family is likely to feel understood.
2. They help create a more positive climate in the family by positively reframing the meaning of the behavior pattern.
3. By accepting the existing behavior and telling the family to continue it for good reason, they reduce feelings of guilt and blame and position the therapist as different from everyone who tells them to stop it. This is also a surprise element.
4. Reframing the meaning of the behavior encourages the family and individuals to develop a new perspective and therefore to begin to see new options.
5. Prescribing the symptom makes the family responsible for their own behavior. It puts them in charge of creating it instead of feeling helpless before it.
6. They are particularly effective in dealing with rigid behavior patterns and a high degree of resistance, which tends to frustrate the success of other therapeutic techniques.
7. The therapist, having joined with the symptoms, is removed from a power play with the family, which is now responsible for any changes that take place.
8. The paradoxical prescription correctly made reveals the secret rules of the family system and makes the whole behavioral process overt.

This chapter includes a sampling of paradoxical techniques such as reframing, the paradoxical letter, pretending to have the symptom, putting the clients in control of the symptom, joining the opposition, contaminating the suicidal fantasy, the winner's bet with adolescents, prescribing indecision, the therapist as director of the family drama, and illusion of alternatives.

RESOURCES

Anderson, S. A. and Russell, C. S. Utilizing process and content in designing paradoxical interventions. *American Journal of Family Therapy*, 1982, *10*(2), 48–60.

Ansbacher, H. L and Ansbacher, R. R. (eds.) *The individual psychology of Alfred Adler*. New York: Harper & Row, 1956.

Andolfi, M. *Family therapy: An interactional approach*. New York: Plenum, 1979.

Andolfi, M. and Zwerling, I. *Dimensions of family therapy*. New York: Guilford Press, 1980.

Andolfi, M., Angelo, C., Menghi, P., and Nicolò-Corigliano, A. M. *Behind the family mask: Therapeutic change in rigid family systems*. New York: Brunner/Mazel, 1983.

Bateson, G. *Steps to an ecology of mind*. New York: Ballantine Books, 1972.

Bergman, J. S. Fishing for barracuda: Pragmatics of brief systemic therapy. New York: W. W. Norton, 1985.

De Shazer, S. *Patterns of brief family therapy: An ecosystemic approach*. New York: Guilford Press, 1982.

Dreikurs, R. *Psychodynamics, psychotherapy and counseling*. Chicago: Alfred Adler Institute, 1967.

Duhl, B. S. *From the inside out: A systems thinking approach*. New York: Brunner/Mazel, 1983.

Four walls treatment. *Time*, October 2, 1972, p. 101.

Frankl, V. E. Paradoxical intention and dereflection. *Psychotherapy Theory, Research and Practice*, 1975, *12*, 226–237.

Haley, J. *Leaving home*. New York: McGraw-Hill, 1980.

Haley, J. *Ordeal therapy*. San Francisco: Jossey-Bass, 1984.

Hill, W. *Learning*. New York: Crowell, 1977.

L'Abate, L. Beyond paradox: Issues of control. *American Journal of Family Therapy*, 1984, *12*(4), 12–20.

L'Abate, L. and Weeks, G. A bibliography of paradoxical methods in psychotherapy of family systems. *Family Process*, 1978, *17*, 95–98.

Madanes, C. *Strategic family therapy*. San Francisco: Jossey-Bass, 1981.

Madanes, C. *Behind the one-way mirror*. San Francisco: Jossey-Bass, 1984.

Mozdzierz, G. J. Paradox. Workshops given at Regional Convention, North American Society of Adlerian Psychology, New York, March 1983.

Mozdzierz, G. J., Macchitelli, F. J., and Lisiecki, J. The paradox in psychotherapy: An Adlerian perspective. *Journal of Individual Psychology*, 1976, *32*(2), 169–184.

Papp, P. *The process of change*. New York: Guilford Press, 1984.

Selvini Palazzoli, M. S., Boscolo, L., Cecchin, C., and Prata, J. *Paradox and counterparadox*. New York: Jason Aronson, 1978.

Stampfl, T. C. and Lewis, D. J. Essentials of implosive: A learning theory based on psychodynamic behavioral therapy. *Journal of Abnormal Psychology*, 1967, *72*, 496–503.

Watzlawick, P. *The situation is hopeless, but not serious*. New York: Norton, 1983.

Watzlawick, P. *The invented reality*. New York: Norton, 1984.

Watzlawick, P., Weakland, J. H., and Fisch, R. *Change: Principles of problem formation and problem resolution*. New York: Norton, 1974.

Weeks, G. R. and L'Abate, L. *Paradoxical psychotherapy*. New York: Brunner/Mazel, 1982.

44 | REFRAMING

Rationale

One of the tasks of Adlerian therapy is to change minuses into pluses. Reframing, or relabeling, is a technique used to change a negative meaning into a positive one. It consists of changing the frame of reference against which a given event is considered or judged, thus changing the meaning and value judgment of the event without changing the facts (Paolino and McGrady, 1978).

The mother accused of nagging is reframed by the therapist as one who is intensely interested and caring. The child who is very anxious and worries a lot is reframed as one who has accepted the very difficult job of being the family's guardian and protector. The husband who accuses his wife of never wanting to do anything and the wife who complains that her husband is never satisfied are relabeled respectively as being in charge of excitement and security in the family.

Having observed the family's language, view of the world, and solution to their problem (the symptom), the therapist feeds back the pattern of behavior in a different, positive frame of reference or context so that the clients will see it differently. Seeing it in another way should offer some new possibilities and help them think and feel differently about it. In turn this may trigger optimism in approaching the situation.

This technique is used by most therapists but is especially important in strategic and Adlerian models. It is the foundation upon which paradoxical interventions can be constructed and it is an essential ingredient in the Adlerian process of encouragement and validation of clients.

Technically, reframing is taking something out of its logical class and putting it into another logical category without changing the facts. Nagging can legitimately be categorized as an effort to teach another new behavior, an expression of caring and concern for the other, a willingness to fight in behalf of the other to mobilize that person more effectively, a desire to seek a cooperative alliance with another, and so on, without changing the facts. But in each category it has a different meaning and usefulness. By converting the family's statement into a more constructive category, the technique helps families to restructure the situation and do something differently. In all teleological theories, the symptom is believed to serve a useful purpose. By reframing the purpose to something that is positive, the climate of the system is changed.

Procedure

The therapist's first problem in joining the family is to define the therapeutic reality. Therapy is a goal-oriented enterprise, to which not all truths are relevant. By observing the family members' transactions in the therapeutic system, the therapist selects the data that will facilitate problem solving.

Therapy starts, therefore, with the clash between two framings of reality. In systems theory, the family's framing is relevant for the continuity and maintenance of the system more or less as it is; the therapeutic framing is related to the goal of moving the family toward a more differentiated and competent dealing with their dysfunctional reality.

Having elicited the pattern through which each person reinforces the behavior of others and understanding the family's complaints, the therapist is now in a position to redefine or reinterpret the meaning of the behavior by reframing it in another constructive category.

Example

This case concerns an acting-out adolescent boy. The therapist says: "It seems to me that there is a lot of loving in this family." She then proceeds to deliver her reframing of the situation indicating the positive usefulness of the symptomatic pattern according to the truth of the family's structure. Father complains mother can't handle the boy and he is too busy.

The therapist might say to the son: "Is it possible, John, that your arguing with Mom helps her clarify exactly what she wants and needs in the family and mobilizes her to fight for what she wants? At the same time, Mom, by making demands on your son you help him to grow up and move toward greater independence by opposing you. When the two of you fight it catches Dad's attention. He cares, so he gets involved. In that way the whole family gets together, which is another thing you all want, because otherwise Dad might feel left out."

The therapist reframes the meaning of the fighting so that everyone is seen as helping someone else and the family is seen as loving and caring; the meaning is changed from hatred and defiance to ultimate family harmony. The therapist thus challenges the family structure by challenging its perception of reality. The family will accept the reframing or challenge it. If challenged, the therapist can indicate that she is merely reporting what she sees them doing or, if she is preparing for a paradoxical prescription, she then delivers it.

A second example is adapted from Herr and Weakland (1982).

The presenting problem is a sharp conflict between an adult daughter and her elderly mother about whether mother can continue driving a car. Mother insists she can and that daughter is unreasonable and bullying her. Daughter insists it's not safe and mother stubbornly refuses to accept the reality of her disabilities.

The therapist observes that in the language of the family mother is stubborn and daughter is a bully. She then reframes the situation.

"Daughter's concern for mother is truly admirable. It is a rare person who would be willing to drive her mother everywhere to assure her safety. Most children would think it is too much. Mother's concern for daughter is also very impressive. She doesn't want to be a burden on anyone and to maintain as much independence as possible, even if there are some serious risks involved. You are both very caring and protective of one another."

Then the therapist suggests that people age at different rates and perhaps a physician could determine after examination how much risk is involved for mother to drive and make a professional recommendation. Each felt better about the other and saw a way of resolving their "war."

In the interchange both daughter and mother are acknowledged as good people with good intentions, each caring about the other. Then a new option is presented for their consideration. The reframing allows them to substitute protective and caring (positives) for stubborn and bullying (negatives) in their view of one another.

Uses

Reframing changes the meaning of what is going on without changing the facts. It helps families and couples stuck in a repeating pattern find new purpose and new hope and better understanding of one another. It redirects the forms of attention from the negative to the underlying positive elements in the relationship. Through reframing the therapist assigns good intention and worthwhile purpose to each participant. This validates all members individually and in terms of their functions in the system, which makes them feel better about themselves and each other and is encouraging to all. Finally, this assists the family in escaping its downward spiral that occurs within the negative frame of meaning and perpetuates the problem.

RESOURCES

Adler, A. *Understanding human nature*. New York: Fawcett, 1954.

Ansbacher, H. L. and Ansbacher, R. R. (eds.) *The individual psychology of Alfred Adler*. New York: Harper & Row, 1956.

Christenson, O. C. and McKay, G. *Adlerian family counseling*. Minneapolis: Educational Media Corp., 1983.

Dinkmeyer, D. C., Pew, W., and Dinkmeyer, D. C., Jr. *Adlerian counseling and psychotherapy*. Monterey, CA: Brooks/Cole, 1979.

Herr, E. and Weakland, J. *Counseling elders and their families*. Rockville, MD: Aspen Press, 1982.

Madanes, C. *Strategic family therapy*. San Francisco: Jossey-Bass, 1981.

Minuchin, S. and Fishman, H. C. *Family therapy techniques*. Cambridge, MA: Harvard University Press, 1981.

Paolino, T. J., Jr. and McGrady, B. S. *Marriage and marital therapy*. New York: Brunner/Mazel, 1978.

Stuart, R. B. *Helping couples change: A social learning approach to marital therapy*. New York: Guilford Press, 1980.

45 | PRETENDING TO HAVE THE SYMPTOM

Rationale

Madanes (1981) developed the "game" of prescribing that the family pretend to behave in the ways they are already behaving symptomatically. Nichols (1984) also describes and discusses her technique. This technique is a paradoxical intervention designed to have a more gentle effect in producing change than relying on the family's defiance of the therapist. It puts the family in the paradoxical position that if they pretend to behave in a certain way they cannot "really" behave that way. You can't pretend to be having a temper tantrum and actually be having a tantrum at the same time. If the reactions of other family members are also a pretense, then the whole situation becomes a game that all are cooperating to play and it becomes less serious. It dramatizes what is actually happening in the family while producing less tension. Because it is a game, the members become more flexible and begin to vary their behaviors, thus bringing about change in the system.

The prescription introduces a process of creative playfulness to replace the former deadly serious interactions. It depends on the willingness of the participants to comply and cooperate in playing the game.

Procedure

The first step is to get a clear picture of the symptomatic pattern of behavior. Who does what, followed by what reaction, followed by what reaction, until the entire pattern is elaborated.

Next the therapist determines if the family is likely to cooperate and perform according to her requests.

The third step is to ask the participants to pretend to enact the scene in the session. The initiator is told to pretend to act as he usually does and the reactors to react as they usually do.

The fourth step is to request that the scene be reenacted. This time, however, the therapist prescribes some additional behavior to modify the sequence or to highlight the meaning of the symptom.

The fifth step is to prescribe that the participants practice this reenactment regularly at home until the next session.

Sixth, during the next session, the family reports what happened. At this point, if significant behavior change has occurred, the therapist may accept that the system has made a permanent change or she may reinforce the change through restraint, cautioning the family against rapid change and prescribing that they continue the assignment.

Example

Madanes (1981, pp. 147–177) reports the following case.

The case concerned a single-parent family of a mother, two older daughters, a baby brother, and a ten-year-old son. The mother sought therapy for the ten-year-old boy, who had night terrors. Madanes hypothesized that the boy was concerned about his mother, who had lost two husbands.

The therapist asked all the members of the family to describe their dreams. Both mother and son had nightmares. "The mother's nightmare was that someone would break into the house, and the boy's was that he was being attacked by a witch. When Madanes asked what the mother did when the boy had nightmares, she said that she took him into her bed and told him to pray to God. She explained that she thought his nightmares were the work of the devil."

The therapist hypothesized that the boy's nightmares were a metaphorical expression of the mother's fears and his desire to help her. When he was terrified, mother had to be adequate, strong, and helpful and did not have time to be afraid for herself. His behavior helped by distracting her. However, her beliefs about the devil frightened him even more. So each was helpful in dysfunctional ways.

For the reenactment, "The family members were told to pretend that they were at home and mother was afraid that someone would break in. The son was asked to protect his mother. In this way the mother had to pretend to need the child's help instead of really needing it. At first the family had difficulty playing the scene because the mother would attack the make believe thief before the son could help. Thus she communicated that she was capable of taking care of herself; she did not need the son's protection. After the scene was performed correctly, with the son attacking the thief, they all discussed the performance. The mother explained that it was difficult for her to play her part because she was a competent person who could defend herself. Madanes sent the family home with the task of repeating the dramatization every evening for a week. If the son started screaming during his sleep, his mother was to wake him up and play the scene again. They were told that this was important to do no matter how late it was or how tired they were. The son's night terrors completely disappeared."

Of course, there was more work to do with this family. But pretending to have the nightmares and adding the dimension of fighting the thief acted paradoxically to eliminate the fears.

Uses
The pretend technique can be used with any family or individual who is willing and able to comply with the request to describe and enact the scene. It puts the participants in charge of the symptom. It enables the therapist to introduce a novel modification in the enactment that dramatizes its meaning and promotes a shift in behaviors. Its effectiveness depends on the therapist being able to properly understand the meaning of the symptom and to invent a prescription which elaborates that meaning in the pretend game. The game transforms the action from the "real" world to the world of playfulness where experimentation is less threatening. Compliance with the therapist who prescribes the symptom as a game ultimately leads to rejection of the symptom.

RESOURCES
Madanes, C. *Strategic family therapy*. San Francisco: Jossey-Bass, 1981.
Nichols, M. *Family therapy: Concepts and methods*. New York: Gardner Press, 1984.

46 | ILLUSION OF ALTERNATIVES

Rationale
Illusion of alternatives is basically a reframing technique that places the symptomatic issue in a new logical category in which all the choices are positive and functional. The reframing places the family system in an

entirely new and more acceptable position. This ancient method was refined by Milton Erickson and Jay Haley (Haley, 1973) and specifically described by Breit, Won-Gi Im, and Wilner (1983). It is based on reframing (see the section on "Reframing" in this chapter for an explanation of that process) and the power of suggestion derived from work in hypnotherapy and the use of power.

Because people generally find choice more palatable than mandate, this strategy provides a choice in a way that bypasses resistance. Most parents with challenging children know this technique, which shifts the focus from whether the patient will cooperate to how or when he will cooperate. The therapist, taking for granted that the patient will cooperate, offers an apparent choice. Erickson learned about illusory choices as a boy when his father would ask, "Do you want to feed the chickens first or the hogs first?" (Haley, 1973).

Procedure

The therapist obtains a diagnostic understanding of the system and how the symptom functions in the system. She then reframes the symptom in a new logical category that is more acceptable in terms of the values and metaphors of the family. For example, the acting-out adolescent is characterized as practicing new skills to become more independent and self-sufficient. The therapist then prescribes positive choices: "Do you want this week to become more independent by doing all your homework by yourself, volunteering for a variety of household chores, or by getting a part-time job?" By making a choice, the client assumes responsibility for his behavior and is doing what he wants. His oppositional behavior is therefore channeled into constructive directions. At the same time, since the adolescent is doing something approved by the parents, the parents are urged to disengage from the activity so the child can be more independent. This breaks the circular, self-reinforcing pattern that keeps the symptom going. The child now has nothing to oppose and is engaged in a productive activity pleasing to him and his parents.

Example

Breit et al. (1983) report the following case.

A 12-year-old girl, a good student, popular, and highly valued in her family, had become school phobic following an appendectomy which had unexpectedly also entailed the removal of an ovary. Her recovery was complicated by postsurgical infection. Once her physical ordeal was over and she was expected to return to school, she could not. She stayed home month after month in a state of severe depression and psychological paralysis, refusing not only to go to school but also to see friends and relatives. Her distraught parents brought her first to one therapist, then another. The first therapist proved unacceptable to the youngster and her parents because she reportedly "delved into her past," thus implying to the family that she believed the client had been emotionally disturbed before the surgery. The second therapist, in frustration at not being able to return her to school, alienated the girl and her parents by calling her a manipulator.

Based on the drawing this client did of a "perfect family," as well as the mother's stated pride in the psychological strength of her family of origin, it was clear that emotional disturbance was anathema to them. Thus the therapist's first move was to reframe the school phobia as a normal recuperation period. It was explained that people who have suffered the trauma of surgery need a period of time to restore themselves to health. Keeping in mind this client's dread of being considered emotionally disturbed, it was pointed out that if the normal recuperative period lasts too long, one runs the risk of being classified as a psychiatric case. Therefore, the time had come for her to return to school. The only issue to be decided was the school to which she would go. If she felt too embarrassed to return to her old school, she might want to consider a different school in the district, or perhaps a school out of the district, or perhaps even a private school. A discussion of which school to attend, rather than the question of whether to return to school, preoccupied the family for the coming week. After much deliberation, they decided she would live with her grandmother in another neighborhood. She attended school there for the remainder of the term with no recurrence of the school phobia.

Uses
Illusion of alternatives is particularly useful as a means of overcoming resistance. It changes the negative to the positive, ascribes good intention to all family members, particularly the client, and provides positive choices to help improve the family's functioning. This detoxifies hostility and conflict. The power of suggestion coming from an authority who utilizes the family metaphor is a forceful stimulant to action. Because choices are given, the family feels as though it is being empowered.

RESOURCES
Breit, M., Won-Gi Im, Wilner, S. Strategic approaches with resistant families. *American Journal of Family Therapy*, 1983, *11*, 51–58.
Haley, J. *Uncommon therapy*. New York: Norton, 1973.
Lankton, S. R. and Lankton, C. H. *The answer within*. New York: Brunner/Mazel, 1983.
Rossi, E. L. (Ed.) *The collected papers of Milton Erickson*, Vols. 1 and 4. New York: Irvington, 1980.
Zeig, J. K. *A teaching seminar with Milton H. Erickson*. New York: Brunner/Mazel, 1980.

47 | THE PARADOXICAL LETTER: BRINGING A RESISTANT FAMILY MEMBER TO THERAPY

Rationale

The paradoxical letter is designed to put a family member who refuses to come to therapy sessions in a double bind that will encourage him to come. Weeks and L'Abate (1982) indicate that letters have been used in psychotherapy for many years. Ellis (1965) wrote about the uses of written communication in therapy after a case of laryngitis made it necessary for him to write down interpretations for clients in therapy when he found the clients progressed faster than with verbal ones. Strategic therapists such as Selvini Palazzoli, Boscolo, Cecchin, and Prata (1978) and Weeks and L'Abate (1982) have been strong advocates of the use of written paradoxical communications in therapy.

Clients frequently claim that they are unable to enlist family members to attend. A therapist might choose not to see a client if he doesn't bring in the rest of his family. This tests the client's commitment to the therapy; if he is truly interested in working, then he will find a way to bring his family in. The demand to bring in the spouse makes the therapist's commitment conform to her theoretical beliefs, which in itself can be an important statement to the client. However, it may also intensify the existing power play between the client and other members of the family.

If a client is willing to accept the therapist's assignment to bring in the spouse, there would be no need for a paradoxical intervention. However, when straightforward intervention by the client and therapist does not work, it may be interpreted as a form of resistance by the spouse, and a paradoxical intervention might be more successful.

Procedure

While there are many types of paradoxical letters (see Weeks and L'Abate, 1982, Chapter 9, and Selvini Palazzoli et al., 1978, Chapter 13), the technique described here is the paradoxical letter as a method to bring in an absent member of a family. A therapist must have a hypothesis concerning the reason a given member does not join the sessions. A straightforward request to join the sessions may be easy to refuse if the "resister" does not wish to facilitate the therapeutic process. Therefore, the therapist phrases the letter to make it appear that not coming is causing exactly the effect that the resister was fearful of if he did attend sessions. The resister is then less certain that abstaining from the sessions is a productive way to reach his goals.

For instance, if a therapist senses that a wife is not joining in the therapy because she is trying to make a statement about her own power and ability to control her husband's behavior in session, a paradoxical intervention might be called for. Rather than requesting the wife to join the therapy as a member who would be helpful in the progress (which is just what the wife does not want to do), a therapist might intimate through the use of a paradoxical letter that it is appreciated that the wife does not want to join as she understands that the husband will be able to work on marital issues more effectively without her presence.

Paradoxical letters are usually started with some kind of reframing, whereby the therapist ascribes positive intent for the refusal to join the therapy. This is followed by a prescriptive statement that places the noncooperating spouse in a bind, namely, that the person continue to behave the same way. The therapist has joined with the oppositional behavior and instructed the person to continue it. If the person obeys the therapist, he admits to his behavior and is part of the therapeutic process. If he rejects the prescription, he continues his opposition by coming to the session. The letter is worded to imply that refusal to come defeats the noncooperating person's goals. As a result there is greater incentive to be present than absent.

Letters are kept within one page and are targeted on one or two major objectives. Clients obviously must be able to read the letter and understand its subtlety. It may take up to an hour to carefully prepare such a letter.

Example

A young woman was in therapy for marriage problems but reported that her husband was unwilling to come. Through work with the client, the therapist hypothesized that the husband felt threatened by his wife's work in sessions. He believed that his wife would not be able to deal with marital issues in his absence and so hoped to sabotage her progress by continued refusal to join her.

The following is a letter constructed by the therapist and mailed to Joe, the husband, after the third session with Joyce:

> Dear Joe,
>
> I am very impressed with your deep commitment to your marriage and your assurance that everything is as it should be. You are to be commended on your willingness to sacrifice some of your own needs and your willingness to have your wife work ardently on her own development and independence. I also appreciate that you are able to encourage Joyce to present her issues in dealing with your marriage, trusting the accuracy of her perceptions about you and the marriage, without feeling the need to come in and discuss your side.
>
> Since Joyce has informed me that you are paying for the counseling jointly, I thought that you would like to know that she is making good progress in her development and clarifying what she wants in the marriage.
>
> Joyce told me that you do not wish to join our sessions and I respect your stand and the firmness with which you adhere to it. Your continued sacrifice in not coming has been very helpful.

Of course, whenever you feel that she has made sufficient individual progress, you are welcome to join us.

Sincerely,

When Joe read this letter, he asked Joyce if the therapist was "for real." Joyce responded that, indeed, that's how things were going and she appreciated her own progress. After the next session, Joyce called saying Joe wanted to know if it would be all right for him to come along next time just to see. He participated fully in subsequent sessions.

Uses
The principal use of the technique is to overcome resistance by paradoxically prescribing "continued resistance." Writing a paradoxical letter forces the therapist to carefully think through how the system works. Putting the information into writing allows the participants to read about it and perhaps perceive it differently in the role of observers rather than as immediate actors. Seeing it written also makes it harder to deny. The technique can be used with any resistant member who can read or who can understand what is read to him. A letter would not be used in any situation in which paradoxical work is contraindicated.

RESOURCES
Ellis, A. The use of printed, written and recorded words in psychotherapy. In L. Peason (ed.), *The use of written communication in psychotherapy*. Springfield, IL: Charles C Thomas, 1965.

Pearson, L. (ed.) *The use of written communication in psychotherapy*. Springfield, IL: Charles C Thomas, 1965.

Selvini Palazzoli, M., Cecchin, G., Prata, G., and Boscolo, L. *Paradox and counterparadox*. New York: Jason Aronson, 1978.

Weeks, G. and L'Abate, L. *Paradoxical psychotherapy*. New York: Brunner/Mazel, 1982.

48 | CONTAMINATING THE SUICIDAL FANTASY

Rationale
Whitaker (in Held and Bellows, 1983) defines contamination as an exploration of the fantasy pursued in detail in order to destroy it as a worthwhile solution. Adler (in Dinkmeyer, Pew, and Dinkmeyer, 1979) used it as a way of "spitting in the client's soup."

Many suicidal people create elaborate fantasies involving the people with whom they are most involved. The suicidal patient may create a fantasy in which all the teachers at school or associates at work are shocked and remorseful when they hear of his death. The fantasy may involve grieving parents and relatives who are sorry about all the unhappiness that they have caused this poor person. Another fantasy may involve the suicide's death as being helpful to the family. Upon his demise, they will have less of a burden. Adler (in Ansbacher and Ansbacher, 1956) sees most suicides as acts of spite or nobility, designed to attain personal superiority in relation to others.

The therapist would explore the fantasy in detail in order to contaminate the fantasy. The basic idea would be to help the suicide-prone individual see that suicide is not a solution to his or the family's problems and that a further exploration of the problems is needed.

The technique requires sensitivity and skill so that the therapist does not become one of those who encourages the suicide.

It is wise at the outset to acknowledge to the patient that indeed he does have the power to kill himself and that option is open to him at any time. But after the suicide option is exercised there are no others; therefore, it would be useful to experiment with some others first since he can always kill himself.

Procedure

The session is based on the fact that the patient has threatened suicide and possibly has inflicted some harm on himself before this interview. The therapist acknowledges that the patient has tried to harm himself. The therapist will have some knowledge of the family structure before this interview. She may have already interviewed other members of the client's family.

The therapist indicates to the client that he may have envisioned what effect his suicide would have on those around him. The therapist suggests that the client imagine the reactions of other people upon hearing of his death, then at the funeral, and then later on. The client is asked to describe the fantasies in detail. Who is involved? How are they dressed? Where are they? What do they do? What do they say? What do they eat and drink? What is the weather? Will there be an obituary in the paper?

The description will allow the therapist to assess the purpose of the suicide. If it is indeed spite or nobility, she can proceed to contaminate the fantasy. Asking for mundane details in itself deglorifies and demystifies the experience.

Next the therapist can ask the client to enact the fantasy and play all the parts. This active process may provide relief from the pressures exerted toward suicide. She can interpret back the goals of spite or nobility which were just vividly dramatized. Sometimes when the client sees his purpose described to him while reviewing the action in the fantasy it is sufficient to enable him to see the need for other solutions. The therapist may describe what happens to the body in the ground as the worms crawl in and out; she may mention that the newspaper containing the obituary is used to wrap garbage and is burned; she can suggest that those close to him will quickly forget him after the mourning period.

The therapist can use a guilt trip on the client. If his purpose is to instill guilt in other family members, she can grossly exaggerate the harm the patient will do to them, thus raising the price of his action higher than he intends. The opposite is also possible; she can greatly minimize the impact his action will have and make it seem not worth the price.

Another procedure is to redirect the patient to verbal expressions of anger or even pillow beating directed toward those people who the client wishes to spite. If he wants to be noble and relieve them of burdens, it might be suggested that a hug or a present would be more appreciated than the cost of burying him.

Example

Laura is a recently widowed woman in her thirties with a 12-year-old child. Her husband dominated her and she took a passive role. Her husband's death left her with no money and little confidence and forced her to reorganize her life. She changed her part-time clerical job into a full-time job. Her boss was very kind to her through her crisis period and ultimately signaled his sexual interest. She accepted and they had a liaison. He then treated her in a hot and cold, moody way, leading her on and cutting her off.

In session, Laura admitted that she was depressed, frustrated with all that she had to cope with, and would like to commit suicide. When asked how, she said she would take an overdose of pills, but didn't yet have them and didn't know which ones.

Therapist: Laura, how do you think your death would affect those close to you? Could you please picture the scene? (Laura thinks about the scene silently.) Now, please describe the scene.

Laura: I see my boss, all my in-laws, and my mother standing around my grave. They are all crying and feeling very sorry that they didn't help me when I needed help!

Therapist: So you'll kill yourself, and boy will they be sorry. Just like a five-year-old when she's mad at her parents.

Laura: (Laughs)

Therapist: Could you picture your boss standing over the grave? (She signals yes.) Tell him how angry you are with the way he behaves toward you.

Laura: You're a real pig, you know. I love you and you're playing with me. You come on, get cold feet, and then pull back. I'm willing to take the risks; why are you so frightened?

Therapist: It sounds as if you are the strong one and he the weaker one. Is it possible that you're not allowed to be stronger than the men you like and so you better kill yourself?

Laura: I never thought of myself as strong.

Therapist: Well, you're the one willing to take the risks and he doesn't have the courage to kill himself!

Laura: I don't know what to do. I really like him, but I can't stand this!

Therapist: What happens after the funeral? Can you imagine that?

Laura: They all go home. My boss to his wife and kids and my mother to Florida and my in-laws to their homes.

Therapist: And what happens next.

Laura: They talk about me and how they miss me.

Therapist: Are you kidding? When they get home they're going to put on the television set, take off their shoes, enjoy a cup of coffee and a drink. What will you be doing?

Laura: Nothing.

Therapist: It's really very nice of you to sacrifice yourself for this man who makes you angry. Yet, you're so angry you'll give him your life to upset him. So which is it? Do you want to give him a present of your dead body or do you want to hurt him? Do you think that there might possibly be some other ways of being angry besides killing yourself?

Laura: I guess so, but I don't know how.

Therapist: Would you be interested in learning.

Laura: Yes.

In this excerpt Laura's purpose is revealed by the fantasy. It is to spite those who are not giving her what she wants. When confronted with her purpose, its childishness, and her own anger she is able to see that she can consider other alternatives.

Uses

Dealing with a suicidal patient requires courage on the part of the therapist. The ability to elicit the fantasy enables the therapist to understand the underlying drive toward suicide. By joining in with the fantasy, the therapist can turn it sour in the client's mouth. This technique is to be used selectively with suicidal patients who are likely to recoil from their act when confronted with their true purpose.

RESOURCES

Adler, A. *Understanding human nature*. New York: Guilford Press, 1981.

Ansbacher, H. L. and Ansbacher, R. R. (eds.) *The individual psychology of Alfred Adler*. New York: Harper & Row, 1956.

Dinkmeyer, D. C., Pew, W. L., and Dinkmeyer, D. C., Jr. *Adlerian counseling and psychotherapy*. Monterey, CA: Brooks/Cole, 1979.

Held, B. S. and Bellows, D. C. A family systems approach to crisis reactions in college students. *Journal of Marital and Family Therapy*, 1983, *9*(4), 365–373.

Ross, M. Suicide among college students. *American Journal of Psychiatry*, 1969, *126*, 220–225.

49 | THE THERAPIST AS DIRECTOR OF THE FAMILY DRAMA

Rationale

Andolfi and Angelo (1982) describe this technique within the context of strategic family therapy: "The therapist enters the family system in the role of theatrical director who revises a play, . . . the family drama" (p. 119). The therapist is invited to accept the family's paradoxical request to help them change without changing. It is theorized that this dilemma occurs as a result of the family system's need for greater stability so that interactional patterns and individual functions become progressively more rigid and pathological.

The therapist seeks to provoke a change in values: "The values in this theory are the totality of cognitive and emotional meanings that the family attributes to its own reality. The therapist becomes concerned with how to change those meanings that have led to the formation and maintenance of pathological behaviors including both the mental disturbance expressed by the identified client and the reactive behaviors of the others" (Andolfi and Angelo, 1982, p. 121). The purpose is to "reedit" and "revise" the actual family "drama" that they live daily. The differentiation of family members and flexibility in their interactional patterns are catalyzed by the directions of the therapist entering the drama and the reinterpretations of meanings that she presents.

The technique teaches family members new roles or teaches how to view established roles in a new way. Dysfunctioning families generally have rigidly assigned roles and have lost their capacity for playing creative games. The therapeutic situation differs from the family's daily life because, with the introduction of the therapist, functions are redistributed and a new entity, the therapeutic system, is created. Some of the functions originally assigned within the family system are now projected onto the therapist (e.g., judge, savior, expert) so that performance seen in therapy is not identical with what would be seen if the family were acting for its own members.

As director, the therapist takes part in the action. He has to redefine each player's role (including his own) and alter the timing and modality of each sequence of behavior, introducing new ways of playing the game.

Procedure

The therapist proposes a different version of the family's script. She amplifies the significance of the various functions. She seeks out what appear to be the critical elements around which the family organizes its behavior and then devises an alternative structure. These nodal elements appear in the context of the manner in which the members interact and the relation each seeks with the therapist. A few of these elements are chosen and utilized by the therapist; magnified, these serve as structural supports for an alternative script. These elements are perceived by the therapist as a comprehensive "gestalt" on which she bases her effort to redefine and reorganize the situation. A new framework is gradually built on during the course of the session as new information emerges.

In the therapeutic drama the individual family actors are encouraged to perform, utilizing parts of their self which they had hoped to keep concealed, fearing their strong emotional implications. For this game or re-composition to take place, the therapist also risks exposure, utilizing her own fantasies in her relation with her family. These fantasies, in which the elements supplied by the family are reintroduced in the form of images, actions, or scenes, stimulate the others to offer new information or to make further associations in a circular process. The therapeutic relationship becomes intensified as the critical elements of the family script are brought together and organized by the therapist's suggestions. She emphasizes some elements which have previously gone unnoticed, relegates to the background others which have been overemphasized, or alters their sequential positions.

Examples

The following examples are adapted from Andolfi and Angelo (1982, pp. 124–129).

A 50-year-old woman, married for the second time, telephoned the therapist requesting an appointment. She wanted help in curing a 20-year depression. Efforts by her family and friends to draw her out of her apathy had failed. She described her life as that of a "hermit" avoiding outside contacts and completely losing interest in life. She spoke in a mournful and theatrical tone punctuated by weeping and sobbing. She insisted that only the therapist could "save" her.

The therapist concluded that the patient's magical expectations concerning him concealed an attempt to induce him to play the role of "impotent hero" previously played by other therapists and probably by all of the men in her life. Her message seemed to be "you act for me; I am helpless."

The therapist, after gathering information on the present and previous family composition, told the patient that since there was clearly nothing that could be done to help her, he was willing to see her only if she brought in her family to help make them feel less imprisoned by her depression. The client complained that she no longer had the strength to live but the therapist encouraged "her to find the energy to bring in her family so that they might liberate themselves from her. In this way the therapist prepared the script for the first session and forced her, contrary to her expectations, to mobilize her latent resources" (p. 124).

"On the appointed day, the client appeared with her family consisting of her first and second husbands . . . and her two daughters" (p. 124), one from each marriage. "The general atmosphere suggested a group of people who had fallen under the curse of some malign fate" (p. 125).

The therapist addressed this view in his script as he directed the client to sit on a chair in a corner of the room while the remaining members form and close the circle forgetting about the client. The therapist pointed out that there was no "hope" in the direction where the client was seated and that the meeting would be useless unless the remaining individuals could escape the "curse."

The therapist began by asking the family members whether there was any hope left for them. Each daughter expressed her longtime suffering because of the mother's condition and the resulting family atmosphere. When asked where the men stood in this situation, both replied that they felt detached from the situation; they felt outside this "curse" even though they felt sorry for the client and her daughters. The therapist then suggested to the first husband that he saved himself but not his daughter and that perhaps she might have escaped the "curse" if she lived with him. The husband replied that he never thought about this seriously because he was an "egotist" and wanted to be independent.

The second husband replied that although he was suffering in some ways, he managed to keep detached from what was happening.

The therapist stated that according to what everyone told him it seemed that the first husband escaped intact because he was egotistic and independent — lucky for him — but the daughters seemed to be imprisoned in jail. The therapist suggested that the two husbands "passed an injection of egotism" from one to another and that the only way they could be saved was to continue being egotistic and ignore what was happening to all these women, otherwise the "curse" would get them also.

In this example, the few elements supplied by the family were magnified and served as structural supports for an alternative script. Emphasis was placed on the functions of these various members, for example, posture, physical characteristics, spatial positioning. The historical and emotional elements that characterized the various functions were gradually added as the therapist called attention to them in order to provoke personal responses from each member. Instead of depending on the men, the women were encouraged to become more "egotistical" and independent.

Detachment, a major theme in this family, has been redefined both as a "curse" to be escaped and positively as egotism and independence. The therapist will continue to revise the family drama in succeeding sessions.

A family with a 26-year-old psychotic son, Georgio, came for treatment. The client's father, 72 years old, who had lost his hearing, sat at a considerable distance from the others, slumped over, giving the appearance of a dead man whose position in the family has been replaced by his own ghost. The mother sat with an expression of suffering. The older brother and his wife took responsibility for relating the client's history of "illness," emphasizing the organic aspect, tracing the origin to a head injury caused by an automobile accident. The brother spoke with an air of competence using the appropriate medical and psychiatric terms and detailing the various diagnoses, prescribed drugs, and so on. A medical context had emerged in this family scene in which symptoms discussed were seen as organically caused.

The therapist interrupted this sequence to disrupt the script proposed by the family. In redefining the context, the therapist introduced a new language which translated and reintegrated the various important elements, viewing interactions in a manner not discerned by the family and about which they were now forced to furnish new information. Once this occurred, the family had to recognize this new viewpoint and, as such, became the basis for change.

The therapist asked the client when his father had "died"; before or after Georgio became sick. The question perplexed James at first but he then responded that it happened after he got sick. The brother began to respond to Georgio's "illness" again in terms of psychiatric interpretations; the therapist interrupted by stating that he was not concerned with Georgio; the therapist was asking how long the father was "dead"; the brother replied that his father "died" about a year ago when he completely lost his hearing. The therapist asked the mother whether he might have "died" of heartbreak; the mother replied that he had; the therapist asked whether there was a new head of the family; the mother replied that this was the problem; she needed to find the "right medicine"; the therapist took out his prescription pad as though intending to comply with her request to prescribe an effective medication. The therapist asked the mother whether he should prescribe medication for a crazy person who suddenly had to take over his father's place or medication for a crazy person who purposely "killed" his father so he could take his place. The therapist emphasized the importance of dealing with this question and stated that therapy could not continue until he got an answer.

In this example, as in the preceding one, it can be seen how the family selected from its entire history only those elements that conformed to its preferred script. The elements it selected, diagnoses, medication, head trauma, became the framework. The therapist tried to change the significance of those elements of the script and introduce other elements which modified their original framework by redefining the function of each member in the system.

Uses
This technique is helpful for families who are "stuck" and feeling hopeless after many years of dysfunctional behavior and after other attempts at therapy which have failed. It shifts the ground of the interactions and forces the family to attend in new ways to the same or different elements of family life and meanings. They can no longer try harder to enact the same drama.

RESOURCES
Andolfi, M. Redefinition in family therapy. *American Journal of Family Therapy*, 1979, *7*, 5–15.
Andolfi, M. and Angelo, C. The therapist as director of the family drama. In F. W. Kaslow (ed.), *The international book of family therapy*. New York: Brunner/Mazel, 1982.
Andolfi, M., Menghi, P., Nicolo, A. M., and Saccu, C. Interaction in rigid systems: A model for intervention in families with a schizophrenic patient. In M. Andolfi and I. Zwerling (eds.), *Dimensions of family therapy*. New York: Guilford Press, 1980.
Angelo, C. The use of the metaphoric object in family therapy. *American Journal of Family Therapy*, 1981, *9*, 69–78.
Ferreira, A. J. Family myths and homeostasis. *Archives of General Psychiatry*, 1963, *9*, 457–473.
Hoffman, L. Deviation-amplifying processes in natural groups. In J. Haley (ed.), *Changing families*, New York: Grune & Stratton, 1971.

50 | PRESCRIBING INDECISION

Rationale
When a couple or family is stuck in indecision, the therapist may also become stuck. She cannot get them to make up their minds and does not want to favor one decision over another. One technique to use when

such impasses occur is to prescribe indecision. Todd (1984) describes this technique.

Keller (1981) stresses that paradoxical techniques do not need to be aggressive, confrontational, or adversarial and do not have to elevate conflict. Prescribing indecision reinforces the existing negative double bind and increases the cost of maintaining it. It has an effect similar to those created by Haley (1984) in his ideas about ordeals in therapy. It also puts the clients in charge of their symptoms. They are asked to carefully describe the existing roles played by each participant. Those behaviors are then identified as important rules of keeping things as they are so as not to increase upsets by changing anything. The impasse in deciding whether to divorce or commit to the marriage is an example of indecision that frequently occurs.

Procedure

After unsuccessfully trying various nonparadoxical strategies in helping clients make a choice or a decision this paradoxical procedure may be useful. The therapist tells the client(s) that she finally realizes that they are right and she is wrong for trying to make them decide. She backs this statement up with various supportive arguments: (1) They know what is good for them and she was not listening correctly. (2) There are systemic reasons why changing the present status quo would result in problems. (3) There is merit to making careful and slow choices rather than hasty and rushed ones. (4) They functioned reasonably well with their dysfunction, but there is no telling how incapable they might be to deal with a changed situation. The effect of these statements is a powerful joining of the clients as well as the foundations of a therapeutic double bind.

In addition to the support for indecision, the therapist recommends that the client(s) spell out the exact terms of the indecision. They might even be asked to write out a list or shake hands over a contract which describes just how they should continue to not decide. The therapeutic double bind is formed. If the clients resist the therapist they will make a decision. If they acquiesce to her wishes, they will also make decisions about how to not decide. In both cases, they are making decisions and affecting their situations actively. An added result is that they may feel as if they made up their minds without the therapist trying to get them to do that.

Examples

The following is an example provided by Todd (1984, pp. 373–379).

A couple is not able to decide whether to get a divorce, although they claim it is intolerable for them to stay married. Whenever asked what is holding them back from divorce, they provide a hefty list of problems regarding finances, possessions, and the children.

After nonparadoxical attempts have failed to bring change, the therapist finally remarks that she realizes there are very good reasons they have resisted all of her efforts to reach a decision. She now understands this. At this point, the systemic reasons for maintaining the status quo are explained by her. She adds that they should continue to put off a decision. At times, this may cause them to come to a decision. However, in this case they continue to be unable to decide. An even stronger prescription to be indecisive is recommended to them by the therapist.

The therapist suggests a contract for a de facto divorce. Since they are not really married and not really divorced, they should stay in this situation, but with clearly spelled out terms regarding their interactions. The terms will indicate living arrangements, contacts, visits, and finances. When they ask her if she believes they should get a divorce, she tells them the many reasons they have for not being able to do that. They are in a bind in which they must either overtly live their indecisiveness and settle their affairs that way, or they must reject the prescription and make a decision about the divorce. As a result of this technique, they decide one way or another and have no sense of having been pressured by the therapist to do so.

In an example provided by Weisz (personal communication, 1985), a couple cannot come to a decision about their style of raising their daughter. They both state that they know they are spoiling their child just as they were spoiled as children by their parents. They also are irritated by her constant demands for things and at times her lack of interest in them once they are bought for her. The therapist points out their own statements of knowing that spoiling their child could cause problems for her in growing up. However, their inability to deny her anything puts them in a dilemma. They added that it was getting almost unbearable. After talking and using nonparadoxical techniques, the couple reaches an impasse. They agree that they know they should find new ways to raise their child, but they cannot actually make the decision to do it. The therapist decides to use the strategy of prescribing indecision.

She tells them that she has tried various things and finally realizes that she was completely wrong in trying to change their situation. They had good reasons for not listening to her suggestions of change. She explains that they were not able to decide how they would continue to raise their daughter, but they will be when and if they become ready. Until then, it was wisest for them to continue to think and agonize about it, changing nothing. They are to spell out in writing all the things they will do for their daughter, describe all her reactions to it, tell her she is to continue reacting that way, then carefully describe their pleasure and sense of being good parents in doing what daughter wants, and finally write out all their misgivings about the outcomes for her. They listened respectfully to her, and then meekly asked if it wouldn't be useful for them to try to change just a little. The therapist tells them not to until they are very sure they are ready. She does not feel that they are yet. The therapist drives home this advice with further assurance that often her clients have problems with changing before they are ready, but nobody has had any trouble from changing too slowly. The best course is to put it off and go slowly.

In following sessions, they report various experiences with their daughter where they are firmer or where they have fun without spending money. The therapist warns them that they should not go too fast because of the upsets that may result.

Uses
Prescribing indecision is useful in situations where the clients and the therapist are feeling stuck trying to come to a decision. A signal for the therapist to think about this procedure is when she is feeling frustrated or impatient with her client's indecisiveness. This technique will allow her to not push or wish for the client(s) to decide. Paradoxically the "giving in" to the decision is helpful for both the clients' and the therapist's well-being. A therapist need not be using a strategic orientation prior to this technique. She may use various other kinds of interventions up to this point. This paradoxical technique is not very aggressive, confrontational, or conflict-increasing.

Specific situations where indecision becomes a problem can involve marriage, divorce, childrearing, and finances among other things. Whatever the content, the choosing can become more of a problem than living with either choice because it means giving up something important.

RESOURCES
Haley, J. *Ordeal therapy*. San Francisco: Jossey-Bass, 1984.
Keller, J. F. Therapist adjustments for adapting therapy models to varied clinical settings. In A. Gurman (ed.), *Questions and answers in the practice of family therapy*. New York: Brunner/Mazel, 1981, pp. 482–485.
Todd, T. C. Strategic approaches to marital stuckness. *Journal of Marital and Family Therapy*, 1984, *10*(4), 373–379.

51 | THE WINNER'S BET WITH ADOLESCENTS

Rationale
The therapist bets the adolescent that he will continue his misbehavior. To prove the therapist wrong, the adolescent must abandon the misbehavior. Williams and Weeks (1984) describe some paradoxical techniques in a school setting with preadolescents and adolescents. There are various

advantages in using a strategic model with such a population. With paradox, there is less need for verbal ability or insight (Jessee and L'Abate, 1980). In addition, Weeks and Wright (1979) advocate the use of paradox with people who are having difficulty in a life-cycle transition, which often describes adolescents who appear in guidance and counseling offices. Paradox is considered to be effective for use with people who are low in motivation and high in resistance and opposition, typical of many adolescents (Papp, 1981). For these reasons, the use of paradox with children around the age of adolescence is highly recommended.

Procedure
In the winner's bet technique, the authority figure describes the misbehavior, predicts its continuation, and challenges the child to prove her wrong. A bet is made, in which the therapist loses if the child does *not* misbehave. The therapist takes the position that the adolescent cannot control his misbehavior. The therapist expects that the adolescent will give up his formerly oppositional behavior in order to oppose the therapist's present beliefs about him. Therefore, if the adolescent does misbehave again, it confirms that the authority figure has figured out his game. Rather than be under the authority figure's control, the adolescent is likely to choose his behavior. He then opposes the authority figure by not misbehaving.

What appears to be manipulative is actually a technique to help the child gain self-control. His misbehavior is not independence, but often a misguided attempt to gain independence. The bet can be made with a wager or not. It is most important that a challenge be made, where the child wins when he behaves appropriately.

Examples
An example is provided by Williams and Weeks (1984). In a school situation, two seventh grade students are sent to a guidance counselor after they have had a fight with each other. They each blame the other for starting the fight. As the counselor begins to ask them about the fight, they both say that they weren't doing anything wrong. It was, in fact, their teacher who overreacted and so they shouldn't be punished.

The counselor thoughtfully remarks that she cannot disagree with their story if they will prove that their teacher overreacted. She asks them to act the same way in their next class as they just did in the previous one. If the second teacher does not send them to her office, then clearly the first teacher was wrong in her judgment of what misbehavior is. However, if they get into trouble again, then she cannot accept their view of the teacher; they will have proven that it was their misbehavior and not the teacher's unfairness that caused the trouble. In that case they will be punished for misbehaving.

The students are incredulous when the counselor continues to emphasize that she wants them to argue or fight in the same way in their next class as they just have done. However, several months went by and the students did not reappear in the counselor's office.

Another example is provided by Weisz (personal communication, 1985). Two brothers in a family counseling session each accuse the other of being argumentative. Each says that he argues only because the other starts. The counselor challenges them to prove to her and each other who is the one who can not control himself. The counselor says a bet is one way that they will be able to find out. After a long discussion, the terms of the bet are clarified. Whoever contradicts or disagrees with a statement that the other made immediately before will have to give a dollar to his brother.

In the next session, the brothers bashfully admit that they both lost within the first 15 minutes of the bet. However, after losing a few times, they got the hang of abiding by the bet. In this way, they gained control over their style of interaction. On their own initiative they later made their own bet about losing weight and thus gained some control over their weight. Meanwhile, the parents were not so involved in dealing with their children's arguments and talked more about their marital issues with the counselor.

Uses

This procedure is ideal for use with students in school or youngsters in counseling. The paradox reframes their opposition to authority into compliance with authority. They are challenged in a bet, where they are winners if they behave appropriately. This technique is suitable for the child who has a strong dislike for compliance with authority and a strong desire to win competitions.

Williams and Weeks (1984) recommend that in using this technique some care should be taken. If a school counselor recommends that a student misbehaves in his next class, she should be certain that she will not be perceived as being delinquent by her colleagues. It helps to have a good relationship with the faculty and to let them know what kinds of counseling techniques she is using.

RESOURCES

Jessee, E. and L'Abate, L. The use of paradox with children in an inpatient treatment setting. *Family Process*. 1980, *19*, 59–64.

Papp, P. Paradoxical strategies and countertransference. In A. Gurman (ed.), *Questions & answers in the practice of family therapy*. New York: Brunner/Mazel, 1981, pp. 201–203.

Weeks, G. and Wright, L. Dialectics of the family life cycle. *American Journal of Family Therapy*. 1979, *7*, 85–91.

Williams, J. M. and Weeks, G. Use of paradoxical techniques in a school setting. *American Journal of Family Therapy*, 1984, *12*(3), 47–56.

52 | JOINING THE OPPOSITION: PARADOX WITH AN OPPOSITIONAL ACTING-OUT CLIENT AND HIS COMPLIANT FAMILY

Rationale

This technique applies the therapeutic paradox to an acting-out, resistant identified patient and his more cooperative family so that the family joins with his oppositional behavior instead of opposing it.

The object is to prescribe a way in which the family accepts the oppositional stance of the client so that he is no longer against them. Their compliance eliminates the power play and the purpose of the negative behavior is defused. If the identified client accepts their compliance, then the fight is over and the family reorganizes. For the client to continue his oppositional pattern, he must give up his acting-out activities that are now approved and do something more constructive in order to remain in opposition. As his behavior improves, the family no longer has incentive to nag, get upset, become more involved, or do whatever it was that maintained the oppositional symptom. Either way, the family reorganizes and gains.

The typical result counts on the resistant child to recoil from the prescription. Success depends on at least one central member of the family being cooperative and willing to use the paradox with the child. Success also depends upon an accurate understanding by the therapist of the correct fomulation of the paradox.

The technique is used primarily by strategic therapists and by Adlerian therapists.

Procedure

Once the hypothesis has been formulated, the therapist reframes the symptomatic pattern of behavior in positive terms (see the technique of "reframing" in this chapter). The compliant family members are seen separately from the child. They are told that if they follow the prescription about to be given, the child is likely to change his behavior, which would create a better climate in the household. The compliant members are then given the paradoxical prescription which they in turn are to follow with the child. They are asked to commit themselves to the suggested behavior. They can role play how to behave until they feel confident. They are to continue with the paradoxical behavior even if the child stops acting out. The therapist reinforces the continuation of the technique in subsequent therapy sessions until the new pattern becomes the family norm.

The temptation is to praise the child for his new behavior and to encourage him to continue with his new behavior. Such praise will eliminate the paradoxical effect and may cause a reversion to the former symptomatic state. The therapist can indicate to the child that of course he does have the option to behave in this new way, but it may be risky and he should proceed with it slowly if that's what he really wants to do.

Example

Peckman provides the following example (personal communication, 1984).

The identified patient in this family is 17-year-old Duane, who was brought in by his mother. Duane has an older sister who is married and is living in North Carolina. Duane's father left the family shortly after he was born and subsequently died about seven years ago. Duane was never a good student, but he did pass most of his classes until about two or three years ago. This coincided with his sister's marriage and leaving home.

Since that time Duane has attended school irregularly. He has managed to accumulate enough credits to allow him to graduate from school by staying one extra year. Duane is not attending classes and is failing everything. He is not sure what he wants to do, but knows that he doesn't want to go to school. Mom is insisting that he remain in school.

The hypothesis formed was that the purpose of this symptom was to keep Duane at home and give Mom a child to care for and look after. The therapist first spoke with the mother alone and then had Duane join them.

Therapist: It seems that Duane is working very hard proving that he can't make it in school.

Mom: I know he could pass if he wanted to.

Therapist: Yes, you're probably right, but apparently he loves you too much to do that.

Mom: What do you mean? If he loved me, he'd make me happy and go to school.

Therapist: Well, that might appear to make you happy, but in the back of his mind he knows you would be very lonely if he graduated and left home.

Mom: My God, that can't really be true!

Therapist: It might possibly be true. Children do those things out of love for their parents. It's not a conscious decision on his part.

Mom: If it is true, what can I do?

Therapist: You can do two very important things. First, you could develop a life apart from your children. You've been a terrific mother and always sacrificed for them. You must get out more with friends and learn to enjoy life again. It's important that Duane believe you can survive without him. Second, I would like you to go along with Duane's wishes and tell him you want him to quit school.

Mom: That's insane!

Therapist: Let's hope it appears that way to Duane, too. Encourage him to leave school and get a job. He will of course have to take extra responsibilities around the house, including donating at least half of his salary to cover household expenses. You will present these conditions to him. Plan some heavy responsibilities for him, the more the better. One of two things can happen. Duane will quit school and become more responsible. Or, more likely, Duane wants to stay in school and succeed there and will fight you for the privilege.

Mom: But I don't need his money or want it and I don't want him around me all the time.

Therapist: Then you can secretly put the money into a savings account for him. Are you willing to do it?

Mom: I'll try almost anything.

Therapist: Here's some paper to write down Duane's responsibilities. (The responsibilities were discussed in detail to determine their appropriateness and to have mother and son in a great deal of contact. They now role play the scene of presenting this to Duane.) Call Duane in now. (Duane enters.) Your Mom and I have been talking about what we can do to help you. As we discussed when we last met, I shared with your Mom that I believe you're working very hard proving you don't want to go to school but would rather take care of your Mom. She decided that it probably would be a good idea to let you drop out of school under certain conditions. What do you think?

Duane: What kind of conditions?

Therapist: Talk to your Mom.

Duane: What kind of conditions?

Mom: Duane, since you don't like school, I would like you to quit and find a full-time job. We will also set up a system of sharing responsibility in the house. It takes most of my salary to support us, so you'll have to give me half of your pay toward household expenses. We'll both be working and we will divide up the cooking, cleaning, and washing jobs. You'll be responsible for your own phone expenses and car insurance and maintenance.

Duane: Hey, there won't be anything left for me! I won't even have time to breathe!

Mom: I never said being an adult was easy; but if you don't want to go to school then I need your help and you'll have to make sacrifices. I would like you to start looking for a job.

Duane: Maybe tomorrow. Do I still have to go to school while I'm looking?
Mom: I'm not sure you could go to school and look for a job at the same time. And tonight we'll work out a schedule of chores that you can begin tomorrow.
Duane: Supposing I don't want to quit school.
Mom: At this point it's probably best that you do.

Duane now begins to fight mother to stay in school, promising to do better. The therapist and Mom exact a promise that if there is no improvement in attendance, behavior, and grades reported by the school within two weeks he must quit and get a job, which would be more in line with his true desires to take care of Mom.

The family subsequently reported that mother developed more interests of her own and a social life outside of her family. Duane was doing better and remained in school.

Another example is reported by Sherman (1983).

George complains that his wife, Martha, is not interested in his family, who live in the same apartment house; he visits them constantly. Martha stays home and is resentful of his overinvolvement with them. They fight often about the situation. The couple are also short of money. The following paradoxical intervention could be used. The compliant wife is instructed without the husband being present to invite her in-laws over for dinner three times during the coming week. She is to buy expensive foods and beverages, using George's bowling money and other essential funds. When George questions her, she is to say, "I have been thinking it over and you are absolutely right. We should be more involved with your family and I realize how important this is for you. Also, what do you think about canceling our plans for Saturday night and spending the evening with your parents?"

As a result George recoiled from too much of a good thing, while Martha got more involved with his family, thus pleasing George.

Uses

The goal in this technique is to reduce the enmeshment and allow the family members to become more differentiated. The process is a way to get both the compliant and defiant members to change their behavior. The compliant ones change in order to overcome the defiant ones. The defiant ones change in order to remain in opposition. The therapist joins the resistance rather than trying to overcome or interpret it.

The meaning of the symptom is reframed from something that is in the way to something that is necessary and useful in the family. At the same time the clients are put in charge of making the symptom happen instead of letting the symptom happen to them. (See the following technique, "Putting the Client in Charge of the Symptom.")

RESOURCES

Haley, J. *Problem solving therapy*. San Francisco: Jossey-Bass, 1976.

Haley, J. *Ordeal therapy*. San Francisco: Jossey-Bass, 1984.

Madanes, C. *Strategic family therapy*. San Francisco: Jossey-Bass, 1981.

Papp, P. *The process of change*. New York: Guilford, 1984.

Rowe, J., Pasch, M., and Hamilton, W. *The new model me*. New York: Teachers' College Press, 1983.

Sherman, R. The power dimension in the family: A synthesis of Adlerian perspectives. *The American Journal of Family Therapy*, 1983, *11*(3), 43–53.

53 | PUTTING THE CLIENT IN CONTROL OF THE SYMPTOM

Rationale

This strategy is motivated by the fact that many families request help but at the same time reject all offers for help. In systemic terms, these contradictory attitudes derive from the dynamic equilibrium existing between the tendency toward change, which is implicit in the request for help at the one level, and the tendency toward homeostasis, which at another level imposes the repetition of the family's habitual rules of interaction. Helping a family gain control of their symptom aids them in gaining a sense of power and order in their life.

This technique is used widely in strategic therapy (Andolfi and Angelo, 1982; Haley, 1973; Haley and Hoffman, 1967). The therapist recommends the continuation of a specific symptom such as worrying, crying, feeling sorry for oneself, or phobic behaviors. This has a paradoxical effect because the family is complaining about the symptom. However, they experience it as being out of their control. They feel helpless.

Once the symptom is prescribed, the members have options of how to carry it out. If the family follows the prescription and continues the symptom under the direction of the therapist, they are in effect taking charge. If the prescription helps the individual or family to sense the absurdity of the situation (e.g., an anxious mother who is told to list 15 fears an hour of things that might happen to her child), then the client has the opportunity to recoil and reject the behavior. Either way, he or she is now in control and responsible for the behavior. Gestalt psychologists would explain the phenomenon as the clients owning their own behavior and integrating the artificial split between what they say they want and what they do.

This technique can be extremely effective in initiating intervention as early as the first or second session. It can be used even if the therapist has not crystalized a working hypothesis; she is not actually depriving the family or individual of their symptom, which may very well be providing needed stability to the system.

Procedure
The therapist invents some way to "box in" the symptom. Both time factors and intensity of the symptom can be varied to limit the symptom's impact on the system. It may mean prescribing that the symptom be limited to certain times of the day, be of limited duration, or be exaggerated and increased in intensity. It is also often helpful to have the clients develop some predictive insights and learn to avoid falling back into old patterns that evoke symptomatic behavior. The therapist may assist the clients to believe that they can contain their symptomatic behavior. She may also create a paradoxical effect by insisting that the clients must not give up the symptom, but merely contain it.

The therapist might sequentially ask, "What is a good time for you to worry? How much time do you need? How hard do you need to worry during that time? Where is a good place for you to worry? Do you worry best sitting, pacing, writing, or beating your breast? Is it better in the light or the dark?" Some therapists attach extremely debilitating symptoms to a particular object, such as a "worry chair." The client is *required* to worry while sitting in that chair. If nonworrisome thoughts enter their minds, they *must* leave the chair. The therapist would end the session by saying, "Will you agree to worry every day under the conditions that you just described until our next meeting?"

Since everyone tells the client to stop worrying and this is what he expects to hear, the prescription comes as a surprise. Meanwhile the client has explored his process of worrying in some detail.

Example
Peckman (1984) provides the following case.

A family of four in its second therapy session relates that every little interaction in the house results in an argument. There is constant shouting back and forth over any and every issue imaginable; indeed, the family members demonstrate their bickering during the session. The following excerpt is from the last few minutes of the session.

Therapist: It seems obvious that this family has a need to shout at each other and argue much of the time. This shows great strength of character. Fighting for what you think is right and being right is an important family value. It also provides a way for family members to get together and really feel one another's presence. Of course, there is a price to pay. It is possible that the arguing may get in the way of the family's functioning and performance of necessary activities. Perhaps we can find some way to confine the fighting to a specific time of the day so that it will cost less and still accomplish the useful things you get out of fighting.

Mom: What do I do in the meantime? If I ask Cathy (her daughter) to set the table for dinner, she's always too busy.

Therapist: You will have to find some way to put off the argument until your "FFT."

Dad: What is "FFT"?

Therapist: Family Fighting Time! I recommend at least one hour of FFT per day. You should set up the FFT to be held at least one hour after dinner, to allow for your dinner to be digested.

Mom: How do we have dinner when nobody ever helps?

Therapist: I would suggest that you each get a small notebook to make notes for FFT so that you won't forget to fight about everything that comes up. Can you (Mom) figure out a way to put off the argument until FFT?

Mom: Well, I could set the table, as usual.

Therapist: Or . . . you might consider calling the family into dinner after you've set only one place for yourself. Of course, you would only serve yourself in that case. (The therapist is testing the resistance.)

Mom: I couldn't do that!

Therapist: You'll just have to find some way of putting off the fight until FFT.

Therapist: In summary, it would be well for you to follow these rules:
1.   Family members will find some way to postpone all arguments until FFT, even if it means giving in that one time.
2.   Family members will make comprehensive notes so that they won't forget the smallest detail to fight about.
3.   The family will spend the entire hour of FFT each day screaming and arguing with each other as loud as they possibly can. It will be important to make your points, so remember to refer to your notes. If you run out of things to fight about, you may have to invent some — just be sure to use up the entire hour.
4.   If someone starts in with you (pushes your button), rather than retaliating simply ask them to save it for FFT. Then you both must make notes in your books.

The hour will take place in the living room with the entire family present so you can fight with anyone you need to. Put on all the lights to see each other well. There will be no interruptions of the fighting and no competition with records or T.V. or telephone. It's important that you carry out this assignment. I'll see you next week.

From the above example one can see the potential effects of putting the family in control of the symptom. The family members are encouraged to examine their positions during a much needed cooling-off period. Their tendency will be to work against the paradox and find other solutions. Often such a technique will help to provide a certain degree of order in the midst of their chaos. The therapist also reframed the fighting as having two useful purposes: to be right and to get together. Achieving these goals costs a price in bad feelings and inconvenience. The reframing forces the family members to take responsibility for the behavior they choose and the price that they are willing to pay for it.

Uses

Prescribing the symptom is a technique most often used in rigid family systems where there is a minimum degree of flexibility and members strive to maintain their existing state.

Creative use of this technique can be applied to a variety of symptoms and family members from about age seven on. Giving permission for the symptom reduces tension and allows the clients to go about the business of living most of the time. Opposition to the prescription reduces or stops the symptomatic behavior. Either way the clients win.

RESOURCES

Andolfi, M. and Angelo, C. The therapist as director of the family drama. In F. Kaslow (Ed.), *The international book of family therapy*. New York: Brunner/Mazel, 1982.

Gaines, T. A technique for reducing parental obsessions. *Family Therapy*, 1978, *5*, 97.

Haley, J. *Uncommon therapy*. New York: Norton, 1973.

Haley, J. *Ordeal therapy*. San Francisco: Jossey-Bass, 1984.

Haley, J. and Hoffman, L. *Techniques of family therapy*. New York: Basic Books, 1967.

Peckman, L. The use of interventive group activities and other techniques in family therapy. Unpublished manuscript, Long Beach, New York, 1984.

7

Alternative Models

INTRODUCTION

Just as there are many different family therapy theories, there are also many different modalities available to encourage behavior change. The modalities are developed by manipulating important variables. Some are made possible by available technology such as videotaping, one-way-vision mirrors, the telephone, the computer, and rapid transportation. Others are created by adding members to the system, as in co-therapy, multiple-couple groups, multiple-family groups, surrogate family groups, and family network groups. Similarly, the model can insist that all attend, work with the family through one individual member, or work with varying subsystems.

We can invent new modalities by varying the time frame. There can be a 50-minute session, a flexible-time session, a weekend group session, and so on. The number of sessions can be varied from a single consultation to contracting a fixed number of meetings to an open-ended series of sessions.

The place in which the therapy is conducted can be varied for different effects. Aside from the therapy office, sessions can take place in the client's home, a community center, school, conference center, church, resort/hotel, or camp.

The activity during which therapy takes place can be altered in order to create a specific therapeutic climate. Having lunch with the family, taking the family out of its usual context and working with the family in a resort hotel, or using "mood" music as a background for specific activities are examples. Playing out a fantasy or drama and playing games are other interesting activities.

The therapist can utilize methods that tap into different levels of consciousness such as meditation, hypnosis, fantasy, and metaphor.

Additional variables such as patterns of communication, ways of engaging clients, homework tasks, and the role of the therapist have been discussed.

This chapter illustrates how these variables can be utilized to create many different models for working with couples and families. Videotape playback, co-therapy, home visits, surrogate families, time-extended family interviewing, and telephone calls within sessions are discussed.

The advantages and uses of alternative modalities revolve around the increased flexibility they provide to the practitioner to alter significant variables described above to meet the needs of the clients. The therapist's creative potential is enhanced because she is not limited to a single textbook format. The problem, as with the use of any technique, is to adapt a particular modality to a specific theoretical model and to the therapist's understanding of the needs of the clients.

54 | CO-THERAPY

Rationale

Co-therapy refers to the simultaneous use of two or more therapists in a counseling setting. It adds greatly to the richness and complexity of what can be done in the session. The assumption is that joint participation facilitates the therapeutic process. Advantages of this technique include mutual support for the therapists, greater objectivity in the evaluation process, and a positive modeling opportunity for the clients. Each therapist may observe different aspects of family functioning or rescue one another when falling into the family's dysfunctional system. When one therapist is stuck, the other might have a good idea. Each could present opposing options to the clients. There are opportunities to form different kinds of alliances or to create boundaries. They can also discuss the case between them allowing the clients to become observers of how they impress others. The therapists can either supplement or complement one another.

Procedure

Effective co-therapy entails more than the simultaneous presence of two therapists. They must work together to facilitate therapeutic change. For example, co-therapists can work together in the use of paradox. One works with the family, helping to bring about change. The other takes the position that change is premature. Additionally, co-therapists can promote therapeutic progress by mirroring the family pattern. The examples of this specific technique that follow are derived from Hannum (1980).

Examples
John and Sue C. came for counseling because of marital discord. They were both in their mid-thirties. They have been married for ten years and had a seven-year-old son and a four-year-old daughter. John is a fairly successful lawyer at a local law firm. After interrupting her education to look after her family, Sue returned to complete doctoral studies at a local university. The presenting problem was general dissatisfaction with the marriage. This is particularly true for Sue. In the session described here they are in the midst of an argument over childcare responsibilities. They are both angry and going around in circles. The co-therapists' initial approach was to mirror the clients' moods. They begin to role play as follows:

Therapist 1: Look John, I have things to do. You'll have to rearrange your schedule so that you can go to Tom's open school program next Thursday. You know that's when Professor Jones is discussing his research.

Therapist 2: I can't. I have a meeting with Jim at 6:00 to discuss that Smith case. Sorry, Sue, I can't help this time.

Therapist 1: Isn't that the way it always is? Your work is always more important than mine.

Therapist 2: Well my work does allow us to pay the bills.

Therapist 1: I knew you would throw that at me. You do it when you can't think of anything else. Look, this anger between us is not getting us anywhere. This is really important to me. Can't we try to resolve it?

Therapist 2: Okay, I can see that. Maybe I can do a bit of rescheduling. I'll ask Jim to meet me at 8:00 in the morning. That way I can leave by 5:00.

Therapist 1: Good, then you'll have plenty of time to get to the school.

Therapist 2: Sue, it would be helpful if you could give me some advance notice. I'm not comfortable with last-minute changes.

Therapist 1: That's reasonable, In fact if you are willing, could we work out a schedule for the next week tonight? I have all my relevant dates.

Therapist 2: We'll work on it after dinner.

(Pause)

Therapist: (to couple) Now, would you two care to solve your problem?

In the first segment of the session described above the co-therapists initially mirrored their clients' moods. This was done to establish alliances. Halfway through, the therapists changed their strategy. They provided an example of tackling the problem differently. The therapists provided an example of a cooperative approach to problem solving. When the couple continued their discussion, they began to look for solutions rather than trying to win points or claiming to be the greater victim.

Therapists may work toward promoting change by blocking communication within the family. This approach might be taken if a member of the family is intruding in other relationships and thereby preventing interaction between members of a dyad. The following case exemplified this point.

Mrs. P., her 12-year-old daughter, and the maternal grandmother entered therapy because of difficulties the daughter was having in school. During the initial meeting it became clear that the grandmother was overinvolved with her granddaughter. As the co-therapists discussed this they agreed on the following strategy. Therapist 1 said to the grandmother, "Mrs. L., today I would appreciate it if you would work with me. As your daughter and granddaughter discuss some of their concerns with Dr. A. (therapist 2), you sit here with me and we will listen and observe." During the session when the grandmother attempted to speak she was firmly told, "Remember, our job is to listen and observe."

This alliance with grandmother that stops her from interfering with the efforts of mother to handle daughter eliminates the triangular relationship in the family and creates a hierarchical boundary between the generations. The grandmother is given a special place alongside therapist 1 so that she is not just kicked out. She is now a special observer. Mother and daughter and therapist 2 then worked out an agreement on an issue between them.

Uses

Co-therapists can work together in most settings. Co-therapy is frequently used with particularly large families and with multiple-family and couple group therapy. In such situations modeling effects may prove beneficial. Clients might particularly benefit from male and female co-therapists. The technique is also used in training centers where co-therapy serves as a training device. The beginner works with her supervisor or two beginners are observed by the supervisor. The assumption is that it provides a sound educational experience for beginning therapists.

There are several possible disadvantages. The most obvious is the cost of providing additional professional personnel. It is also important that the co-leaders be able to "read" one another and not sabotage each other's strategy or tactics. Planning time to discuss the case before and after sessions is a necessary part of this process. It is all right for the therapists occasionally to disagree in session and to genuinely work out their differences, modeling how to do this, with the courage to be imperfect.

Another kind of co-therapy is to have one or more co-therapists behind the one-way-vision mirror communicating with the therapist in session by knocking at the door or by telephone. (See the sections on "Videotape Playback" and "Telephone Calls Within the Session" in this chapter.)

RESOURCES
Goldenberg, I. and Goldenberg, H. *Family therapy: An overview*. Monterey, CA: Brooks/Cole, 1980.
Hannum, J. Some co-therapy techniques with families. *Family Process*, 1980, *19*, 161–168.
Holt, M. and Greiner, D. Co-therapy in the treatment of families. In P. J. Guerin (ed.), *Family therapy: Theory and practice*. New York: Gardner Press, 1976.
Papp, P. The Greek chorus and other techniques of paradoxical therapy. *Family Process*, 1980, *19*, 45–57.
Papp, P. *The process of change*. New York: Guilford Press, 1983.

55 | VIDEOTAPE PLAYBACK

"O wad some pow'r the giftie gie us
to see oursels as others see us!"
To a louse.

Rationale
It is now possible to realize Robert Burns' immortal words: videotape not only is an aid to memory for client and therapist; it can be used as a therapy tool itself. The assumption is that viewing behavior on a screen helps clarify what is going on within the family as well as one's role in the perpetuation of the system. The rationale is that videotape playback prompts self-confrontation inasmuch as it becomes more difficult to engage in denial. It permits the players to become observers and actually see what they are doing. Segments can be discussed, interpreted, analyzed, or reenacted. It may be especially powerful with couples or families in which members differ radically in their perception of events.

Procedure
This procedure is closely taken from Alger (1976).

Videotaping may be initiated during the first session or later in therapy. The family is informed that the therapist plans to tape because she views it as helpful to the therapeutic process and that videotapes will not be seen by others unless the clients have given their written permission.

Clients are also given some orientation about television images to reduce the likelihood that they will be preoccupied with their own physical appearance. They are informed that the television image is not an absolute depiction of how one looks in real life. Emphasis is placed on observing the manner in which the family interacts. It is important for the therapist to appear comfortable with video equipment. Playbacks can be immediate or in subsequent sessions. Additionally, therapists may select the segment to be replayed or may accept suggestions from the family.

Example

Mr. and Mrs. A. came for counseling because of marital difficulties they were experiencing. They have been married for eight years and have a six-year-old son and a three-year-old daughter. The wife complained of being depressed and the husband explained that they would be happier if she would just do what he said. During the session that was taped the therapist elicited information from them about their difficulties.

Therapist: Mrs. A., you mentioned that your husband acts as if he doesn't respect you. Could you tell me more about that?

Mr. A.:   I don't know why she said that. It's stupid and doesn't make sense.

Therapist: Mr. A., I asked your wife that question. Let's give her a chance to respond.

Mrs. A.:   He doesn't value anything I say. He doesn't ask my advice about anything, even things that concern the house.

Mr. A.:   You know why that it is. I'm out in the world. I work. I support the house. I know more about things.

Mrs. A.:   About everything, you mean.

Mr. A.:   Yes, I do. Besides, I'm just trying to look after you and the kids to make things nice for you. I don't know what's bad about that. If you would just do as I say, things would be better. You and the kids are my prize possessions. I don't want anything to happen.

Mrs. A.:   I hate it when you treat me like a child. I just hate it!

Mr. A.:   Look, it's my responsibility to take care of you.

Mrs. A.:   You're not my father. Why do you act. . . .

Mr. A.:   That's ridiculous. It's a stupid thing to say.

The therapist played back the segment presented above to clarify issues between Mr. and Mrs. A. The discussion that followed is presented below.

Therapist: What do you think about what you've just seen?

Mrs. A.:   Do I really look like that?

Therapist: Remember, your image on the screen is not exactly how you appear in real life. People look heavier than they appear in person.

Mrs. A.:   I guess so.

Mr. A.:   I look rather chunky too.

Therapist: What do you think about what you saw on the screen? What do you make of what went on between the two of you?

Mr. A.:   I have to admit I didn't realize that I was so bossy.

Therapist: Bossy in what way?

Mr. A.:   I was doing so much of the talking although you addressed your question to my wife. I was really laying it down hard. I guess I was treating her like a kid. I noticed that I spoke real loud. I guess I didn't have to scream.

Therapist: Was it just how you said things? What about the statements you made?

Mr. A.:   That too. I called her remarks stupid.

Mrs. A.:   You certainly did. I bet you didn't realize how often you do that. Did you also notice that you didn't look at me when you were talking. You were looking at Dr. B. not me.

Therapist: Mrs. A., what about your eye contact? Did you look at your husband when you spoke to him?

Mrs. A.:   I wasn't looking at anyone. That's a good point. I was staring at the floor.

Therapist: What do you think that was all about?

Mrs. A.:   I guess I wasn't standing up to him. I usually cringe and slink away when he takes that tone with me. I really can't do that. I can't buckle under. That means I am acting like a child, but that's how he makes me feel when he yells at me like that.

In this case videotape playback was particularly helpful in clarifying behavior that had been denied. The husband made some progress in recognizing that there was some validity to his wife's complaints. Additionally, the wife made important observations about the impact of her behavior on her husband's mode of treating her.

The therapist asks them to work on the problem again and videotapes it again.

Uses

Videotape playback can be used in virtually all settings where the necessary equipment is available. Therapists could utilize this technique across the range of family problems which are encountered. It need not be limited to adults. It has demonstrated success with children, especially adolescents.

RESOURCES

Alger, I. Integrating immediate video playback in family therapy. In P. J. Guerin (ed.), *Family therapy: Theory and practice*. New York: Gardner Press, 1976.

Lawry, H. F. and Thorp, W. T. (eds.) *An Oxford anthology of English poetry*. New York: Oxford University Press.

Paul, N. Effects of playback on family members on their own previously recorded conjoint therapy material. *Psychiatric Research Reports*, 1966, *20*, 175–165.

Silk, S. The use of videotape in brief joint marital therapy. *American Journal of Psychotherapy*, 1972, *26*, 417–424.

56 | TELEPHONE CALLS WITHIN THE SESSION

Rationale

The use of the telephone in sessions with a family is a technique described by Coppersmith (1980) in the context of strategic therapy. Originally, telephone calls to the therapist in session were used to supervise the therapist. But telephone calls in sessions can have a variety of motives. Phone calls within the session can bring new members into the therapeutic system, including observers behind the one-way-vision mirror or members in another location; change the direction or plan of activity; introduce new content into the session; help the therapist attend to something that she is missing (often observers are able to catch something that a therapist might miss because of her involvement with the family); provide immediate supervision to the worker; arouse curiosity among the other individuals present (this can help direct the focus onto something other than the present discussion); be useful in restructuring the family system; clarify boundaries and the organization of subsystems; facilitate the establishment of alliances; and permit observers to take sides with different members or positions. They also can be used to improve the therapist's chances of joining with the family.

Procedure

Coppersmith (1980) discusses three distinct types of strategic calls. The first type of phone call is to the therapist from the supervisor or another member of the team. This technique involves a phone call from behind a one-way-vision mirror directed to the therapist. The content may be to redirect the therapist. The observers may feel that the therapist is not addressing an important issue, and the call is intended to help the therapist return to the right track. The call may also afford the therapist the opportunity to join with the family. The team might call to convey a feeling of discouragement about the family's progress or commitment. This allows the therapist to take an opposing view from that of the observers, in hope that the family will be interested in supporting her. When the therapist conveys a message to the clients, the tone of the session is broken. The focus switches to what the outside member has said.

The second type of phone call is from a member of the team of observers directly to a member of the family. The result is similar in that it breaks the tone of the session. The phone call becomes the focus. This might be particularly helpful when the therapist is trying to involve a member of the family who has taken the position of an outsider.

A third type of phone call is placed by a family member who has left the session to join the team. Once again this breaks the tone of the session. With this method, the session would refocus on the caller and the person receiving the call.

Examples

Coppersmith (1980) provides the following two examples.

A husband and wife and their two children were engaged in therapy. The focus of the sessions was the delinquent behavior of the daughter. The family paid very little attention to the son. The youngster made little effort to involve himself in the sessions. During one meeting the therapist engaged the boy in an art task while she talked with the parents. Immediately after that assignment was started a member of the team called the youngster and praised him for his work. This appeared to prompt the curiosity of the other family members. In response the boy discussed the call with them. This constituted the beginning of his verbal participation in the sessions. This was followed by a reduction in the distance between the boy and his parents as well as a reduction in the parents' overinvolvement with their daughter.

This example demonstrates communication between a therapist and the supervisor. A therapist was encountering a great deal of resistance with a family. Homework assignments were consistently sabotaged or ignored. The supervisor called the therapist to question the family's willingness to work on the designated problem. The therapist conveyed the message to the family and added that despite her supervisor's point she thought she was the better judge of the family. They seemed to rally around the trainee. Following that conversation, they cooperated with her in terms of assigned tasks.

Uses

The techniques described here are best used in settings in which a therapeutic team is operating. They appear appropriate for all individuals except the very young. They are particularly useful in restructuring the family system. The telephone calls can clarify boundaries and the organization of subsystems. Moreover, they can facilitate the establishment of alliances. Team members can take a position different from the therapist or bet on different actions by the family or a subsystem. This sets up a paradoxical double bind. No matter what they do they have to cooperate with someone. The calls might also be used to improve the therapist's chances for joining the family.

Although structural and strategic therapists might be particularly interested in this approach, depending on the purpose, the techniques can be used by other types of therapists as well.

Telephone calls can also be made to include absent members in the session or to have a member implement an immediate change. For example, a client might make a call for a job interview or connect with a member of the extended family who is cut off from the clients.

RESOURCES
Coppersmith, E. (Imber-Black) Expanding uses of the telephone in family therapy. *Family Process*, 1980, *19*, 411–417.

Papp, P. The Greek chorus and other techniques of paradoxical therapy. *Family Process*, 1980, *19*, 45–57.

57 | HOME VISITS

Rationale
As the term "home visits" implies, the therapist meets with the family in their home rather than in the office. The rationale is that the therapist has a better understanding of family functioning when he or she is able to observe the clients in their own environment. Information which is not readily presented in office visits may come across as the therapist interacts in a setting that is more natural to the family. Arranged home visits have the potential for decreasing family defensiveness and promoting the involvement of the entire family. It is a more natural setting for the family's functioning. It may also be possible that behavior change achieved in the home environment is both more adaptive to the family's reality and more likely to be retained.

Procedure
After the therapist informs the family of her desire to visit the family at home, a mutually acceptable time is agreed upon. It is stressed that this is not a social occasion or an investigation, but a part of the treatment. It is imperative to achieve the family's cooperation in this endeavor. The family's privacy must be respected. There should be no surprise visits.

Once at the home, the family determines where the session will be conducted. Decisions about the frequency of home visits are made by the therapist. Some therapists include one visit in the treatment plan. Others, particularly those in community outreach programs, schedule visits on a regular basis. During these visits the family and therapist may engage in verbally oriented sessions or in activities such as performance of tasks or even games. In any case a major goal is to assess family functioning and help the members adopt more functional behavior. Especially during the first visit, remarking on family artifacts or photographs may assist the therapist in joining with the family.

Example

Mrs. B. is a 30-year-old woman who came for counseling with her 11-year-old son, Todd, who was experiencing difficulty in school. She complained of feeling overwhelmed and out of control. She felt that she was just not managing and viewed her son's difficulties as proof of that. The counselor indicated that she would like to make a home visit and Mrs. B. agreed. They decided on a mutually acceptable time. Although Mrs. B. had described herself as living in a reasonably comfortable neighborhood, the therapist found that it was quite run down. The building was in extremely poor condition and there were numerous empty apartments. Although the building was in horrible condition, Mrs. B.'s apartment was immaculate. The furniture was old but obviously well cared for. A partition had been set up in the living room to create sleeping space for Todd. Mrs. B. had described her mother as ill during therapy sessions, but as a result of the home visit, the therapist found that she was a chronically ill diabetic who had already undergone one leg amputation. As Mrs. B., her mother, and Todd came together in the living room for the sessions, it became clear that the maternal grandmother was the real power broker. She was the authority figure for Todd. She was also very directive in terms of her daughter. The grandmother appeared to be the central figure within the family. Since the amputation of her leg, she has limited her activities to what could be done in the confines of the apartment. She has not kept up friendships, so she relied on her daughter and grandson for just about everything. Before her operation she had been relatively self-sufficient. She had maintained her own apartment and was employed.

Information obtained in the home visit proved invaluable in working with the B. family. The therapist felt that she had a clearer idea about what was going on in the family. Issues that had not been discussed in the office became abundantly clear. The therapist now had new insight into the conditions which Mrs. B. and Todd had to cope with on a daily basis. There was the problem of their place of residence. The counselor learned that Mrs. B. was eligible for subsidized housing but had been unsuccessful in her efforts to negotiate the system. Helping her deal with this became a high-priority issue. Additionally, it was clear that help had to be provided in terms of the grandmother. The importance of identifying strategies for increasing the grandmother's options were discussed. The home visit also served the purpose of identifying strengths which had gone undetected. In spite of the stresses and strains which seemed ever present, Mrs. B. had taken care of her family. She had continued to maintain a neat, attractive apartment in the midst of very unpleasant environmental conditions. She had organized her apartment so that her son had the privacy and space which she viewed as important for healthy development. The identification of these positives was important to the therapeutic process.

Uses
Home visits may be used in a variety of settings. Although most descriptions in the literature are with low-income families where crisis intervention is occurring, there is no reason why it should be limited to this population. Visits can be employed routinely with all families as part of the therapeutic process. However, the technique may be particularly helpful in cases where family members are unable or unwilling to come to the office or where the therapist suspects gross discrepancies between reality and what's reported.

Working in the home can help build trust where there is distrust of the institutions of the "establishment." Behavior changes can be implemented immediately under the conditions in which they will more normally occur. This enhances the likelihood that new learning will actually take place and be incorporated. Being "on the spot" presents opportunities to make structural moves with immediate impact.

RESOURCES
Behrens, M. Brief home visits by the clinic therapist in the treatment of lowerclass patients. *American Journal of Psychiatry*, 1967, *124*, 371–375.

Fish, R. Home visits in a private psychiatric practice. *Family Process*, 1964, *3*(1), 114–125.

Moynihan, S. Home visits for family treatment. *Social Casework*, 1974, *55*, 712–717.

58 | TIME-EXTENDED FAMILY INTERVIEWING

Rationale
Time-extended family interviewing is a technique described by Breslow and Hron (1977). It is designed for those who are prevented from engaging in therapy because they reside a considerable distance from the

therapist, are resistant to regularly scheduled therapy, or find that their work schedule or school hours conflict with ongoing therapy. Most important, time-extended interviewing implies the need for flexibility in viewing the traditional hourly session.

Aside from the "convenience" issues that justify this technique, a major purpose of time-extended family interviewing relates to the particular family and psychodynamics involved. The interview ranges anywhere from three to seven hours and is intended to have the effect of strengthening family life, preventing a breakdown of family structure, and promoting movement and change in family. The problem rather than the clock defines the length of the session. More time together may increase the intensity of the proceedings and facilitate "breakthroughs."

Procedure

The therapist has to assess when it is appropriate to employ the technique, how to schedule the time, and how to structure the use of the time. The need for such a meeting and who is to be there are discussed with the family and an agreement is obtained to do it.

Breslow and Hron (1977) suggest that before implementing the technique it is usually desirable to use traditional length sessions to explore the family situation and needs. They caution it might be inappropriate to use the technique when families require space and time to develop a trusting relationship with the therapist or to adjust to new situations, such as mourning the loss of a loved one. Families who are very intense emotionally may experience too much stimulation in a long session. Young children may become fatigued or very restless.

The therapist suggests several blocks of time during which she could be available. If more than three hours is desired and geographically distant members are invited, a weekend date may turn out to be the most convenient to schedule. The meeting should be scheduled far enough in advance to accommodate those who need to travel. One or more family members assume responsibility for setting up the session if additional persons are to be included. That person may need to rehearse a rationale and strategy for bringing the others in.

Incorporated within the structure of the extended sessions are a variety of therapeutic activities relevant to the theory being used and which are also diagnostically appropriate. Examples are interview techniques, role playing, structural moves, sculpting, or the assignment of tasks. It is usually helpful to vary the activity over time.

Example

The following example is adapted from Breslow and Hron (1977).

Mr. and Mrs. L., each formerly widowed and now married to one another, entered therapy. It was diagnosed that they were operating within an extremely rigid system. Each believed that if the other changed, all of their problems would be solved. These projections continued even after the third hourly session. An extended session was scheduled in order to establish a contract in which each would take responsibility for his or her own behavior. It was observed during this session that interaction between the couple stopped after each demanded change from the other. There were none of the usual arguments that might be expected to follow such demands. Each would retreat feeling frustrated and not heard. The couple seemed to be operating under the myth that in a good marriage there is no conflict. When confronted with this, the couple uncovered the fear that arguing might lead to divorce. This would reignite the terrible feelings of loss and loneliness that they each experienced with the death of their former spouses.

The couple, now recognizing their bind, began to explore their fears. Each began to take responsibility for his or her own behavior and began to relate more effectively with the other.

In an extended session there was sufficient time to discover and work through their dilemma.

Uses

Time-extended interviewing as a technique in family therapy is appropriate when working with:

1. extremely inhibited and defended families;
2. resistant families;
3. families who experience a particular point of impasse as therapy progresses;
4. families who experience a fear of change;
5. families who experience difficulties in integrating intellectual insight and emotions during the therapeutic process;
6. families who express the need for closure on a particular issue;
7. families with scheduling impasses, such as school hours, job hours, inordinate geographic distances;
8. families who tend to repeat dysfunctional patterns of interacting during the ongoing therapeutic situation; and
9. extended families and influential others who would have difficulty attending a session more than once.

RESOURCES

Bach, G. R. The marathon group: Intensive practice of intimate interaction. *Psychological Reports*, 1966, *18*, 995–1000.

Bach, G. R. Marathon group dynamics: Some functions of the professional group facilitator. *Psychological Reports*, 1967, *20*, 995–999.

Breslow, D. B. and Hron, B. G. Time-extended family interviewing. *Family Process*, 1977, *16*, 97–103.

Demos, G. D. Marathon therapy: A new therapeutic modality. *Psychotherapy and Psychosomatics*, 1967, *15*, 14–15.

Gardner, R. A. A four-day diagnostic therapeutic home visit in Turkey. *Family Process*, 1970, *3*, 301–331.

Hansen, C. C. An extended home visit with conjoint family therapy. *Family Process*, 1968, *7*, 67–87.

Landes, J. and Winter, W. A new strategy for treating disintegrating families. *Family Process*, 1966, *51*, 1–20.

MacGregor, R. Multiple impact psychotherapy with families. *Family Process*, 1962, *1*, 15–29.

MacGregor, R., Ritchie, A. M., Serrano, A. C. and Schuster, F. P. *Multiple impact therapy with families*. New York: McGraw-Hill, 1964.

Stroller, F. H. The long week-end. *Psychology Today*, 1967, *1*, 28–33.

59 | THE SURROGATE FAMILY GROUP

Rationale

The surrogate family group is a relatively new approach to group therapy derived from a combination of group therapy and family networking. It is designed and proposed by Lifton, Tavantzis, and Mooney (1979). It places great significance on the contribution of individual differences to the group, which includes children, seniors, single-parent families, and adolescents. It represents a population that one encounters in the real world.

An extended family artificially created by the therapist is designed to provide the support, modeling, and experience ordinarily found in extended and traditional nuclear families. Those cut off for whatever reason from their extended families can particularly benefit from such a group. The growth in the number of single-parent families, the effects of geographic mobility, and the inability of some extended families to provide support for given members impel this movement.

With mothers and fathers being absent and aunts, uncles, and grandparents being underinvolved, children are deprived of the role models these adults provide and of the opportunity to anticipate and to vicariously experience problems related to different stages of life. They struggle as they seek support and help in facing life crises. Children display symptomatic behavior in the classroom and cannot be evaluated in isolation from their family systems. Sometimes it is realistic for the therapist to build surrogate family groups for the atypical family, which may be able to function as the extended family once did (Lifton et al., 1979).

Churches have been active in recognizing the emotional and spiritual needs of the lonely and have formed new family groups (surrogate families), described by Clark (1974) and Crane (1974). Support has been offered by such groups as Parents without Partners and by senior citizen centers. The Havura movement in Judaism brings nonrelated local singles, aging persons, and families together in an ongoing friendship group which shares holidays, joy, grief, study, illness, and social occasions.

The Surrogate Family Group Model described here differs from the efforts just mentioned in that it is a therapeutic group organized by the family therapist to help specific persons in need. The therapist serves as the therapeutic leader of the group she creates to help it become a functional extended family. She uses her professional skills to assist the group in coping with its problems of organization, communication, development through life cycle stages, and existing dysfunctional behavior.

The surrogate family system is advocated as a unit in which an individual can participate, create, share, laugh, live, and die. Participating in a social institution can be a vehicle for a person's need to relate to the infinite and give meaning to life. It is another method of achieving immortality (Woodward, 1978) through the recognition of the self. Quoting from Hillel, "If I am not for myself, who is for me? If I care only for myself, what am I?" (Ethics of the Fathers 1:14). It therefore stimulates development both of a significant differentiated self and a sense of belonging in a group with social feeling and interest in others.

Organizing such a group is time consuming and requires a commitment to reach out in order to recruit the necessary members and bring them together. The method is probably better suited to a community agency or school than to the private practitioner.

Procedure

The therapist identifies several individuals and/or isolated family units for whom a surrogate family would be useful. They are interviewed to determine suitability in terms of willingness to participate, sufficient commonality of background and interests to be congenial, and sufficient individual and subgroup differences to provide as well for complementarity in age, gender, needs, interests, and goals. These will form the nucleus of the new "family." Additional members can be recruited from the community if additional balance is desired. Recruitment methods might be through families formerly treated, church congregations, advertising in local media, discussions in school parent association groups, school counselors, and family education groups.

The therapist convenes the new "family" and uses group dynamic techniques to help the group form and become a group. This involves

1. Getting acquainted, testing oneself out in relation to the others, finding one's place;
2. Deciding on rules, goals, and purposes;

3.   Attending to the components required in an extended family such
     as development of rituals like birthdays, anniversaries, holidays; as-
     sessing and sharing of resources; division of labor; development of
     effective patterns of communication; finding time together; and
     others.
4.   Inventing a process for decision making and negotiation of differ-
     ences; respect for and acceptance of minority and individual needs
     and opinions; and participation in carrying out agreements.

The leader takes the responsibility for the group's development of a
supportive network (Rueveni, 1979), with interventions focusing on the
entire group rather than on the individuals. The therapeutic dimension
begins with acceptance and validation of each person. The group leader
points out common feelings of group members to promote group cohesiveness; teaches positive approaches to confrontations; facilitates membership agreement on group limits for confidentiality and tardiness; interprets idiosyncratic behaviors for the members; and remains aware of
the impact of intervention on the total family system.

The climate is set as the group agrees on limits and develops cohesiveness, which builds a family culture and history. Individual differences
are valued, and interaction among members is fostered. The influence
of the past on present group behavior is reviewed.

The self-disclosure, trust, and willingness to interact with one another
contribute to the development of group cohesion. This helps members
of the group recognize sources of stress, and members may intervene
in crises such as illness or economic need.

The therapeutic dimension includes development of commitment
through the acceptance of emotions and needs, helping people learn the
value of feedback, and pinpointing the rewards one obtains from involvement in a family.

The difficult task is to help members of the family see the value of their
new heritage. Complete commitment to the group involves some loss of
individual autonomy. The acceptance of emotionality, the negotiation
of reciprocity among members, the risk of self-exposure in the presence
of a strange new family are all aspects of commitments.

As the group proceeds, the therapist utilizes any theory of family therapy that is effective with a multigenerational extended family system.

Uses
A lonely or isolated person or family can be incorporated into a larger
system which provides more options than an isolated position can provide. It helps increase a sense of belonging, personal significance, and
social feeling, and thereby overcomes alienation. There are more resources available for support, pursuit of goals, modeling, identification,

and differentiation. Combined resources permit the group to achieve goals that might not be possible for most of its subsystems.

RESOURCES

Clark, R. On accidental extended families. *Journal of Liberal Ministry*, 1974, *14*(2), 17–19.

Crane, J. A., Jr. The extended family in Santa Barbara: A new direction. *Journal of Liberal Ministry*, 1974, *14*(2), 23–25.

Lifton, W. M., Tavantzis, T. N., and Mooney, W. The disappearing family: The role of counselors in creating surrogate families. *Personnel and Guidance Journal*, November 1979, pp. 17–19.

Rueveni, D. *Networking families in crisis*. New York: Garland, 1979.

Woodward, K. The emergence of a new theology. *Psychology Today*. January 1978, p. 47.

8

Epilogue

In researching this book, we in effect observed the present state of the art. What we found was that the field is moving in particular directions.

Directions

1. There is a powerful thrust toward *higher* standards and greater rigor in research and practice. This is promoted by, among others, professional associations, journal editors, the increasing number of family therapy doctoral programs in the universities, and state licensing laws.
2. Practitioners are held increasingly accountable for their work as a result of peer review procedures, third-party payments, and the increase in the number of trained supervisors providing supervision. Also more cases arrive in court in divorce and custody proceedings with marriage and family specialists involved either as evaluators or expert witnesses.
3. Family research centers and universities stimulate an obligation to publish. There is an explosion of new books and journals in the field.
4. Theories and their underlying assumption of knowing are being constantly refined and made clearer.
5. The nature of family therapy training focuses increasingly on live supervision of practice as it is occurring rather than after the fact.

247

One-way-vision rooms and videotape systems facilitate this procedure. While confidentiality is maintained within the system, there is an immediate expanded therapeutic system which includes the clients, therapist, supervisor, and perhaps additional trainees or supervisors.

6. Greater interest in prevention and development processes is stimulated by the difficulties experienced by so many families, the high rate of divorce, single-parent families, and stepfamilies. Church-affiliated centers have been taking a strong lead in this direction and in the formulation of new instruments. Family education centers and formal programs have been increasing steadily in number and clientele. The focus is on normality and development rather than on pathology.

7. A closer connection has been evolving between theory and operational techniques and instruments.

8. The computer provides an instrument for the development of new techniques. It provides more sophisticated methods of data collection and record storage and makes more advanced statistical and research designs possible for the development of instruments and the processing and analysis of data.

9. More techniques are being invented to deal with or assess very specific problems rather than general issues.

10. Studies of interactional analyses in the family have given impetus to the creation of more efficient, measured interpersonal behaviors.

11. The emergence of new technologies provides means for creating new techniques and measurements, evaluating such creations, and educating therapists in their use.

12. Increasing attention is being given to adaptations of hypnotherapy and right-hemisphere brain functioning. This opens up possibilities for new behavior change techniques.

13. Recently, much energy has been devoted to find ways to synthesize the good ideas in the many theories of family therapy and to create new "integrative" theories. The contributions of the individual, past history, and the context of the family within other systems are receiving more attention. As this movement proceeds, it will probably make techniques formulated within one theoretical frame more readily adaptable to other frameworks.

14. There is a great deal of openness in the field. Traditionally, psychotherapists share their work by merely describing it to others. But family therapists, beginning with Adler in 1919, have been willing to work publicly so that colleagues could directly observe what they are doing, sometimes questioning them while they are doing it. This has a tremendous impact on the very nature of the field.

It reduces the subjective perception and editing done by the sharing one. It exposes a much wider range of activity and nuance in how therapy is actually conducted. It reveals the impact of the personality of the worker as well as the theory and techniques utilized. It provides directly observable master models for all of us to consider. It creates the expectation of more openness of the work in training and ongoing supervision. It is a message to the clients that what is happening to them is not so terrible that it must be kept a dark secret, nor are they afflicted by a contagious disease requiring their isolation from others. However, watching the masters perform can also be a humbling experience as we strive for the same levels of success.

15. There is a paradox that exists between the increasing openness in the field and the tightening of standards at the same time. The drive toward greater professionalism requires greater conformity with specified standards for training, certification, supervision, and practice. The interdisciplinary "freshness" of an earlier generation is replaced by a more formal, predetermined set of expectations. Of course, as the field matures, there is a need for continuing professionalization on the one hand and a willingness to accept new ideas and reforms on the other, just as a family must provide for both continuity and change.

We learned that marriage and family therapy is a very productive and creative field that has generated or adapted a wide range of modalities to work with, exemplified by the many chapters of this book. Many of the methods developed are fun to use and are surprising to clients who have come to expect straightforward, interview-type talk therapies.

What Is Needed

1. Greater refinement in all areas.
2. More outcome studies on techniques and instruments being used.
3. More measures of systems rather than individual differences.
4. Attention to methods dealing with very specific problem areas.
5. Constructive ways of defining, viewing and utilizing client resistance in behalf of the client system. Some systems theorists believe that the entire therapy is devoted to overcoming resistance and others that there is no such thing as resistance.
6. Organization of techniques to accomplish a specific therapeutic task or goal such as strengthening boundaries, building family esteem, and increasing differentiation among members.
7. Flexibility to make conceptual changes in the field to adjust to changes taking place in culture and role behavior.

8. Development of concepts, models, techniques, and instruments concerned with the interaction of the family with other families and social institutions.
9. Greater recognition in test development and reference groups of the influence of culture on behavior, values, satisfaction, and expected role.
10. Ways of measuring the therapist variable on the kind of therapeutic system evolved and the outcomes of the therapy.

Practitioners and students express great concern about "how to do it." Observing master therapists in person or on videotape sometimes makes family therapy seem either very simple or pure magic. What is expressed in those demonstrations and case reports in textbooks is the successful integration of theory, empathy, intelligence, and talent. These are well salted by years of experience and creative artistry. They are all incorporated congenially within the personality of the therapist and tailored to benefit that personality. Failures are seldom reported. And what happens after the demonstration is seldom reported.

One of the problems facing any scientist is the ability to formulate a methodology that can be learned and implemented by any reasonably intelligent and interested person independent of most other personality variables. However, in marriage and family therapy — indeed, in psychotherapy in general — therapist variables are vital ingredients in accepting and applying theory and in forming therapeutic relationships with clients. The therapist becomes the refined tool to help bring about change. The most typical path is for each therapist, in one fashion or another, consciously or unconsciously, to invent a personal integrative theory of her own, even as a proponent of a given theoretical school. This takes years to do and continues over the course of one's career.

A technique is a tool, like a hammer or a piano. A hammer can be used as a weapon or to build a house; a piano can make a lot of annoying noise or beautiful music. Its value is determined by how it is used and with what skill.

The techniques available in this book and in the literature are to be examined in that spirit of befitting one's personality, theory, the ethics of the profession, and the specific needs of the clients. Magic is an illusion. Behavior change consists of specific action, thoughts, and feelings. Most techniques can be refined and adapted to meet those criteria.